Napoleon's Marshals
나폴레옹의 원수들

Napoleon's Marshals ❶

초판 1쇄 인쇄 2013년 12월 03일
초판 1쇄 발행 2013년 12월 10일

해설자	조 성 민
지은이	리처드 던-패티슨(R. P. Dunn-Pattison)
펴낸이	손 형 국
펴낸곳	(주)북랩
출판등록	2004. 12. 1(제2012-000051호)
주소	서울시 금천구 가산디지털 1로 168, 우림라이온스밸리 B동 B113, 114호
홈페이지	www.book.co.kr
전화번호	(02)2026-5777
팩스	(02)2026-5747

ISBN   979-11-5585-093-0 04840(종이책)
        979-11-5585-100-5 04840(세트)
        979-11-5585-094-7 05840(전자책)

이 책의 판권은 해설자와 (주)북랩에 있습니다.
내용의 일부와 전부를 무단 전재하거나 복제를 금합니다.

이 도서의 국립중앙도서관 출판시도서목록(CIP)은 서지정보유통지원시스템 홈페이지(http://seoji.nl.go.kr)와
국가자료공동목록시스템(http://www.nl.go.kr/kolisnet)에서 이용하실 수 있습니다.
(CIP제어번호 : 2013026062)

Napoleon's Marshals

나폴레옹의 원수들

리처드 던-패티슨(R. P. Dunn-Pattison) 지음
조성민 해설

나폴레옹을 위대한 영웅으로 만든 숨은 조력자들,
**역사상 가장 위대했던 조연들의 이야기를
원문으로 만나다**

book Lab

해설

영어로 책을 읽는다는 것은 멋진 모험이다. 먼저 방대한 종류의 책들 속에서 하나를 고르는 것부터가 새로운 여행지를 선택하는 것 같은 즐거움을 준다. 그리고 마침내 손에 넣은 원서는 낯선 세계로 안내하는 신비의 열쇠가 되어 우리의 도전욕구를 자극하고, 그 뒤에 펼쳐지는 모험 속에는 쉽게 접근하기 어렵지만 한 번 빠지면 헤어나오기 힘든 묘한 매력이 숨어 있다.

그러나 독자들에 따라 영어 실력에 차이가 있고, 많은 원서들이 초보들이 접근하기에는 다소 어려움이 있는 문장 패턴을 지니고 있어 선뜻 책을 집어 들지 못하는 것도 사실이다. 그렇다고 해서 쉽게 쓰인 책만 찾다보면 성인에게 동화책 수준이나 읽히는 격이 되어 흥미가 떨어지게 된다. 리처드 던-패티슨(R. P. Dunn-Pattison: 1874~1916)이 저술한 이 책《Napoleon's Marshals》는 그런 조건을 모두 충족시켜 주는 쉬우면서도 흥미진진한 책에 속한다.

영국의 군인이자 역사학자였던 던-패티슨은 전쟁사에서 탁월한 인물이었다. 이 책을 저술한 1909년, 35세의 젊은 나이로 옥스퍼드 대학에서 역사교수로 재직하고 있었던 전도유망한 학자였다. 그러나 1916년 1차 대전에 대위로 참전한 그는 불행히도 메소포타미아에서 전사하고 만다. 학계로서는 참으로 안타까운 손실이 아닐 수 없다.

《Napoleon's Marshals》는 제목 그대로 나폴레옹 휘하에서 활약하던 26명의 원수(元帥)들의 삶에 대해 적은 책이다. 비록 저자 자신이 뛰어난 전쟁사학자였지만 이 책은 전문가보다는 일반인을 위한 교양서로 저술되었다. 그 내용도 군사적인 전술보다는 원수들의 성격과 삶에 더 초점이 맞춰져 있어 읽는 데 전혀 부담이 없다.

다만 이 책의 저자는 서문에서부터 나폴레옹을 심하게 폄하하면서 출발한다. 뛰어난 재능은 인정하지만, 유럽의 평화를 어지럽힌 악의 상징 정도로 그리고 있다. 나폴레옹을 좋아하는 독자들에게는 다소 불편한 부분일지도 모른다. 그러나 한편으로는 나폴레옹이 워낙 대단한 인물이다 보니 글 속에서 조금씩 그를 비판하는 것이 26명의 원수들의 모습을 더욱 부각시키는 데에 도움이 되는 것 같다.

1권의 주인공은 베르티에, 뮈라, 마세나, 베르나도트 네 사람이다. 나폴레옹이라는 인물을 구심점으로 모인 다른 원수들과 마찬가지로 이들도 각각의 개성이 다르고 나름대로의 장·단점을 지닌 인물들이다. 우직하고 성실하지만 스스로 2인자의 역할로 한정해 버린 베르티에, 최고의 기병사령관이었지만 허영심 때문에 모든 것을 망친 뮈라, 나폴레옹도 인정한 뛰어난 전략가임에도 탐욕스럽고 인색했던 마세나, 뛰어난 통찰력과 매력으로 사람들을 사로잡았지만, 교활하게 기회만 엿보았던 베르나도트. 이들의 삶을 통해 독자들은 다양한 인간 군상을 엿볼 수 있다.

나폴레옹 전쟁의 결말 때문인지 이 책에서 원수들의 삶이 다소 불운하게 그려지는 경향이 있다. 그런 경향은 스웨덴의 왕이 되어 후손들에게 왕관을 물려주는 데에 성공한 베르나도트에게도 예외가 아니다. 그러나 던-패티슨은 전통적인 영국 사학자다운 태도로 엄격한 사료와 철저한 고증을 통해서만 이야기할 뿐, 결코 감정적으로나 의도적으로 이들의 삶을 왜곡한 것은 아니다.

치밀한 내용 구성뿐만 아니라 강약을 조절하고 흡인력 있는 문장력은 100년 이상이 지난 지금도 읽는 데에 전혀 손색이 없다. 오히려 현대에 출판된 다른 책들보다도 뛰어난 면이 많다. 이제 던-패티슨의 유려한 문장력과 함께 나폴레옹의 원수들 중 4명과 만나는 모험을 떠나보기로 하자.

2013년 겨울, 鳥川에서

나폴레옹 휘하 26명의 원수

이름	출생	사망	대표 작위
Louis Alexandre Berthier 루이 알렉상드르 베르티에	1753	1815	바그람 공작
Joachim Murat 조아생 뮈라	1767	1815	나폴리 왕
Bon Adrien Jeannot de Moncey 봉 아드리앙 자노 드 몽시	1754	1842	코네글리아노 공작
Jean Baptiste Jourdan 장 바티스트 주르당	1762	1833	백작
André Masséna 앙드레 마세나	1756	1817	에슬링 공작
Charles Pierre François Augereau 샤를 피에르 프랑수아 오주로	1757	1816	카스티글리오네 공작
Jean Baptiste Jules Bernadotte 장 바티스트 쥘 베르나도트	1763	1844	스웨덴 왕
Jean de Dieu Nicolas Soult 장 드 듀 니콜라 술트	1769	1851	달마티아 공작
Guillaume Marie Anne Brune 기욤 마리 안 브륀	1763	1815	백작
Jean Lannes 장 란	1769	1809	몬테벨로 공작
Adolphe Édouard Casimir Joseph Mortier 아돌프 에두아르 카시미르 조제프 모르티에	1768	1835	트레비소 공작
Michel Ney 미셸 네	1769	1815	모스크바 공작
Louis Nicolas Davout 루이 니콜라 다부	1770	1823	에크뮐 공작
Jean Baptiste Bessières 장 바티스트 베시에르	1768	1813	이스트리아 공작
François Christophe Kellermann 프랑수아 크리스토프 켈레르망	1735	1820	발미 공작
François Joseph Lefèbvre 프랑수아 조제프 르페브르	1755	1820	단치히 공작
Dominique Catherine de Pérignon 도미니크 카트린 드 페리뇽	1754	1818	백작
Jean Mathieu Philibert Serurier 장 마티유 필리베르 세뤼리에	1742	1819	백작
Claude Victor Perrin 클로드 빅토르 페랭	1764	1841	벨루노 공작
Jacques Étienne Joseph Alexandre Macdonald 자크 에티엔 조제프 알렉상드르 막도날	1765	1840	타렌툼 공작

이름	출생	사망	대표 작위
Nicholas Charles Oudinot 니콜라 샤를 우디노	1767	1847	레지오 공작
Auguste Frédéric Louis Viesse de Marmont 오귀스트 프레데릭 루이 비스 드 마르몽	1774	1852	라구사 공작
Louis Gabriel Suchet 루이 가브리엘 쉬셰	1770	1826	알부페라 공작
Laurent Gouvion St. Cyr 로랑 구비옹 생-시르	1764	1830	백작
Prince Joseph Poniatowski 유제프 포니아토프스키 왕자	1762	1813	-
Emmanuel de Grouchy 에마뉘엘 드 그루시	1766	1847	백작

※ Prince와 Duke는 미묘한 차이가 있지만 자주 혼용되어 사용되므로 원칙적으로는 '공작' 으로 통일해서 번역한다. 다만 상황에 따라 '왕자', '왕세자' 등으로 번역해야 할 경우에는 그에 따른다.

CONTENTS

INTRODUCTION
서문
010

1
034

LOUIS ALEXANDRE BERTHIER
루이 알렉상드르 베르티에

◆

2
100

JOACHIM MURAT
조아생 뮈라

◆

3
176

ANDRÉ MASSÉNA
앙드레 마세나

◆

4
244

JEAN BAPTISTE JULES BERNADOTTE
장 바티스트 쥘 베르나도트

INTRODUCTION

It is a melancholy but instructive fact to remember that, in the opinion of him whom nature had adorned with the greatest intellect that the world has yet seen, selfishness and self-interest lie at the root of all human action. "For," as Napoleon said, "in ambition is to be found the chief motive force of humanity, and a man puts forth his best powers in proportion to his hopes of advancement." It was on this cynical hypothesis therefore, with a complete disregard of those higher aspirations of self-sacrifice and self-control which raise man above the mere brute, that the Corsican adventurer waded through seas of blood to the throne of France, and then attempted, by the destruction of a million human beings, to bind on his brow the imperial crown of Western Europe. In spite of loud-sounding phrases and constitutional sleight-of-hand, none knew better than Napoleon that by the sword alone he had won his empire and by the sword alone he could keep it. Keen student of history, it was not in vain that again and again he had read and re-read the works of Cæsar, and pondered on the achievements of Charlemagne and the career of Cromwell. The problem he had to solve was, how to con-

- **melancholy** [mélənkàli/-kɔ̀li] 명 우울, 울적함
- **instructive** [instrʌ́ktiv] 형 교훈적인, 본받을 점이 많은
- **adorn** [ədɔ́:rn] 통 꾸미다, 장식하다, 광채를 더하다
  - the opinion of him whom nature had adorned with the greatest intellect that the world has yet seen
    조물주가 지금까지 세상이 본 적 없는 가장 뛰어난 지능으로 그를 꾸며 주었다는 견해
- **selfishness and self-interest lie at the root of all human action**
  이기심과 사리추구는 모든 인간의 행동에 근본적으로 존재한다
- **put forth** 발휘하다
- **in proportion to** ~에 비례하여
  - a man puts forth his best powers **in proportion to** his hopes of advancement
    사람은 성공에 대한 희망에 비례해서 자신의 능력을 최고로 발휘한다
- **cynical hypothesis** 냉소적인 가정
- **aspiration** [æ̀spəréiʃən] 명 열망, 포부, 큰 뜻
- **a complete disregard of those higher aspirations of self-sacrifice and self-control**
  자기희생과 자기절제의 더 높은 포부를 완전히 무시하는 것
- **which raise man above the mere brute**
  단순한 짐승들보다 인간을 더 높은 위치에 올려놓은
- **wade** [weid] 통 힘들여 나아가다, 애써서 나아가다
  - **waded** through seas of blood to the throne of France
    프랑스의 왕위를 향해 피바다를 헤쳐나갔다
- **to bind on his brow the imperial crown of Western Europe**
  이마에 서유럽 황제의 관을 쓰기 위해
- **sleight-of-hand** 명 교묘한 속임수
  - loud-sounding phrases and constitutional **sleight-of-hand**
    화려한 말솜씨와 헌법주의자라는 속임수
- **none knew better than Napoleon that**
  나폴레옹이 ~이상은 아니라는 것을 모두가 알았다
- **Keen student of history** (나폴레옹은) 예리한 역사학도로서
- **ponder** [pándər/pɔ́n-] 통 깊이 생각하다, 숙고하다

ceal from his lieutenants that his dynasty rested purely on their swords, to bind their honours so closely to his own fortune that they should ever be loyal; so to distribute his favours that his servants should never become so great as to threaten his own position. It was with this object in view that at the time he seized for himself the imperial crown he re-established the old rôle of Marshal of France, frankly confessing to Roederer that his reason for showering rewards on his lieutenants was to assure to himself his own dignity, since they could not object to it when they found themselves the recipients of such lofty titles. But, with the cunning of the serpent, while he gave with one hand he took away with the other. He fixed the number of Marshals at sixteen on the active list and added four others for those too old for active service. Hence he had it in his power to reward twenty hungry aspirants, while he robbed the individuals of their glory, since each Marshal shared his dignity with nineteen others. Plainly also he told them that, lofty though their rank might appear to others, to him they were still mere servants, created by him and dependent for their position on him alone. "Recollect," he said, "that you are soldiers only when with the army. The title of Marshal is merely a civil distinction which gives you the honourable rank at my court which is your due, but it carries with it no authority. On the battlefield you are generals, at court you are nobles, belonging to

- **conceal** [kənsíːl] 동 숨기다
  - to **conceal** from his lieutenants that his dynasty rested purely on their swords
  그의 부관들에게 어떻게 하면 자신의 왕조가 단순히 무력에 의지하고 있다는 것을 숨길지
- **to bind their honours so closely to his own fortune that they should ever be loyal**
  그들의 영광을 자기 자신의 운명에 결부시켜 영원히 충성하게 만드는
- **so to distribute his favours that his servants should never become so great as to threaten his own position**
  호의를 신하들에게 베풀어 절대 자신의 위치를 넘보지 못하도록 하는
- **with this object in view** 이런 목적을 위해서
- **the old rôle of Marshal of France** 프랑스 원수라는 유서 깊은 지위
- **frankly confessing to Roederer that** 뢰데레르 백작에게 솔직하게 고백했듯이
- **showering rewards** 보상을 듬뿍 주는 것
- **assure to himself his own dignity** 자신의 권위를 확인하다
- **object to** ~에 반대하다
- **recipient** [risípiənt] 명 수상자, 수령인
- **lofty** [lɔ́ːfti/lɔ́fti] 형 높은, 고위의
- **with the cunning of the serpent** 뱀처럼 교활하게
- **while he gave with one hand he took away with the other**
  한 손으로는 주고 다른 손으로는 빼앗아 갔다
- **at sixteen on the active list** 현역 장교 중에는 16명으로
- **added four others for those too old for active service**
  현역으로 복무하기에는 너무 나이가 든 이들 4명을 추가했다
- **twenty hungry aspirants** 높은 지위를 간절히 원하는 20인
- **lofty though their rank might appear to others**
  높은 지위에 걸맞는 모습을 다른 사람들에게 보여야 한다
- **recollect** [rèkəlékt] 동 기억하다, 명심하다
- **merely a civil distinction** 단순히 민간적으로 구분 짓는 것
- **it carries with it no authority** 아무런 권한이 수반되지 않는다

the State by the civil position I created for you when I bestowed your titles on you." It was on May 19, 1804, that the Gazette appeared with the first creation of Marshals. There were fourteen on the active list and four honorary Marshals in the Senate. Two bâtons were withheld as a reward for future service. The original fourteen were Berthier, Murat, Moncey, Jourdan, Masséna, Augereau, Bernadotte, Soult, Brune, Lannes, Mortier, Ney, Davout and Bessières; while on the retired list were Kellermann, Lefèbvre, Pérignon, and Serurier. The list caused much surprise and dissatisfaction. On the one hand there were those like Masséna who received their congratulations with a grunt and "Yes, one of fourteen." On the other hand were those like Macdonald, Marmont, Victor, and many another, who thought they ought to have been included. An examination of the names soon explains how the choice was made. Except Jourdan, who was too great a soldier to be passed over, all those who could not forget their Republican principles were excluded. Masséna received his bâton as the greatest soldier of France. Berthier, Murat, and Lannes had won theirs by their talents, as much as by their personal devotion. Soult, Ney, Davout, and Mortier were Napoleon's choice from among the coming men, who in the camps of the Army of the Ocean were fast justifying their selection. Bessières was

- **the civil position I created for you** 내가 그대들을 임명한 민간지위
- **bestow** [bistóu] 동 주다, 수여하다
- **the Gazette** the Gazette 라 가제트(또는 가제트 드 프랑스, 1631년 테오프라스트 르노도가 창간한 프랑스 최초의 주간지)
- **There were fourteen on the active list and four honorary Marshals in the Senate.**
  14명의 현역과 상원에 소속된 4명의 명예원수가 있었다.
- **Two bâtons were withheld as a reward for future service.**
  2개의 지휘봉은 앞으로 공을 세울 자들을 위해 남겨두었다.
- **dissatisfaction** [dissætisfǽkʃən] 명 불만, 불평
  - The list caused much surprise and **dissatisfaction**.
  그 명단은 많은 놀라움과 불만을 야기했다.
- **grunt** [grʌnt] 명 불평
  - On the one hand there were those like Masséna who received their congratulations with a **grunt** and "Yes, one of fourteen."
  한편에서는 마세나처럼 축하인사에 대해 "그래, 14명 중에 하나란 말이지"라며 불만스럽게 받아들인 이들도 있었다.
- **On the other hand were those like Macdonald, Marmont, Victor, and many another, who thought they ought to have been included.**
  다른 한편에서는 막도날, 마르몽, 빅토르 등 많은 이들이 마땅히 자신이 포함되어야 한다고 여기는 이들도 있었다
- **An examination of the names** 그 명단에 대한 검토
- **pass over** 그냥 지나가다
  - Except Jourdan, who was too great a soldier to be **passed over**
  주르당과 같이 그냥 넘어가기에는 너무 대단한 군인을 제외하고는
- **all those who could not forget their Republican principles were excluded**
  공화주의 신념을 잊지 못하는 이들은 모두 배제되었다
- **coming man** 전도유망한 사람
- **were fast justifying their selection** 그들의 선발이 정당함이 빨리 확인되었다

included because he would never win it at any later date, but his doglike devotion made him a priceless subordinate. Augereau and Bernadotte received their bâtons to keep them quiet. The names of Moncey, Brune, Kellermann, Pérignon, and Serurier were intimately connected with glorious feats of the republican armies, and so, though only fortunate mediocrities, they were included in the first creation, while Lefèbvre, the republican of republicans, now under the glamour of Napoleon's power, was placed on the list as a stalking-horse of the extreme members of his party. At the time of the first creation, of the great soldiers of the Republic, Moreau was branded as a traitor; Hoche, Marceau, Kléber, Desaix, and Pichegru were dead; Carnot, the organiser of victory, was a voluntary exile; while staunch blades like Leclerc, Richepanse, Lecourbe, Macdonald, Victor, St. Cyr, and Suchet were all more or less in disgrace. By the end of the Empire, death and the necessity of rewarding merit added to the list of Marshals until in all twenty-six bâtons were granted by the Emperor. In 1808 Victor was restored to favour and received his bâton. After Wagram, Macdonald, Oudinot, and Marmont received the prize, while the Spanish War brought it to Suchet, and the Russian campaign to St. Cyr. In 1813 the Polish prince, Poniatowski, was sent his truncheon on the field of Leipzig, while last of all, in 1815, Grouchy was promoted to one of the vacancies caused by

- **at any later date** 훗날에도
- **doglike** 형 개 같은, 충실한
  - Bessières was included because he would never win it at any later date, but his **doglike** devotion made him a priceless subordinate.
  베시에르는 앞으로도 결코 그런 지위를 얻을만한 공적이 없을 터였지만, 그의 충실한 헌신 덕택에 중요한 신하로 여겨져 명단에 포함되었다
- **to keep them quiet** 그들의 불만을 잠재우기 위해
- **feat** [fiːt] 명 위업, 공적
- **fortunate** [fɔ́ːrtʃənit] 형 운이 좋아
- **mediocrity** [mìːdiákrəti/-ɔ́k-] 명 평범, 평범한 사람
- **glamour** [glǽmər] 명 매력, 매혹, 마법
- **stalking-horse** 명 (사냥용) 은신마(隱身馬), 구실, 위장
  - Lefèbvre, the republican of republicans, now under the glamour of Napoleon's power, was placed on the list as a **stalking-horse** of the extreme members of his party.
  이제는 나폴레옹의 능력에 홀려 있었던 공화주의자들 중의 공화주의자 르페브르는 극단적인 공화주의자들을 달래기 위한 위장용으로 명단에 올라가 있었다.
- **be branded as** ~로 낙인찍히다
- **Carnot, the organiser of victory, was a voluntary exile**
  승리를 만드는 자, 카르노는 자발적으로 망명 중이었다
- **staunch** [stɔːntʃ, staːntʃ] 형 철두철미한, 완고한
- **blade** [bleid] 명 기세 있는 사내
- **were all more or less in disgrace** 대부분 눈 밖에 나 있었다
- **death and the necessity of rewarding merit**
  (원수들의) 죽음과 공적을 치하할 필요성
- **while the Spanish War brought it to Suchet, and the Russian campaign to St. Cyr**
  반면 스페인 전쟁에서는 쉬셰에게, 러시아 원정에서는 생시르에게 수여되었다
- **truncheon** [trʌ́ntʃən] 명 지휘봉
- **caused by the refusal of many of the Marshals** 많은 원수들이 사퇴했기 때문에

the refusal of many of the Marshals to cast off their allegiance to the Bourbons.

It was a popular saying in the Napoleonic army that every private soldier carried in his knapsack a Marshal's bâton, and the early history of many of these Marshals bears out this saying. But while the Revolution carried away all the barriers and opened the highest ranks to talent, be it never so humble in its origin, the history of the Marshals proves that heaven-born soldiers are scarce, and that the art of war, save in the case of one out of a million, can only be acquired by years of patient work in a subordinate position. Of the generals of the revolutionary armies only four, Moreau, Mortier, Suchet, and Brune, had no previous military training, and of these four, Moreau and Suchet alone had claim to greatness. The rough unlettered generals of the early years of the war soon proved that they could never rise above the science of the drill-sergeant. Once discipline and organisation were restored there was no room for a general like the gallant Macard, who, when about to charge, used to call out, "Look here, I am going to dress like a beast," and thereon divest himself of everything save his leather breeches and boots, and then, like some great hairy baboon, with strange oaths and yells lead his horsemen against the enemy. A higher type was required

- **cast off** ~을 던져버리다
  - to **cast off** their allegiance to the Bourbons 부르봉가에 충성을 바치기 위해
- **knapsack** 몡 배낭
  - every private soldier carried in his **knapsack** a Marshal's bâton
    모든 병사들이 원수의 지휘봉을 배낭에 싣고 있다(누구나 원수가 될 수 있다는 뜻)
- **bear out** 옳음이 입증되다, 사실임을 증명하다
  - the early history of many of these Marshals **bears out** this saying
    초기 임명된 많은 원수들의 경우에는 그들의 업적을 통해 이 말이 사실임이 입증되었다
- **carry away** 휩쓸어 가다
  - while the Revolution **carried away** all the barriers and opened the highest ranks to talent
    혁명이 모든 장벽을 휩쓸어 가버리고 재능에 능력에 따라 높은 계급으로 승진할 수 있는 길이 열렸는데도
- **be it never so humble in its origin** 그 출신이 미천한 사람은 하나도 없었다
- **heaven-born** 몡 천부적으로 재능을 타고난
  - **heaven-born** soldiers are scarce 천부적으로 재능을 타고난 군인은 드물었다
- **only four, Moreau, Mortier, Suchet, and Brune, had no previous military training**
  이전에 군사적 훈련을 받지 않은 사람은 모로, 모르티에, 쉬세, 브륀 4명밖에 없었다
- **Moreau and Suchet alone had claim to greatness**
  위대하다고 말할 수 있는 사람은 모로와 쉬세밖에 없었다
- **rough unlettered generals** 거칠고 무식한 장군들
- **science of the drill-sergeant** 훈련받은 부사관들의 기량
- **Once discipline and organisation were restored** 일단 규율과 조직이 회복되자
- **gallant** [gǽlənt] 몡 용감한
  - there was no room for a general like the **gallant** Macard
    용맹한 마카르 같은 장군들에게는 기회가 없었다
- **when about to charge** 돌격할 때
- **Look here, I am going to dress like a beast,** 잘 봐, 나는 야수처럼 입겠다
- **divest onself of** ~을 벗어버리다
- **breeches** [brítʃiz] 몡 (승마용) 반바지
  - save his leather **breeches** and boots 가죽으로 된 반바지와 부츠만 남기고

나폴레옹의 원수들 **19**

than this Macard, who could not understand that because an officer could sketch mountains he could not necessarily measure a man for a pair of boots.

'General Macard', 1895. Artist: E Chaperon

※ **마카르 장군:** 전장에서 용맹을 과시하기 위해 바지와 부츠를 제외하고는 모두 벗어버리고 싸웠다. 화려한 복장을 즐겨 입었던 기병사령관 뮈라와 대조된다.

- **baboon** [bæbúːn/bə-] 명 비비, 개코원숭이
- **oath** [ouθ] 명 저주, 욕설
  - with strange **oaths** and yells 괴이한 저주와 함께 괴성을 지르며
- **A higher type was required than this Macard**
  이 마카르보다는 더 높은 수준이 요구되었다
- **who could not understand that because an officer could sketch mountains he could not necessarily measure a man for a pair of boots**
  장교라면 산세(山勢)를 스케치할 수 있어야 하는 것이지, 부츠 한 켤레 신고 용맹을 과시할 필요는 없다는 사실을 이해하지 못하는

Of the twenty-six Marshals, nine had held commissions ranging from lieutenant-general to lieutenant in the old royal army, one was a Polish Prince, an ex-Austrian officer, while one had passed the artillery college but had refused to accept a commission; eleven had commenced life as privates in the old service, and of these, nine had risen to the rank of sergeant; and four had had no previous military training. It must also be remembered that the standard of the non-commissioned rank in the royal army just before the Revolution was extremely high. The reforms of St. Germain and the popularity of the American War had enticed into the ranks a high class of recruits, with the result that the authorities were able to impose tests, and no private could rise to the rank of corporal, or from corporal to sergeant, without passing an examination. Further, since the officers of the ancient régime left the entire organisation, discipline, and control in the hands of the non-commissioned officers, and seldom, if ever, visited their companies either in barracks or on the parade ground, the non-commissioned officers, in everything save actual title, were really extremely well-trained officers. It was this class which really saved France when the old officers emigrated and the incapable politicians in Paris did their best to ruin the army. Hence it was that, without prejudice to the service, a sergeant might one day be found quietly obeying the orders of his com-

- **commission** [kəmíʃən] 명 장교직
- nine had held commissions ranging from lieutenant-general to lieutenant in the old royal army
  9명은 옛 왕실 군대에서 중장에서 중위까지 다양하게 복무했다
- one had passed the artillery college but had refused to accept a commission
  한 명은 포병 학교를 졸업했지만 임관을 거부했다
- **commence** [kəméns] 동 시작하다, 개시하다
  - eleven had **commenced** life as privates in the old service
    11명은 옛 군대에서 사병으로 삶을 시작했었다
- of these nine had risen to the rank of sergeant
  이들 중 9명은 병장까지 승진했다(영·미에서는 병장부터 부사관으로 봄)
- non-commissioned rank 부사관
- reforms of St. Germain 생제르맹 백작(루이 16세의 군사장관)의 개혁
- **entice** [entáis] 동 유혹하다, 부추기다
  - **enticed** into the ranks a high class of recruits
    부사관에 상류층 출신의 신병들이 지원하도록 부추겼다
- no private could rise to the rank of corporal, or from corporal to sergeant, without passing an examination
  시험을 통과하지 않고서는 일병에서 상병으로, 상병으로 병장으로 승진할 수 없었다
- left the entire organisation, discipline, and control in the hands of the non-commissioned officers
  편제와 규율, 통제 그 모든 것을 부사관에게 일임했다
- and seldom, if ever, visited their companies either in barracks or on the parade ground
  그리고 병영이든 연병장에서든 그들의 부대를 거의 방문하지 않았다
- **emigrate** [émɘgrèit] 동 타국으로 이주하다
- the incapable politicians in Paris did their best to ruin the army
  파리의 무능한 정치가들이 군대를 엉망으로 만드는 데 혈연이 되어 있었다
- without prejudice to service 복무에 대한 편견 없이

pany officer, and the next day with the rank of lieutenant-colonel commanding his battalion.

The art of war can only be truly learned in the field, and the officers of the French army had such an experience as had never fallen to the lot of any other nation since the days of the Thirty Years' War. With continuous fighting winter and summer, on every frontier, military knowledge was easily gained by those who had the ability to acquire it, and the young generals of brigade, with but three years' service in commissioned rank, had gone through experiences which seldom fall to the lot of officers with thirty years' service. The cycle of war seemed unending. From the day on which, in 1792, France hurled her declaration of war on Austria, till the surrender of Paris, in 1814, with the exception of the year of peace gained at Amiens, war was continuous. It began with a light-hearted invasion of France by Austria and Prussia in September, 1792, which ended in the cannonade of Valmy, when Dumouriez and Kellermann, with the remnant of the old royal army, showed such a bold front that the Allies, who had never expected to fight, lost heart and ran home. The Austro-Prussian invasion sealed the King's death-warrant, and France, in the hands of republican enthusiasts, went forth with a rabble of old soldiers and volunteers to preach the doctrine of the Equal-

- The art of war can only be truly learned in the field
  진정한 전술은 전장에서만 배울 수 있다
- such an experience as had never fallen to the lot of any other nation since the days of the Thirty Years' War
  30년 전쟁 이후로 다른 나라들이 결코 얻을 수 없었던 그런 경험들
- military knowledge was easily gained by those who had the ability to acquire it
  습득할 수 있는 능력이 있는 자라면 쉽게 군사적 지식을 쌓을 수 있었다
- the young generals of brigade, with but three years' service in commissioned rank
  고작 3년간 장교로 복무하는 젊은 여단장들도
- **go through** (고난을) 경험하다, 견디어 내다
  - had **gone through** experiences which seldom fall to the lot of officers with thirty years' service
    다른 많은 장교들이 30년이 걸려서도 얻기 어려운 경험을 쌓았다
- **hurl** [həːrl] 통 집어 던지다
  - France **hurled** her declaration of war on Austria
    프랑스는 오스트리아에게 전쟁을 선포했다
- **light-hearted** 형 낙천적인, 쾌활한, 걱정 없는
  - a **light-hearted** invasion of France by Austria and Prussia
    오스트리아와 프로이센의 낙관적인 프랑스 침공
- **cannonade** [kænənéid] 명 포격, 포성
  - **cannonade** of Valmy 발미의 포성(발미전투에서의 승리)
- **showed a bold front** 대담한 모습을 보였다
- **lost heart and ran home** 사기를 잃고 본국으로 도망쳤다
- **seal** [síːl] 통 날인하다, 도장을 찍다
- **death-warrant** 명 사형 집행장
  - The Austro-Prussian invasion sealed the King's **death-warrant**
    오스트리아-프로이센 연합군의 침공은 왕(루이 16세)을 처형하라는 사형 집행장에 날인하는 계기가 되었다
- **rabble** [rǽbəl] 명 폭도, 어중이떠중이, 하층민

ity of Man and the Brotherhood of Nations. But the sovereigns of Europe determined to fight for their crowns, and the licence of the French soldiers and the selfishness of these prophets of the new doctrine of Equality soon disgusted the people of the Rhine valley; so the revolutionary mob armies were driven into France, and for two years she was busy on every frontier striving to drive the enemy from her soil. It was during these years that the new French army arose. The volunteers were brigaded with the old regular battalions, the ranks were kept full by calling out all fit to bear arms, and the incompetent and unfortunate were weeded out by the guillotine. By 1795 France had freed her own soil and had forged a weapon whereby she could retaliate on the Powers who had attempted to annex her territory in the hour of her degradation. The Rhine now became her eastern frontier. But Austria, whose Archduke was Emperor of the Holy Roman Empire, would not give up the provinces seized from her; so from 1795 to 1797, on the headwaters of the Danube and in Italy, the representative of the Feudal Ages fought the new democracy. It was the appearance of the great military talent of Bonaparte which decided the day. On the Danube the Austrians had found that under the excellent leading of the Archduke Charles they were fit to defeat the best French troops under capable generals like Jourdan and Moreau. But the military genius of Bonaparte

- volunteers to preach the doctrine of the Equality of Man and the Brotherhood of Nations
  평등과 박애의 이념을 설교하는 의용병들
- licence [láisəns] 명 멋대로 함, 방자함
- disgusted the people of the Rhine valley
  라인 계곡의 국민들(오스트리아인과 프로이센인)을 혐오스럽게 했다
- the revolutionary mob armies were driven into France
  혁명을 일으킨 폭도들의 군대는 프랑스 내로 쫓겨나게 되었다
- strive [straiv] 동 노력하다, 애쓰다
- to drive the enemy from her soil 프랑스에서 적들을 내쫓기 위해
- brigade [brigéid] 동 여단으로 편성하다
- the ranks were kept full by calling out all fit to bear arms
  싸울 수 있는 사람들은 모두 소집해 병사들은 충분했다
- weed [wi:d] 동 잡초를 뽑다, 제거하다
  - the incompetent and unfortunate were **weeded** out by the guillotine
    무능력하거나 운이 나쁜 자들은 단두대에서 사라져갔다
- retaliate [ritǽlièit] 동 보복하다, 앙갚음하다
- degradation [dègrədéiʃən] 명 하강, 하락
  - the Powers who had attempted to annex her territory in the hour of her **degradation**
    프랑스가 혼란스러운 시기를 틈타 영토를 병합하려고 시도했던 열강들
- The Rhine now became her eastern frontier.
  라인 강은 이제 프랑스의 동쪽 경계가 되었다(영토를 다시 회복함).
- seize [si:z] 동 빼앗다, 강탈하다
  - the provinces **seized** from her 프랑스로부터 빼앗은 지역
- headwaters 명 상류, 수원(水源)
- the representative of the Feudal Ages fought the new democracy.
  봉건시대의 대표(오스트리아)는 새로운 민주주의(프랑스)와 싸웠다.
- It was the appearance of the great military talent of Bonaparte which decided the day. 승리할 수 있었던 것은 보나파르트의 위대한 군사적 재능이 출현했기 때문이었다.
- were fit to defeat ~을 무찌를 것처럼 보였다

overbore all resistance, and when peace came, practically all Italy had been added to the dominion of France. Unfortunately for the peace of Europe, the rulers of France had tasted blood. They found in the captured provinces a means of making war without feeling the effects, for the rich pillage of Italy paid the war expenses. But, grateful as the Directors were to Bonaparte for thus opening to them a means of enriching themselves at the expense of Europe, they rightly saw in him a menace to their own power, and gladly allowed him to depart on the mission to Egypt. From Egypt Bonaparte returned, seized the reins of government, and saved France from the imbecility of her rulers, and, by the battle of Marengo, assured to her all she had lost in his absence. Unfortunately for France the restless ambition of her new ruler was not satisfied with re-establishing the Empire of the West and reviving the glories of Charlemagne, but hankered after a vast oversea dominion, to include America and India. Hence it was that he found in Great Britain an implacable enemy ever stirring up against him European coalitions. To cover his failure to wrest the dominion of the sea from its mistress, Napoleon turned his wrath on Austria, and soon she lay cowed at his feet after the catastrophe at Ulm and the battle of Austerlitz. Austria's fall was due to the lethargy and hesitation of the courts of Berlin and St. Petersburg. But once Austria was disposed of, Prussia and Rus-

- **overbear** 동 압박하다, 눌러 으깨다
  - the military genius of Bonaparte **overbore** all resistance
  보나파르트의 군사적인 천재성은 모든 저항을 제압했다
- **practically** [præktikəli] 부 사실상, ~나 다름없이
  - **practically** all Italy had been added to the dominion of France
  사실상 이탈리아 전역이 프랑스의 지배에 들어갔다
- **taste blood** 피 맛을 알다, 첫 성공에 맛 들다
- **a means of making war** 전쟁을 일으킬 수단
- **without feeling the effects** 효용을 느껴보지도 못하고
- **pillage** [pílidʒ] 명 약탈, 강탈
- **grateful as the Directors were to Bonaparte for thus opening to them a means of enriching themselves at the expense of Europe**
  총재정부는 이렇게 유럽을 희생해서 그들을 부자로 만드는 길을 열어준 보나파르트에게 고마워했다
- **rein** 명 지휘권, 지배권
- **imbecility** [ìmbəsíləti] 명 우둔함, 무능함
  - seized the reins of government, and saved France from the **imbecility** of her rulers
  보나파르트는 돌아와 정권을 탈취하고 프랑스를 무능한 지배자들로부터 구해냈다
- **by the battle of Marengo, assured to her all she had lost in his absence**
  마렝고 전투를 통해 프랑스는 보나파르트가 없는 사이 잃었던 것을 회복할 수 있었다
- **hanker** [hæŋkər] 동 동경하다, 갈망하다
- **implacable** [implǽkəbəl, -pléik-] 형 화해할 수 없는
- **stir up** 일으키다, 선동하다
- **coalition** [kòuəlíʃən] 명 연합, 합동
- **wrest** [rest] 동 억지로 빼앗다
  - To cover his failure to **wrest** the dominion of the sea from its mistress
  해외의 영토를 그 주인(영국)으로부터 빼앗는데 실패한 것을 만회하기 위해
- **lethargy** [léθərdʒi] 명 무기력, 무감각
- **dispose of** 처분하다, 패배시키다
  - But once Austria was **disposed of** 그러나 일단 오스트리아가 패배하자

sia met their punishment for having given her secret or open aid. The storm fell first on Prussia. At one fell swoop on the field of Jena, the famed military monarchy of the great Frederick fell in pieces like a potter's vessel. From Prussia the invincible French legions penetrated into Poland, and after Eylau and Friedland the forces of Prussia and Russia could no longer face the enemy in the field. The Czar, dazzled by Napoleon's greatness, threw over his ally Prussia and at Tilsit made friends with the great conqueror. In June, 1807, it seemed as if Europe lay at Napoleon's feet, but already in Portugal the seeds of his ruin had been sown. The Portuguese monarch, the ally of Great Britain, fled at the mere approach of a single Marshal of the Emperor. The apparent lethargy of the inhabitants of the Iberian Peninsula and the unpopularity of the Spanish Bourbons tempted Napoleon to establish his brother on the throne of Spain. It was a fatal error, for though the Spanish people might despise their King, they were intensely proud of their nationality. For the first time in his experience the Corsican had to meet the forces of a nation and not of a government. The chance defeat of a French army at Baylen was the signal for a general rising throughout the Peninsula, and not only throughout the Peninsula, but for the commencement of a national movement against the French in Austria and Germany. England gladly seized the opportunity of injuring her enemy and

- **Prussia and Russia met their punishment for having given her secret or open aid**
  프로이센과 러시아는 비밀리에 또는 공개적으로 오스트리아를 지원한 대가를 톡톡히 치렀다
- **in pieces** 산산이 부서져서, 산산조각으로
- **like potter's vessel** 도공의 그릇처럼
- **invincible** [invínsəbəl] 형 무적의, 정복할 수 없는
- **after Eylau and Friedland the forces of Prussia and Russia could no longer face the enemy in the field**
  아일라우 전투와 프리틀란트 전투 이후 프로이센과 러시아의 군대는 더 이상 전장에서 적과 대적할 수 없었다
- **dazzle** [dǽzəl] 동 감탄시키다, 압도하다
  - The Czar, **dazzled** by Napoleon's greatness, threw over his ally Prussia and at Tilsit made friends with the great conqueror.
    나폴레옹의 위대함에 감탄한 차르는 프로이센과의 동맹을 내던져버리고, 위대한 정복자와 틸지트에서 화약을 맺었다.
- **but already in Portugal the seeds of his ruin had been sown**
  그러나 이미 포르투갈에서 그의 파멸의 씨앗은 뿌려졌다
- **fled at the mere approach of a single Marshal of the Emperor**
  황제가 보낸 일개 원수의 진격에 달아나버렸다
- **tempt** [tempt] 동 유혹하다, 부추기다
- **It was a fatal error** 그것은 치명적인 실수였다
- **for though the Spanish people might despise their King**
  비록 스페인인들이 그들의 왕을 경멸하기는 했었지만
- **For the first time in his experience the Corsican had to meet the forces of a nation and not of a government.**
  처음으로 그 코르시카인은 정부가 아닌 민족과 대적하는 경험을 겪어야 했다.
- **a general rising throughout the Peninsula** 반도 전역에 걸친 대대적인 봉기
- **a national movement against the French** 프랑스에 대항하는 민족주의 운동
- **gladly** [glǽdli] 부 즐거이, 기꺼이
- **seized the opportunity of injuring her enemy**
  그의 적이 상처입고 있는 기회를 놓치지 않았다

sent aid to the people of Spain. Austria tried another fall with her conqueror, but was defeated at Wagram. Wagram ought to have taught the Emperor that his troops were no longer invincible as of old, but, blind to this lesson, he still attempted to lord it over Europe and treated with contumely his only friend, the Czar. Consequently, in 1812, while still engaged in attempting to conquer Spain, he found himself forced to fight Russia. The result was appalling; out of half a million troops who entered Russia, a bare seventy thousand returned. Prussia and Austria at once made a bid to recover their independence. Napoleon, blinded by rage, refused to listen to reason, and in October, 1813, was defeated by the Allies at Leipzig. Even then he might have saved his throne, but he still refused to listen to the Allies, who in 1814 invaded France, and, after a campaign in which the Emperor showed an almost superhuman ability, at last by sheer weight of numbers they captured Paris. Thereon the French troops refused to fight any longer for the Emperor. Such is a brief outline of what is called the Revolutionary and Napoleonic Wars, the finest school the world has yet seen for an apprenticeship in the trade of arms.

- **Austria tried another fall with her conqueror**
  오스트리아는 한 번 더 정복자를 몰락시키려고 시도했다
- **Wagram ought to have taught the Emperor that this troops were no longer invincible as of old**
  바그람 전투에서 황제는 그의 군대가 더 이상 옛날처럼 무적이 아니라는 것을 배웠어야 했다 (프랑스군도 피해가 많았었다는 뜻)
- **blind to this lesson** 이런 교훈을 무시하고
- **lord it** 마구 뽐내다, 건방을 떨다
- **contumely** [kəntjúːməli, kántu-/kɔ́n-] 명 오만무례
- **appalling** [əpɔ́ːliŋ] 형 섬뜩하게 하는, 질색인
- **bare** [bɛər] 형 겨우 ~한, ~뿐인, 가까스로
  - out of half a million troops who entered Russia, a **bare** seventy thousand returned
  러시아에 진입한 50만 명의 병사 중 겨우 7만 명만 살아 돌아왔다
- **make a bid to** ~하려고 노력하다
- **refused to listen to reason** 이성적인 판단을 거부했다
- **even then** 그렇다 해도
- **might have** ~했을지도 모를 텐데
  - Even then he **might have** saved his throne
  그렇다 해도 왕관은 보전했을지도 몰랐다
- **he still refused to listen to the Allies**
  그는 여전히 연합국들의 말을 듣기를 거부했다
- **by sheer weight of numbers** 순전히 수적 우세로
- **the finest school the world has yet seen for an apprenticeship in the trade of arms**
  무기거래상의 견습생에게는 유례없이 훌륭한 학교(온갖 무기가 총동원되었다는 뜻)

1. LOUIS ALEXANDRE BERTHIER

*MARSHAL, PRINCE OF WAGRAM,
SOVEREIGN PRINCE OF NEUCHÂTEL AND VALANGIN*

To be content ever to play an inferior part, to see all honour and renown fall to the share of another, yet loyally to efface self and work for the glory of a friend, denotes a sterling character and an inflexibility of purpose with which few can claim to be endowed. Nobody doubts that, if it had not been for Napoleon, Berthier, good business man as he was, could never have risen to the fame he attained; still it is often forgotten that without this admirable servant it is more than doubtful if the great Emperor could have achieved all his most splendid success. Berthier, controlled by a master mind, was an instrument beyond price. Versed in the management of an army almost from his cradle, he had the gift of drafting orders so clear, so lucid, that no one could possibly mistake their meaning. His memory was prodigious, and his physical endurance such that he appeared never to require rest. But above all he alone seemed to be able to divine the thoughts

- **content to do** 기꺼이 ~하려 하는
- **inferior** [infíəriər] 형 낮은
- **play a part(=act a part)** 역할을 맡다
  - To be content ever to **play an inferior part**
    보잘 것 없는 역할을 수행하는 것에 항상 만족하고
- **renown** [rináun] 명 명성
- **fall to the share of another** 다른 사람의 몫이 되다
- **efface self** 눈에 띄지 않게 하다, 자신을 지우다
- **denote** [dinóut] 동 나타내다, 보여주다
- **sterling** [stə́ːrliŋ] 형 훌륭한
- **inflexibility** [inflèksəbíləti] 명 강직함, 단호함
- **purpose** [pə́ːrpəs] 명 결단력
- **with which few can claim to be endowed**
  아무나 타고났다고 쉽게 말할 수 없는
- **if it had not been for Napoleon, Berthier, good business man as he was, could never have risen to the fame he attained**
  나폴레옹이 아니었더라면, 베르티에가 제 아무리 수완이 있었다고 하더라도 그런 명성을 얻을 수 없었을 것이다
- **attain** [ətéin] 동 이루다, 획득하다, 얻다
- **without this admirable servant** 이 훌륭한 심복이 없었더라면
- **it is more than doubtful** 더더욱 모르는 일이다
- **splendid** [spléndid] 형 훌륭한, 멋진
- **a master mind** 걸출한 인물, 위인
- **beyond price** 값을 따질 수 없는, 매우 귀중한
- **versed in** ~에 정통한, 조예가 깊은
- **gift** [gift] 명 재능, 재주
- **draft** [dræft, drɑːft] 형 (원고를) 작성하다, 입안하다
- **lucid** [lúːsid] 형 명쾌한, 명료한, 알기 쉬운
- **prodigious** [prədídʒəs] 형 엄청난, 굉장한
- **he appeared never to require rest** 피곤한 기색을 보이지 않았다
- **divine** [diváin] 동 (남의 마음속을) 간파하다

of his great master before they were spoken, and this wonderful intuition taught him how, from a few disjointed utterances, to unravel Napoleon's most daring conceptions and work out the details in ordered perfection. Napoleon called his faithful Achates a gosling whom he had transformed into an eagle, but history proclaims that long before the name of Bonaparte was known beyond the gate of the military academy at Brienne, Berthier had established a record as a staff officer of the highest promise; while, before the young Corsican first met him in Italy, the future major-general of the Grand Army had evolved that perfect system of organisation which enabled the conqueror of Italy to control every movement and vibration in the army, to be informed of events as soon as they happened, and to be absolutely sure of the despatch and performance of his orders.

Alexandre Berthier had seen twenty-three years' service in the old royal army before the Revolution broke out in 1789. Born on November 20, 1753, at the age of thirteen he received his commission in the engineers owing to his father's services in preparing a map of royal hunting forests. But the boy soon forsook his father's old regiment, for he knew well that the highest commands in the army seldom if ever fell to the scientific corps. When in 1780 the French Government decided to send

- **intuition** [ɪntjuíʃən] 몡 직관력
- **disjointed** [dɪsˈdʒɔɪntɪd] 휑 일관성이 없는, 연결이 되지 않는
- **utterance** [ˈʌtərəns] 몡 표현, 입 밖에 냄
- **unravel** [ʌnˈrævl] 동 (이해하기 어려운 것을) 풀어내다
- **daring** [ˈderɪŋ] 휑 대담한
- **work out** 계산하다, 해결하다, 계획해내다
- **Achates** [əkéitiːz] 몡 (그리스·로마 신화의) 아카테스, 신실한 친구
- **gosling** [ˈgɑːzlɪŋ] 몡 거위새끼
- **military academy at Brienne**
  브리엔 군사학교(나폴레옹이 어린 시절을 보낸 군사전문학교)
  - long before the name of Bonaparte was known beyond the gate of the **military academy at Brienne**
  나폴레옹이 브리엔 군사학교의 문 너머로 이름이 알려지기 훨씬 전부터
- **of the highest promise** 매우 전도유망한
- **Corsican** [kɔ́ːrsikən] 몡 코르시카인
- **organisation(=organization)** 몡 조직, 체계성
- **every movement and vibration in the army** 군대 내의 모든 움직임
- **to be informed of events** 사건이 전달될 수 있도록
- **commission** [kəˈmɪʃn] 몡 (군대의) 장교직
- **prepare** [prɪˈper] 동 준비하다, 준비시키다
- **forsake** [fərséik] 동 내버리다, 포기하다
- **regiment** [ˈredʒɪmənt] 몡 (군대의) 연대
- **the highest commands** 최고위직 사령관들
- **seldom if ever** 비록 있다고 해도 극히 드문
- **scientific corps** 공병대
  - for he knew well that the highest commands in the army seldom if ever fell to the **scientific corps**
  최고위직 사령관들 중에서 공병대 출신은 거의 없다는 것을 알았기 때문에

out an expeditionary corps to assist the revolted colonies in their struggle with Great Britain, Berthier, after serving in the infantry and cavalry, was employed as a staff captain with the army of Normandy. Eager to see active service, he at once applied to be attached to the expedition, and offered, if there was no room for an extra captain, to resign his rank and serve as sub-lieutenant. Thanks to powerful family influence and to his record of service his desire was gratified, and in January, 1781, he found himself with the French troops in America employed on the staff of General Count de Rochambeau. Returning from America in 1783 with a well-earned reputation for bravery and ability, Captain Berthier was one of the officers sent to Prussia under the Marquis de Custine to study the military organisation of the great Frederick. Continuously employed on the staff, he had the advantage of serving as brigade major at the great camp of instruction held at Saint Omer in 1788, and in that year received as a reward for his services the cross of Saint Louis. The year 1789 saw him gazetted lieutenant-colonel, and chief of the staff to Baron de Besenval, commanding the troops round Paris.

When, after the capture of the Bastille, Lafayette undertook the work of organising the National Guard, he at once bethought him of his old comrade of American days, and appointed Berthier assistant quartermaster-general. Berthier found the post well suited

- **expeditionary** [èkspədíʃənèri] 형 원정의, 탐험의
  - decided to send out an **expeditionary** corps to assist the revolted colonies in their struggle with Great Britain
  대영제국에 대항해 반란을 일으킨 식민지들을 지원하기 위해 원정군을 보내기로 결정했다
- **Eager to see active service** 실전을 경험하고 싶었기 때문에
- **apply to** 신청하다, 지원하다
- **be attached to** ~에 소속하다
- **there is no room for** ~할 여지가 없다, ~할 곳이 없다
  - offered, if **there was no room for** an extra captain, to resign his rank and serve as sub-lieutenant
  만약 대위로 남는 자리가 없다면, 강등해서 소위로 복무하겠다고 제안했다
- **Thanks to powerful family influence and to his record of service**
  집안의 강한 영향력과 그의 근무 성적 때문에
- **gratified** [grǽtəfàid] 형 만족한, 기뻐하는
- **Returning from America in 1783 with a well-earned reputation for bravery and ability** 용맹하고 유능하다는 명성을 얻으며 1783년 아메리카에서 돌아오자
- **military organisation** 군사조직
  - sent to Prussia under the Marquis de Custine to study the **military organisation** of the great Frederick
  위대한 프리드리히 왕의 군사조직을 공부하기 위해 프로이센에 있는 퀴스틴 후작의 휘하로 보내진
- **brigade major** 명 여단 부관
- **the cross of Saint Louis**
  생루이 훈장, 루이 14세가 만든 훈장으로 레지옹 도뇌르 훈장의 전신)
- **be gazetted to** (장교가) ~에 임명되었음이 관보에 발표되다
- **lieutenant-colonel** 명 중령
- **bethink** [biθíŋk] 동 숙고하다, 생각해내다
  - **bethought** him of comrade of American days
  그가 아메리카 독립전쟁 시절의 전우였다는 것을 생각해냈다
- **assistant quartermaster general** 부(副)병참감
- **post** [póust] 명 지위, 직책
  - the **post** well suited to him 그에게 잘 맞는 직책

to him; inspired by the liberal ideas which he had gained in America, he threw himself heart and soul into the work. Soon his talent as an organiser became widely recognised; many prominent officers applied to have him attached to their command, and, after holding several staff appointments, he was entrusted in 1791 with the organisation and instruction of the thirty battalions of volunteers cantonned between the Somme and Meuse. When war broke out in 1792 he was despatched as major-general and chief of the staff to his old friend Rochambeau, and when the Count resigned his command Berthier was specially retained by Rochambeau's successor, Luckner. But the Revolution, while giving him his chance, nearly brought about his fall. His intimate connection with the nobles of the old royal army, his courage in protecting the King's aunts, and his family connections caused him to become "suspect." It was in vain that the leaders at the front complained of the absolute disorder in their forces, of the necessity of more trained staff officers and of their desire for the services of the brilliant soldier who had gained his experience in war time in America and in peace time in Prussia. In vain Custine wrote to the Minister of War, "In the name of the Republic send Berthier to me to help me in my difficulties," in vain the Commissioners with the army reported that "Berthier has gained the esteem and confidence of all good patriots." Vain also was

- **heart and soul** 열과 성을 다해
- **be widely recognised** 널리 인정받다
- **prominent** [prámənənt/prɔ́m-] 형 중요한, 유명한
- **hold an appointment** 직책을 맡다
    - after **holding** several staff **appointments** 여러 참모직을 두루 섭렵한 뒤
- **battalion** [bətǽljən] 명 대대(大隊)
- **canton** [kæntán, -tóun/kəntúːn, kæn-] 동 (군대가) 주둔하다
- **major-general** 명 소장
- **retain** [ritéin] 동 보유하다, 유지하다
    - Berthier was specially **retained** by Rochambeau's successor, Luckner.
    로샹보의 후임인 뤼크네는 특별히 베르티에가 그 직위를 유지할 수 있도록 해 주었다.
- **while giving him his chance** 그에게 기회를 준 반면에
- **bring about** 야기하다, 초래하다
    - nearly **brought about** his fall 거의 그를 파멸시킬 뻔했다
- **intimate connection** 친밀한 관계
    - His **intimate connection** with the nobles of the old royal army, his courage in protecting the King's aunts
    옛 왕실군대 귀족들과의 친밀한 관계, 왕의 숙모들을 보호하려던 용기
- **caused him to become "suspect,"** '의심스러운 자'로 만들었다
- **the leaders at the front complained of the absolute disorder in their forces**
전방에 있는 지휘관들이 군 내의 심각한 무질서를 불평했다
- **more trained staff officers** 더 숙련된 참모들
- **In the name of the Republic send Berthier to me to help me in my difficulties**
공화국의 이름으로 베르티에를 나에게 보내 나의 어려움을 도울 수 있도록 해주시오
- **esteem** [istíːm] 명 존경

the valour and ability he showed in the campaign against the Royalists in La Vendée. Bouchotte, the incapable, the friend of the brutish, blockheaded Hébert, the insulter of the Queen, the destroyer of the army, decreed that his loyalty to the Republic was not sincere, and by a stroke of the pen dismissed him; thus during the whole of the year 1793 the French army was deprived of the service of an officer who, owing to his powers of organisation, was worth fifty thousand of the butcher generals.

In 1795, with the fall of the Jacobins, Berthier was restored to his rank and sent as chief of the staff to Kellermann, commanding the Army of the Alps, and before the end of the year the staff work of Kellermann's army became the pattern for all the armies of the Republic. When in March, 1796, Bonaparte was appointed commander of the Army of Italy, he at once requisitioned Berthier as the chief of the staff, and from that day till April, 1814, Berthier seldom if ever left the future Emperor's side, serving him with a patience and cheerfulness which neither ill-will nor neglect seemed to disturb. Though over forty-two years of age and sixteen years older than his new chief, the chief of the staff was still in the prime of his manhood. Short, thick-set and athletic, his frame proclaimed his immense physical strength, while his strong alert face under a mass of thick curly hair foretold at a

- Vain also was the valour and ability he showed

  그가 보여준 용맹과 능력도 역시 소용이 없었다
- **campaign** [kæmpéin] 명 군사작전
- **brutish** [brúːtiʃ] 형 잔인한, 야만적인
- **decree** [dikríː] 동 판결하다, 결정하다
- **sincere** [sinsíər] 형 진심어린, 진정한
- **by a stroke of the pen** 펜 놀림 한 번으로
- with the fall of the Jacobins, Berthier was restored to his rank and sent as chief of the staff to Kellermann

  자코뱅당이 몰락하자 베르티에는 직위를 회복하고 켈레르망 장군의 수석참모로 임명되었다
- **pattern** [pǽtərn] 명 모범, 본보기, 귀감
  - became the **pattern** for all the armies of the Republic

  공화국 모든 군대의 귀감이 되었다
- at once requisitioned Berthier as the chief of the staff

  베르티에를 즉시 수석참모로 임명했다
- Berthier seldom if ever left the future Emperor's side

  베르티에는 미래의 황제 곁을 거의 떠나지 않았다
- **disturb** [distə́ːrb] 동 방해하다, 흩뜨리다
- which neither ill-will nor neglect seemed to disturb

  악감정이나 무시에도 전혀 흔들림 없어 보였다
- **prime** [praim] 명 전성기, 한창때
- **thick-set** 형 몸집이 떡 벌어진
- **athletic** [æθlétik] 명 (몸이) 탄탄한
- **frame** [freim] 명 체격
- **proclaim** [proukléim, prə-] 동 증명하다, 분명히 나타내다
- **immense** [iméns] 형 엄청난, 어마어마한
- his strong alert face under a mass of thick curly hair foretold at a glance his mental capacity

  풍성한 곱슬머리에 강하고 빈틈없어 보이는 얼굴은 한눈에도 그가 얼마나 대단한 정신력을 가지고 있는지 말해주었다

glance his mental capacity.

A keen sportsman, in peace he spent all his leisure in the chase. Hard exercise and feats of physical endurance were his delight. Fatigue he never knew, and on one occasion he was said to have spent thirteen days and nights in the saddle. To strangers and officials he was silent and stern, but his aloofness of manner hid a warm heart and a natural sincerity, and many a poor officer or returned émigré received secret help from his purse. Though naturally of a strong character, his affection and respect for his great commander became the dominating note in his career; in fact, it might almost be said that, in later years, his personality became merged to such an extent in that of Napoleon that he was unable to see the actions of the Emperor in their proper perspective. From their first meeting Bonaparte correctly guessed the impression he had made on his new staff officer, and aimed at increasing his influence over him. Meanwhile he was delighted with him, he wrote to the Directory, "Berthier has talents, activity, courage, character—all in his favour." Berthier on his side was well satisfied; as he said to a friend who asked him how he could serve a man with such a temper, "Remember that one day it will be a fine thing to be second to Bonaparte." So the two worked admirably together.

- **in peace he spent all his leisure in the chase**
  평화로울 때에는 사냥하는 것으로 여가를 모두 보냈다
- **delight** [diláit] 몡 기쁨, 즐거움
- **Fatigue he never knew** 그는 지칠 줄 몰랐고
- **in the saddle** 말안장 위에서
- **official** [əfíʃəl] 몡 관리, 공무원
- **stern** [stəːrn] 휑 근엄한, 엄격한
- **aloofness** [əlúːfnis] 몡 무관심, 냉담
- **sincerity** [sinsérəti] 몡 성실, 정직
  - To strangers and officials he was silent and stern, but his aloofness of manner hid a warm heart and a natural **sincerity**
  낯선 사람이나 관리에게 그는 과묵하고 근엄한 사람이었지만, 그의 무관심한 태도 뒤에는 따뜻한 마음과 성실함을 감추고 있었다
- **returned émigré** 다시 돌아온 (혁명기의) 망명 귀족
- **dominating** 휑 지배적인, 우세한
- **merge** [məːrdʒ] 동 (서로 구분이 되지 않게) 어우러지다
- **to such an extent ~that** ~할 정도까지 되다
- **perspective** [pəːrspéktiv] 몡 관점, 시각, (사물의) 균형
  - he was unable to see the actions of the Emperor in their proper **perspective**
  그는 황제의 행동을 객관적인 시각에서 바라볼 수가 없었다
- **From their first meeting Bonaparte correctly guessed the impression he had made on his new staff officer**
  첫 만남에서부터 보나파르트는 그가 새로 참모로 삼은 자의 인상을 정확하게 예측했다
- **aim at** 겨냥하다, 작정하다, 목표로 삼다
  - **aimed** at increasing his influence over him
  그를 자기의 사람으로 만들기로 마음먹었다

다음 장에 해설 계속

나폴레옹의 원수들 **45**

ALEXANDRE BERTHIER, PRINCE OF WAGRAM
FROM AN ENGRAVING AFTER THE PAINTING BY PAJOU FILS

- **Directory** [diréktəri, dai-] 명 (프랑스 혁명기의) 총재정부
- **on his side** 그의 편에 선 것에 대해서
- **how he could serve a man with such a temper**
  그렇게 화를 잘 내는 사람을 어떻게 섬길 수 있느냐
- **be second to** ~에 버금가다
  - Remember that one day it will be a fine thing to **be second to** Bonaparte.
    언젠가는 보나파르트의 2인자가 된다는 것이 얼마나 좋은 일인지 기억하게 될 것이다.
- **admirably** 부 감탄할 만하게, 훌륭히
- **work together** 함께 일하다

Bonaparte kept in his own hands the movement of troops, the direction of skirmishes and battles, commissariat, discipline, and all communications from the Government. Berthier had a free hand in the organisation and maintenance of the general staff, the headquarter staff, and the transmission of orders, subject to inspection by Bonaparte; he also had to throw into written form all verbal orders, and he alone was responsible for their promulgation and execution. It was his ability to work out in detail and to reduce into clear, lucid orders the slightest hint of his commander which, as Napoleon said later, "was the great merit of Berthier, and was of inestimable importance to me. No other could possibly have replaced him." Thanks to Berthier's admirable system, Bonaparte was kept in touch with every part of his command. One of the first principles laid down in the staff regulations was, "That it was vital to the good of the service that the correspondence of the army should be exceedingly swift and regular, that nothing should be neglected which might contribute to this end." To ensure regularity of communication, divisional commanders and officers detached in command of small columns were ordered to report at least twice a day to headquarters. With each division, in addition to the divisional staff, there were officers detached from the headquarters staff. All important despatches had to be sent in duplicate; in times of great danger commanding

- **keep in his own hand** 직접 관여하다
- **skirmish** [skə́ːrmiʃ] 몡 소규모 접전
- **commissariat** [kàməsɛ́əriət/kɔ̀m-] 몡 병참부, 식량보급
- **discipline** [dísəplin] 몡 규율
- **have a free hand** 자유롭게 행동할 수 있다
- **transmission** [trænsmíʃən, trænz-] 몡 전파, 전달
- **subject to** ~을 조건으로
- **inspection** [inspékʃən] 몡 점검
- **throw into written form all verbal orders** 구두 명령을 문서로 작성하다
- **promulgation** [prɑ̀məlgéiʃən, pròu-] 몡 공포, 선포
- **It was his ability to work out in detail and to reduce into clear, lucid orders the slightest hint of his commander**
  사령관이 주는 약간의 암시를 상세하게 이해해서 간단명료한 명령으로 요약하는 것이 그의 능력이었다
- **inestimable** [inéstəməbl] 혱 헤아릴 수 없이 큰
- **No other could possibly have replaced him**
  그 어느 누구도 그를 대신할 수 없었을 것이다
- **keep in touch with** ~과 연락을 취하다
- **regulation** [règjəléiʃən] 몡 (주로 복수 형태) 규정
- **contribute** [kəntríbjuːt] 혱 기여하다
  - nothing should be neglected which might **contribute** to this end
    이 목적을 달성하기 위해서는 어느 것도 소홀히 해서는 안 된다
- **divisional commander** 사단장
- **in command of** ~을 지휘하여, ~을 마음대로 하여
- **detach** [ditǽtʃ] 동 (군인 등을) 파견하다
- **headquarters** [hédkwɔ̀ːrtərz] 몡 본부, 사령부
- **With each division, in addition to the divisional staff**
  각 사단에는 사단참모 이외에도
- **in duplicate** 2통으로, 사본을 만들어서
- **despatch(=dispatch)** [dispǽtʃ] 몡 파견, 공문

officers had to send as many as eight different orderly officers each with a copy of despatches.

But it was not only as an organiser and transmitter of orders that Berthier proved his usefulness to his chief. At Lodi he showed his personal courage and bravery among the band of heroes who forced the bridge, and Bonaparte paid him a fine tribute when he wrote in his despatches, "If I were bound to mention all the soldiers who distinguished themselves on that wonderful day, I should be obliged to mention all the carabiniers and grenadiers of the advance guard, and nearly all the officers of the staff; but I must not forget the courageous Berthier, who on that day played the part of gunner, trooper, and grenadier." At Rivoli, in addition to his staff duties, Berthier commanded the centre of the army, and fought with a stubbornness beyond all praise. By the end of the campaign of 1796 he had proved that he was as great a chief of the staff as Bonaparte was a great commander. Doubtless it is true that before the commencement of a campaign an army possesses in itself the causes of its future victory or defeat, and the Army of Italy, with its masses of enthusiastic veterans and the directing genius of Bonaparte, was bound to defeat the Austrians with their listless men and incompetent old generals; but, without the zeal, activity, and devotion which Berthier transfused

- **among the band of heroes** 영웅들 무리 중에서
- **be bound to** ~할 의무가 있다, 반드시 ~하다
- **distinguish oneself** 뛰어나다, 공을 세우다
  - If I were bound to mention all the soldiers who **distinguished themselves** on that wonderful day
  그 멋진 날 뛰어난 공을 세운 병사들을 모두 거론해야 한다면
- **carabinier(=carabineer)** [kæ̀rəbiníər] 명 용기병(龍騎兵)
- **grenadier** [grènədíər] 명 척탄병(擲彈兵)
- **advance guard** 전위대, 선봉대
- **stubbornness** [stʌ́bərnis] 명 완고함, 완강함
- **beyond all praise** 이루 다 칭찬할 수 없는
  - in addition to his staff duties, Berthier commanded the centre of the army, and fought with a stubbornness **beyond all praise**
  베르티에는 참모 직책에 더해서 중앙군을 이끌고 이루 말할 수 없을 정도로 강력하게 싸웠다
- **commencement** [kəménsmənt] 명 시작, 개시
- **an army possesses in itself the causes of its future victory or defeat**
  군대 그 자체에 이미 장래에 승리할 것인지 패배할 것인지의 원인이 있다
- **masses of** (수·양이) 많은
- **enthusiastic** [enθùːziǽstik] 형 열광적인, 열정적인
  - with its masses of **enthusiastic** veterans and the directing genius of Bonaparte
  수많은 열정적이고 노련한 군인들과 보나파르트의 천재적인 지휘능력으로
- **listless** [listləs] 형 무기력한, 열의가 없는
- **incompetent** [inkɑ́mpətənt/-kɔ́m-] 형 무능한, 쓸모없는
- **was bound to defeat the Austrians with their listless men and incompetent old generals**
  무기력한 병사와 무능한 늙은 장군들로 이루어진 오스트리아군에게는 승리할 수밖에 없었다
- **devotion** [divóuʃən] 명 헌신, 몰두
- **transfuse** [trænsfjúːz] 동 주입하다, 수혈하다, 불어넣다

through the whole of the general staff, success could not have been so sudden or so complete.

After Leoben the conqueror of Italy employed his trusty friend on numerous diplomatic missions in connection with the annexation of Corfu and the government of the Cisalpine republic. Meanwhile he was in close communication with him in regard to the proposed descent on England and the possible expedition to the East. To Berthier, if to any one, Bonaparte entrusted his secret designs, for he knew that he could do so in safety. Accordingly, in 1798, finding an invasion of England impossible at the moment, he persuaded the Directory to send Berthier to Italy as commander-in-chief, his object being to place him in a position to gather funds for the Egyptian expedition. From Italy Berthier sent his former commander the most minute description of everything of importance, but he found the task difficult and uncongenial, and prayed him "to recall me promptly. I much prefer being your aide-de-camp to being commander-in-chief here." Still he carried out his orders and marched on Rome, to place the eight million francs' worth of diamonds wrung from the Pope to the credit of the army. From Rome he returned with coffers well filled for the Egyptian expedition, but leaving behind him an army half-mutinous for want of pay; his blind devotion to

- **success could not have been so sudden or so complete**
  그렇게 놀랍고 완벽하게 승리할 수 없었을 것이다
- **After Leoben** 레오벤 조약 후
- **annexation** [ænekséiʃən] 명 합병
- **descent** [disént] 명 강하, 엄습
  - the proposed **descent** on England 영국 기습 계획의 제안
- **expedition to the East** 동방원정
- **if to any one** 만약 누구에게 ~한다면
- **entrust A (to) B(= entrust B with A)** A에게 B를 맡기다
  - To Berthier, if to any one, Bonaparte **entrusted his secret designs**
  만약 보나파르트가 누구에게 그의 비밀 계획을 맡긴다면 그것은 베르티에가 될 것이었다
- **commander-in-chief** 총사령관
- **gather fund for the Egyptian expedition** 이집트 원정을 위한 자금을 모으다
- **minute** [mainjúːt, mi-] 형 대단히 상세한
- **description** [diskrípʃən] 명 서술, 묘사
  - the most minute **description** of everything of importance
  중요한 모든 것들에 대한 가장 상세한 설명
- **uncongenial** 형 마음에 들지 않는, 자신에게 안 맞는
  - but he found the task difficult and **uncongenial**
  그러나 그 임무가 어렵고 자신에게 맞지 않다는 것을 알았다
- **aide-de-camp** [éiddəkæmp, -káːŋ] 명 (군대에서의) 부관
- **wring from** ~에게서 억지로 뜯어내다
  - to place the eight million francs' worth of diamonds **wrung from** the Pope to the credit of the army
  교황에게서 뜯어낸 8백만 프랑 어치의 다이아몬드들을 군대의 금고에 넣어두었다
- **coffer** [kɔ́ːfər, káf-] 명 돈궤, 금고
- **mutinous** [mjúːtənəs] 형 반항적인
- **for want of pay** 급여를 제대로 지불하지 않아서
- **blind devotion** 맹목적인 헌신

Bonaparte hid this incongruity from his eyes.

As in Italy in 1795 so in Egypt, Berthier was Bonaparte's right-hand man, methodical, indefatigable, and trustworthy. But even his iron frame could scarcely withstand the strain of three years' continuous active service, the incessant office work day and night, and the trials of an unaccustomed climate. After the battle of the Pyramids he fell sick, and before the Syrian expedition, applied to return to France. Unkind friends hinted that he longed for his mistress, Madame Visconti, but Bonaparte, knowing that it was not this but sheer overstrain which had caused his breakdown in health, gave him the desired leave and made all arrangements for his journey home. However, at the moment of departure Berthier's love for his chief overcame his longing for rest, and, in spite of ill-health, he withdrew his resignation and set out with the army for Syria. As ever, he found plenty of work, for even in the face of the ill-success of the expedition, Bonaparte determined to administer Egypt as if the French occupation was to be for ever permanent; and Berthier, in addition to his ordinary work, was ordered to edit a carefully executed map from the complete survey which was being made of the country.

- **incongruity** [ìnkəngrúːəti, -kəŋ-] 명 부조화, 모순
  - his blind devotion to Bonaparte hid this **incongruity** from his eyes
    보나파르트에 대한 맹목적인 충성 때문에 그는 이런 모순을 볼 수 없었다
- **right-hand man** 오른팔, 중요한 인물
- **methodical** [məθádikəl/miθɔ́d-] 형 체계적인, 꼼꼼한
- **indefatigable** [ìndifǽtigəbəl] 형 지칠 줄 모르는
- **trustworthy** [trʌ́stwəːrði] 형 신뢰할 수 있는
- **even his iron frame could scarcely withstand**
  그의 강인한 체력도 견디기가 쉽지 않았다
- **strain** [strein] 명 부담감, 압박
- **incessant** [insésənt] 형 끊임없는, 쉴 새 없는
- **trial** [tráiəl] 명 시련, 골칫거리
- **unaccustomed** 형 익숙하지 않은
- **long for** 그리워하다, 열망하다
- **mistress** [místris] 명 정부(情婦), 애첩, 애인
- **sheer** [ʃiər] 형 순수한, 순전한
  - it was not this but **sheer** overstrain
    그런 이유가 아니라 순수하게 과로로 인한
- **breakdown in health** 건강이 아주 악화됨
- **make arrangements for** ~을 준비하다
- **at the moment of departure Berthier's love for his chief overcame his longing for rest**
  출발할 시점에 베르티에는 쉬고 싶다는 생각이 간절했지만, 그의 사령관에 대한 애정으로 그것을 극복했다
- **set out** 출발하다, 나서다
- **administer** [ædmínəstər, əd-] 동 관리하다
- **as if the French occupation was to be for ever permanent**
  프랑스의 지배가 영원히 계속될 것처럼(완전한 영토로 편입시켜)

It was to Berthier that Bonaparte first divulged his intention of leaving Egypt and returning to France, and his determination to upset the Directory. Liberal by nature, but essentially a man of method and a disciplinarian, the chief of the staff was quite in accord with his commander's ideas on the regeneration of France, and loyally supported him during the coup d'état of the 18th Brumaire. Thereafter the First Consul appointed his friend Minister of War, a position that gave full scope to his talents. All the administrative services had at once to be reorganised, the frontier fortresses garrisoned and placed in a state of defence, and the army covering the frontiers supplied with food, pay, equipment, and reinforcements, while the formation of the secret Army of Reserve was a task which alone would have occupied all the attention of an ordinary man; in fact, the safety of France hung on this army. Consequently, since, by the constitution, the First Consul was unable himself to take command in the field, in April, 1800, he transferred Berthier from the War Office to the head of this most important force. It is not generally known that the idea of the passage of the Alps by the St. Bernard Pass actually originated with Berthier, and had first been projected by him as early as 1795. So it was at the execution of what was really his own idea that for two months Berthier slaved. At times even his stout heart quailed, as when he wrote to the First Consul,

- **divulge** [divʌldʒ, dai-] 동 (비밀을) 알려주다, 누설하다
- **leaving Egypt and returning to France** 이집트를 떠나 프랑스로 돌아올
  (나폴레옹은 이집트 원정에서 군대를 버리다시피 하고 혼자 돌아왔음)
- **his determination to upset the Directory**
  그의 결정은 총재정부를 화나게 했다
- **essentially** [isénʃəli] 부 근본적으로, 본질적으로
- **a mand of method** 매사에 착실한 사람
- **disciplinarian** [dìsəplənέəriən] 명 엄격한 사람, 규율가
- **quite in accord with his commander's ideas**
  그의 사령관의 생각에 매우 부합하는
- **regeneration** [ridʒènəréiʃən] 명 재건, 부흥
- **coup d'état of the 18th Brumaire** 브뤼메르(안개달) 18일의 쿠데타
  (나폴레옹이 쿠데타를 일으켜 독재체제를 구축한 사건)
- **First Consul** 제1집정관(쿠데타 후 권력을 장악한 나폴레옹의 직위)
- **a position that gave full scope to his talents**
  그의 재능을 모두 발휘할 수 있는 직책
- **Army of Reserve** 예비군
- **while the formation of the secret Army of Reserve was a task which alone would have occupied all the attention of an ordinary man**
  은밀히 예비군을 조직하는 것 하나만으로도 보통 사람들이라면 온 정력을 다 쏟아야 하는 임무이지만
- **constitution** [kɑ̀nstətjúːʃən/kɔ́n-] 명 헌법
- **transfer** [trænsfə́ːr] 동 (권력 등을) 넘겨주다
- **It is not generally known that** ~한 사실은 그렇게 잘 알려져 있지 않다
- **had first been projected by him** 그가 최초로 계획했었다
- **slave** [sleiv] 동 노예처럼 고되게 일하다
- **stout heart** 용기, 강심장
- **quail** [kweil] 명 메추라기, 동 겁을 먹다

"It is my duty to complain of the position of this army on which you have justly spent so much interest, and which is paralysed because it can only rely on its bayonets, on account of the lack of ammunition and means to transport the artillery." Incessant work and toil were at last rewarded; but when the Army of the Reserve debouched on the Austrian lines of communication, the First Consul appeared in person, and, though nominally in command, Berthier once again resumed his position of chief of the staff. Without a murmur he allowed Bonaparte to reap all the glory of Marengo, for he knew that without the First Consul, however excellent his own dispositions were, they would have been lacking in the driving power which alone teaches men how to seize on victory. After Marengo, Berthier was despatched as Ambassador Extraordinary to Madrid, "to exhort Spain by every possible means to declare war on Portugal, the ally of England." The result of this mission was eminently successful; a special treaty was drawn up and Spain sold Louisiana to France. By October the ambassador was once again back in Paris at his old post of Minister of War—a post which he held continuously during peace and war till August, 1807. The position was no light one, for even during the short years of peace it involved the supervision of the expedition to San Domingo, the defence of Italy, the reorganisation of the army, and the re-armament of the artillery,

- **paralyse(ze)** [pǽrəlàiz] 동 마비시키다, 무력화 시키다
  - which is **paralysed** because it can only rely on its bayonets
    의지할 것이 총검밖에 없어 무력화된
- **bayonet** [béiənit, -nèt, bèiənét] 명 총검, 동 총검으로 찌르다
- **ammunition** [æmjuníʃən] 명 탄약
  - on account of the lack of **ammunition** and means to transport the artillery
    탄약이 부족하고 대포를 이동시킬 수단이 없었기 때문에
- **toil** [tɔil] 명 노역, 고역, 힘들게 일함
- **debouch** [dibúːʃ, -báutʃ] 동 (길·군대 등이) 넓은 곳으로 나오다
- **lines of communication** 통신선, 연락선
- **though nominally in command** 비록 명목상으로는 지휘관이었지만
- **without a murmur** 군말 없이, 순순히
- **he allowed Bonaparte to reap all the glory of Marengo**
  마렝고 전투의 영광을 보나파르트가 모두 차지하는 것을 받아들였다
- **disposition** [ˌdɪspəˈzɪʃn] 명 타고난 기질, 역량
- **driving power** 전진력, 추진력
- **exhort** [igzɔ́ːrt] 동 열심히 권하다, 촉구하다
  - to **exhort** Spain by every possible means to declare war on Portugal, the ally of England
    영국과 동맹을 맺고 있는 포르투갈에게 선전포고를 하도록 가능한 모든 수단을 동원해 스페인을 부추기 위해
- **a special treaty was drawn up and Spain sold Louisiana to France.**
  특별조약이 체결되고 스페인은 루이지애나를 프랑스에 매각했다.
- **supervision** [sùːpərvíʒən] 명 감독, 관리
  - it involved the **supervision** of the expedition to San Domingo
    산토도밍고 원정의 감독업무를 수반했다
- **re-armament** [riːɑ́ːrməmənt] 명 재무장, 재군비

in addition to the ordinary routine of official work. Moreover, the foundations of the Consulate being based on the army, it was essential that the army should be efficient and content, and consequently the French soldier of that day was not, as in other countries, neglected in peace time. The officers in command of the troops were constantly reminded by the War Minister that "the French soldier is a citizen placed under military law"—not an outcast or serf, whose well-being and comfort concern no one.

On the establishment of the Empire Berthier, like many another, received the reward for his faithfulness to Napoleon. Honours were showered upon him. The first to receive the Marshal's bâton, he was in succession created senator by right as a dignitary of the Empire, grand officer of the palace and grand huntsman to the crown, while at the coronation he carried the imperial globe. But though the Emperor thus honoured, and treated him as his most trustworthy confidant, the cares of state to some extent withdrew Napoleon from close intimacy with his old companion. At the same time the Marshal was insensibly separated from his former comrades-in-arms by his high rank and employment, which, while it tended to make him more the servant than the friend of the Emperor, also caused him to be regarded as a superior to be obeyed by those who were formerly his equals. At

- in addition to the ordinary routine of official work
  일상적으로 반복되는 공직 업무까지 더해서
- Consulate [kánsəlit/kɔ́nsju-] 명 프랑스 집정 정부(1799~1804)
- French soldier of that day was not neglected in peace time
  당시 프랑스 군인들은 평화 시에도 그냥 방치되지 않았다
- a citizen placed under military law 군법의 적용을 받는 시민
- outcast 명 따돌림 받는 사람, 부랑자
- not an outcast or serf, whose well-being and comfort concern no one
  아무도 그들의 행복과 편의를 신경써주지 않는 부랑자나 농노가 아닌
- shower upon ~에게 듬뿍 주다
- Marshal's bâton 원수의 지휘봉
- create senator 상원의원이 되다
- by right 공정하게, 정당하게, 당연히
- dignitary [dígnətèri/-təri] 명 고위관리
- imperial globe
  십자가 달린 보주(寶珠: 대관식 때 쓰이는 물건으로 왕권의 상징)
- trustworthy [trʌ́stwə̀ːrði] 형 신뢰할 수 있는
- care of state 정사(政事)
- to some extent 얼마간, 어느 정도까지
- intimacy [íntəməsi] 명 친밀함
- withdraw 동 물러나다, 철회하다
  - *withdraw* ~from close intimacy (가까운 사이의) 거리를 멀어지게 하다
- insensibly [insénsəbəli] 부 (눈에 띄지 않을 정도로) 서서히
- comrades-in-arms 전우
- employment [emplɔ́imənt] 명 직장, (개인의) 고용
- while it tended to make him more the servant than the friend of the Emperor
  황제의 친구로서보다는 하인으로서의 위치에 더 가깝게 되었지만
- superior [səpíəriər, su-] 명 윗사람, 상급자
  - also caused him to be regarded as a **superior** to be obeyed by those who were formerly his equals
    그 역시도 한 때 동등한 위치에 있었던 이들이 볼 때 복종해야 하는 상급자로 여겨지게 되었다

all times a strict disciplinarian, and one who never passed over a breach of orders, the Marshal, as voicing the commands of the Emperor, gradually began to assume a stern attitude to all subordinates, and spared neither princes or marshals, when he considered that the good of the service required that they should be reprimanded and shown their duty. So strong was the sense of subordination in the army and the desire to stand well with Napoleon, that even the fiery Murat paid attention to orders and reprimands signed by Berthier in the name of the Emperor.

Meanwhile the work of the War Minister increased day by day. The organisation and supervision of the Army of the Ocean added considerably to his work, which was much interfered with by visits of inspection in company with the Emperor, or far-distant expeditions to the frontiers and to Italy for the coronation at Milan.

On August 3rd, 1805, the Emperor created the Marshal major-general and chief of the staff to the Army of the Ocean, and himself assumed command of the Army and held a grand review of one hundred thousand men. Everybody thought that the moment for the invasion of England had arrived. Berthier, and perhaps Talleyrand, alone knew that Austria, not England,

- **disciplinarian** [dìsəplənéəriən] 명 엄격한 사람, 규율가
- **breach** [briːtʃ] 명 위반
  - never passed over a **breach** of orders
    명령을 위반한 이들을 절대 그냥 넘어가지 않았다
- **as voicing the commands of the Emperor** 황제의 명령을 대변하면서
- **assume** [əsjúːm] 통 (특질·양상을) 띠다
- **subordinate** [səbɔ́ːrdənit] 명 부하, 하급자
- **spared neither princes or marshals** 공작들이나 원수들도 예외가 아니었다
- **stand well with** ~와 사이가 좋다, 평판이 좋다
  - So strong was the sense of subordination in the army and the desire to **stand well with** Napoleon
    군대 내에서 철저한 복종이 이루어지고 있었고, 나폴레옹을 기꺼이 따르려는 분위기가 강했기 때문에
- **even the fiery Murat paid attention to orders and reprimands signed by Berthier in the name of the Emperor**
  다혈질인 뮈라까지도 황제의 이름으로 베르티에가 내리는 명령이나 질책에 신경을 쓸 정도였다
- **which was much interfered with by visits of inspection in company with the Emperor**
  황제를 모시고 시찰을 다녀야 하기 때문에 (본연의) 업무에만 몰두할 수 있는 것도 아니었다
- **far-distant expedition** 머나먼 원정
- **review** [rivjúː] 명 (군대의) 사열
  - held a grand **review** of one hundred thousand men
    10만 명의 병사들을 대대적으로 사열했다

was the immediate quarry, and all through August the major-general was busy working out the routes for the concentration of the various corps in the valley of the Danube; whilst at the same time as War Minister he was responsible for the supervision of all the troops left in France and in garrison in Italy, Belgium, Holland, and Hanover. Consequently he had to divide his staff into two sections, one of which he took with him into the field, the other remaining in Paris under an assistant who was capable of managing the ordinary routine, but who had to forward all difficult problems to the War Minister in the field. Even during the drive to the frontier there was no abatement of the strain; during the journey the Emperor would give orders which had to be expanded and written out in the short stoppages for food and rest. By day the major-general travelled in the Emperor's carriage; at night he always slept under the same roof with him, to be ready at any moment, in full uniform, to receive his commands and expand and dictate them to his clerks. Everyone knew when the major-general was worried, for he had a habit of biting his nails when making a decision or trying to solve a problem, but otherwise he never showed any sign of feeling, and whether tired or troubled by the Emperor's occasional outbursts of temper, he went on with his work with the methodical precision of an automaton. To belong to the general staff when

- **quarry** [kwɔ́:ri, kwári] 몡 사냥감
  - Berthier, and perhaps Talleyrand, alone knew that Austria, not England, was the immediate **quarry**
  베르티에, 그리고 아마도 탈레랑 정도는 당장의 목표는 영국이 아니라 오스트리아라는 것을 알고 있었다
- **concentration** 몡 (병력의) 집중
- **in garrison** 수비를 맡고
- **who had to forward all difficult problems to the War Minister in the field**
  전장에서 생기는 어려운 문제는 모두 전쟁장관에게 떠넘겨야만 했다
- **abatement** [əbéitmənt] 몡 감소, 감퇴
  - during the drive to the frontier there was no **abatement** of the strain
  전선으로 향하는 와중에도 부담은 전혀 줄어들지 않았다
- **write out** (상당히 긴 내용을) 세세하게 작성하다
- **stoppage** [stápidʒ/stɔ́p-] 몡 중단, 멈춤
  - in the short **stoppages** for food and rest
  식사를 하거나 잠을 자기 위해 잠깐 멈추기만 하고
- **to be ready at any moment, in full uniform**
  제복을 완전히 갖춰 입은 채 항상 대기한 상태로
- **a habit of biting his nails when making a decision or trying to solve a problem**
  결정을 내리거나 문제를 해결하려 할 때 손톱을 물어뜯는 습관
- **but otherwise he never showed any sign of feeling**
  그러나 그 외의 상황에서 그는 결코 감정을 드러내지 않았다
- **methodical** [məθádikəl/miθɔ́d-] 혱 체계적인, 꼼꼼한
- **precision** [prisíʒən] 몡 정확성, 신중함
- **expand** [ikspǽnd] 동 말을 덧붙이다, 더 상세히 하다

Berthier was major-general was no bed of roses, no place for gilded youth, for with Napoleon commanding and Berthier directing, if there was often fighting there was plenty of writing; if there was galloping on horseback by day, to make up for it by night there were hours of steady copying of orders and no chance of laying down the pen until all business was finished. Thanks to this excellent staff work, Napoleon's ambitious plans were faithfully accomplished, the Austrians were completely taken in by the demonstration in the Black Forest, the French columns stepped astride of their communications on the Danube, and Mack was forced to surrender at Ulm. But Ulm was only the commencement of the campaign, and even after Austerlitz Napoleon pursued the enemy with grim resolution. This was one of the secrets of his success, for, as Berthier wrote to Soult, "The Emperor's opinion is that in war nothing is really achieved as long as there remains something to achieve; a victory is not complete as long as greater success can still be gained."

After the treaty of Pressburg, on December 27, 1805, Napoleon quitted the army and returned to Paris, leaving the major-general in command of the Grand Army with orders to evacuate the conquered territory when the terms of the treaty had been carried

- **gilded youth** 상류층 젊은이들, 귀공자들
- **gallop** [gǽləp] 통 (말 등이) 전속력으로 질주하다
- **to make up for it by night** (낮에 못한 것을) 밤에 일해서 보충해야 하는
- **no chance of laying down the pen** 펜을 내려놓을 시간이 없는
- **be taken in** 속임수에 넘어가다
    - the Austrians were completely **taken in** by the demonstration in the Black Forest
      오스트리아군은 검은 숲 지역에 나타난 적군의 유인에 완전히 속아 넘어갔다
- **step** [step] 통 움직이다
- **astride** [əstráid] 부 양쪽으로 쫙 벌리고
- **commencement** [kəménsmənt] 명 시작, 개시
    - But Ulm was only the **commencement** of the campaign.
      그러나 울름은 전투의 서막에 불과했다
- **grim** [grim] 형 무자비한, 냉혹한
- **resolution** [rèzəlúːʃən] 명 결의
    - pursued the enemy with grim **resolution**
      단호한 결의로 적군을 추격했다
- **in war nothing is really achieved as long as there remains something to achieve**
  전쟁에서 무언가 이룰 것이 남아있다면 실제로는 아무것도 이루지 못한 것이다
- **evacuate** [ivǽkjuèit] 통 떠나다, 비우다
    - **evacuate** the conquered territory 점령한 영토에서 떠나다
- **when the terms of the treaty had been carried out by the Austrians**
  오스트리아인들이 조약내용을 이행한다면

out by the Austrians; but the Emperor retained the real control, and every day a courier had to be despatched to Paris with a detailed account of every event, and every day a courier arrived from Paris bearing fresh orders and instructions. For Napoleon refused to allow the slightest deviation from his orders: "Keep strictly to the orders I give you," he wrote; "execute punctually your instructions. I alone know what I want done." Meanwhile the major-general was still War Minister and had to supervise all the more important business of the War Office; while he also found time to edit an official history of the campaign of 1805, and to superintend the execution of a map of most of the Austrian possessions. The work was immense, but Berthier never flagged, and the Emperor showed his appreciation of his zeal when on March 30th, 1806, he conferred on him the principality of Neuchâtel with the title of Prince and Duke, to hold in full possession and suzerainty for himself, his heirs and successors, with one stipulation, that he should marry. He added that the Prince's passion for Madame Visconti had lasted too long, that it was not becoming to a dignitary of the Empire, and that he was now fifty years old and ought to think of providing an heir to his honours. The Prince Marshal never had time to visit personally his principality, but he sent one of his intimate friends, General Dutaillis, to provide for the welfare of his new subjects, and

- **courier** [kúriər, kə́:ri-] 명 특사, 급사(急使)
- **slightest deviation** 아주 작은 일탈
- **I alone know what I want done.**
  오직 나만이 내가 하고자 하는 것을 알고 있다.
- **had to supervise all the more important business of the War Office**
  전쟁부의 더욱 중요한 업무를 감독해야 했다
- **find time** 틈이 있다, 짬을 내다
- **superintend** [sù:pərinténd] 동 관리하다, 감독하다
- **execution** [èksikjú:ʃən] 명 제작
- **possession** [pəzéʃən] 명 영토, 소유지
  - a map of most of the Austrian **possessions**
    대부분의 오스트리아 영토가 그려진 지도
- **flag** [flæg] 동 축 늘어지다, (기력이) 떨어지다
- **conferred on him the principality of Neuchâtel with the title of Prince and Duke**
  그에게 공작의 작위와 함께 뇌샤텔 공국을 수여했다
- **hold in full possession and suzerainty for himself**
  그 자신이 완전히 소유하고 지배하다
- **with one stipulation** 한 가지 조건을 붙여서
- **the Prince's passion for Madame Visconti had lasted too long**
  비스콩티 부인에 대한 공작의 열정이 너무 오래 계속되었다
- **becoming to** ~에게 어울리는
  - it was not **becoming to** a dignitary of the Empire
    제국의 고위 관리에게 어울리지 않는다
- **intimate** [íntəmit] 형 친밀한, 가까이 지내는
- **to provide for the welfare of his new subjects**
  그의 새로운 신민들이 평안하게 지낼 수 있도록

to the best of his ability he saw that they were well governed, while a battalion of picked troops from Neuchâtel was added to the Imperial Guard. But, orders or no orders, the Prince could never break himself free from the trammels of his mistress, and Napoleon gave him but little leisure in which to find a congenial partner, so that it was not till after Tilsit, in the brief pause before the Peninsular War, that Berthier at last took a wife. His chosen Princess was Elizabeth, the daughter of William, Duke of Bavaria, brother of the King. She was married with all due solemnity in March, 1808, and though the exigencies of war gave her but little opportunity of seeing much of her husband, affection existed between them, as also between Berthier and his father-in-law, the Duke of Bavaria. All cause of difficulty was smoothed over by the fact that in time the Princess herself conceived an affection for Madame Visconti.

By September, 1806, the Grand Army had evacuated Austria, and the Prince Marshal was hoping to return to Paris when suddenly he was informed by the Emperor of the probability of a campaign against Prussia. On the 23rd definite orders arrived indicating the points of assembly; by the next day detailed letters of instructions for every corps had been worked out and despatched by the headquarters staff. Napoleon himself arrived

- **to the best of** ~이 미치는 한, ~하는 한
- **while a battalion of picked troops from Neuchâtel was added to the Imperial Guard**
  한편 뇌샤텔 출신으로 이루어진 대대가 황제의 근위대에 추가로 편입되었다
- **break free** 떨치다, 떨쳐 풀다
- **trammel** [trǽməl] 명 (움직임·활동 등의) 구속, 속박
  - could never break himself free from the **trammels** of his mistress
  애인의 품속에서 벗어나질 못했다
- **but little** 거의 없는
- **congenial** [kəndʒíːnjəl] 형 마음이 맞는, 마음에 드는
- **in the brief pause before the Peninsular War**
  반도전쟁(1808~1814) 전의 짧은 휴지기 동안에
- **Berthier at last took a wife** 베르티에는 마침내 결혼을 했다
- **due** [djuː] 형 적절한, 마땅한
- **solemnity** [səlémnəti] 명 의식 절차, 엄숙함
- **exigency** [éksədʒənsi] 명 급한 볼일, 긴급 사태
  - and though the **exigencies** of war gave her but little opportunity of seeing much of her husband, affection existed between them
  급박한 전시상황 때문에 남편을 자주 볼 기회가 거의 없었지만, 둘은 서로를 사랑했다
- **smooth over** (문제 등을) 해결하다, 바로잡다
- **conceive an affection for** ~에게 호감을 가지다
  - in time the Princess herself **conceived an affection for** Madame Visconti
  곧 공작비(妃) 자신이 비스콩티 부인에게 호감을 가지게 되면서
- **By September, 1806, the Grand Army had evacuated Austria**
  1806년 대육군이 오스트리아를 떠났다
- **be informed of** ~을 들어서 알게 되다
  - when suddenly he **was informed** by the Emperor of the probability **of** a campaign against Prussia
  갑자기 황제가 프로이센에 대한 전쟁의 가능성을 알려 주었을 때
- **indicating the points of assembly** 집결 장소를 가리키는

at Würzburg on October 2nd, and found his army concentrated, but deficient of supplies. At first his anger burst out against the chief of the staff, but a moment's reflection proved to him that there was not sufficient transport in Germany to mass both men and supplies in the time he had given, and he entirely exonerated Berthier, who by hard work contrived in three days to collect sufficient supplies to allow of the opening of the thirty days' campaign which commenced with Jena and ended by carrying the French troops across the Vistula. The fresh campaign in the spring of 1807 was attended by an additional difficulty, there existed no maps of the district, and the topographical department of the staff was worked off its legs in supplying this deficiency. Meanwhile, during the halt after Pultusk, the major-general was busy re-clothing and re-equipping the army and hurrying up reinforcements; while in addition to the work of the War Office he had to supervise the French forces in Italy and Naples. After Tilsit, as after Pressburg, Napoleon hurried back to France and left the Prince of Neuchâtel to arrange for the withdrawal of the Grand Army, and it was not till July 27th that Berthier at last returned to Paris.

The Prince came back more than ever dazzled by the genius of the Emperor; not even Eylau had taught him that there were lim-

- **deficient** [difíʃənt] 헹 부족한, 결함이 있는
  - found his army concentrated, but **deficient** of supplies
    병력은 집결되었지만, 보급이 부족하다는 것을 알게 되었다
- **At first his anger burst out against the chief of the staff**
  처음에 그는 수석참모에게 불같이 화를 냈다
- **reflection** [riflékʃən] 명 심사숙고
  - a moment's **reflection** 잠시 깊이 생각함
- **prove** [pruːv] 동 판명되다, 드러나다
- **there was not sufficient transport in Germany**
  독일에는 충분한 운송수단이 없었다
- **mass** [mæs] 동 모으다, 운집시키다
- **exonerate** [igzánərèit/-zɔ́n-] 동 무죄임을 밝혀주다
- **contrive** [kəntráiv] 동 용케 ~하다, 성사시키다
- **campaign which commenced with Jena and ended by carrying the French troops across the Vistula**
  예나에서 시작해 프랑스군이 비스툴라까지 진격한 것으로 끝난 전투
- **topographical** [tàpəgrǽfikəl/tɔ́p-] 헹 지형학의, 지형상의
- **be worked off its legs** 혹사당하다
- **the major-general was busy re-clothing and re-equipping the army**
  소장(베르티에)는 군인들의 옷을 다시 갈아입히고 장비를 갈아주는 일로 바빴다
- **hurried back to France** 프랑스로 급히 돌아갔다
- **it was not till July 27th that Berthier at last returned to Paris**
  7월 27일이 되서야 베르티에는 마침내 파리로 돌아올 수 있었다
- **more than ever** 더욱 더, 점점 더
- **dazzle** [dǽzəl] 동 눈이 부시게 하다, 황홀하게 하다
- **not even Eylau had taught him that there were limits to his idol's powers**
  에일라우 전투조차도 그로 하여금 자신의 우상의 능력에도 한계가 있다는 것을 가르쳐 주지 못했다(1807년 폴란드 에일라우에서 나폴레옹은 러시아를 상대로 전투를 벌였지만, 2만 5천여 명의 병력을 잃고 사실상 무승부로 끝남)

its to his idol's powers. But with more than eight hundred thousand men on a war footing, with divisions and army corps scattered from the Atlantic to the Niemen, from Lübeck to Brindisi, it was impossible for one man to be at once chief of the staff and Minister of War. Accordingly, on August 9th the Emperor made General Clarke Minister of War, and, to show that this was no slight on his old friend, on the same day he created the Prince of Neuchâtel Vice-constable of France. For the next three months Berthier was able to enjoy his honours at his home at Grosbois, or in his honorary capacity at Fontainebleau, but in November the Emperor carried him off with him to Italy on a tour of inspection. During the whole of this holiday in Italy the Prince was busy elaborating the details of the coming campaign in Spain, and it was the Spanish trouble which cut short his honeymoon, for on April 2nd he had to start with the Emperor for Bayonne. From the outset the Prince warned the Emperor that the question of supplies lay at the root of all difficulties in Spain; but Napoleon clung to his idea that war should support war, and Berthier knew that it was hopeless to attempt to remove a fixed idea from his head, and, still believing in his omnipotence, he thought all would be well. Meanwhile, as the summer went on, it was not only Spain that occupied the Prince's attention, for the conquest of Denmark had to be arranged, and the passes in Silesia and

- **a war footing** 전시 편제
- **scattered from the Atlantic to the Niemen, from Lübeck to Brindisi**
  대서양에서 니멘까지, 뤼벡에서 브린디시까지 산재되어 있는
- **it was impossible for one man to be at once chief of the staff and Minister of War** 한 명이 수석참모와 전쟁장관을 동시에 맡는 것은 불가능했다
- **slight** [slait] 명 모욕, 무시
  - to show that this was no **slight** on his old friend
  그의 옛 친구를 조금도 무시하는 것이 아니란 것을 보여주기 위해
- **Vice-constable of France** 프랑스 부(副) 총사령관
- **honorary capacity** 명예직
- **elaborate** [ilǽbərèit] 동 (계획·사상을) 정교하게 만들어내다
  - the Prince was busy **elaborating** the details of the coming campaign in Spain
  공작은 다가올 스페인 원정의 세부계획을 치밀하게 작성하느라 여념이 없었다
- **it was the Spanish trouble which cut short his honeymoon**
  그의 달콤한 시간은 스페인 문제로 갑자기 끝나버렸다
- **outset** [áutsèt] 명 착수, 시작
  - From the **outset** the Prince warned the Emperor
  처음부터 공작은 황제에게 경고했다
- **lie at the root of** ~의 근본을 이루다, ~의 원인이다
  - the question of supplies **lay at the root of** all difficulties in Spain
  보급의 해결이 스페인에서의 모든 어려움의 원인이다
- **cling** [kliŋ] 동 (생각 등을) 고수하다, 집착하다
- **war should support war**
  전쟁으로써 전쟁을 지원해야 한다(보급은 현지에서 해결해야 한다는 뜻)
- **it was hopeless to attempt to remove a fixed idea from his head**
  그의 머릿속에 확고히 잡은 생각을 바꾸는 것은 거의 불가능했다
- **Meanwhile, as the summer went on, it was not only Spain that occupied the Prince's attention**
  게다가 여름이 지나면서 공작은 스페인에만 신경 쓰고 있을 수 없었다

Bohemia carefully mapped, in view of hostilities with Prussia or Austria. Early in August Berthier was at Saint Cloud making arrangements to reinforce Davout in Silesia, owing to the growing hostility of Austria, when, on the 16th, arrived the news that Joseph had had to evacuate all the country west of the Ebro. But Napoleon and Berthier could not go to his help until after the imperial meeting at Erfurt in September. However, on reaching Spain, the magic of the Emperor's personality soon restored the vigour and prestige of the French arms. Still the Prince Marshal could not hide from himself that all was not as it used to be; Napoleon's temper was more uncertain, and the Marshals, smarting under reprimands, were not pulling together. When the Emperor returned to France, after having missed "the opportunity of giving the English a good lesson," he left Berthier behind for a fortnight "to be sure that King Joseph had a proper understanding of everything." But trouble was bound to come, for the Emperor himself was breaking his own canon of the importance of "the unity of command" by nominally leaving Joseph in control of all the troops in Spain, but at the same time making the Marshals responsible to himself through the major-general.

In 1809 Napoleon made another grave mistake. He had calculated that Austria could make no forward movement before April

- **in view of** ~을 고려하여
  - **in view of** hostilities with Prussia or Austria
  프로이센과 오스트리아의 적개심을 고려하여
- **magic of the Emperor's personality** 황제의 존재로 인한 마법
- **vigour** [vígər] 명 활기, 활력
- **all was not as it used to be** 모든 것이 예전에 그랬던 것이 아니다
- **Napoleon's temper was more uncertain**
  나폴레옹의 성격을 더욱 알 수 없었다
- **smart** [smɑːrt] 동 (비난·실패 등으로) 속상해하다
- **pull together** (조직적으로 다툼 없이) 함께 일하다
  - Marshals were not **pulling together**.
  원수들은 서로 협력이 되지 않고 있었다.
- **the opportunity of giving the English a good lesson**
  영국인들에게 따끔한 맛을 보여줄 기회
- **fortnight** [fɔ́ːrtnàit] 명 2주일
- **King Joseph** 나폴레옹의 형인 스페인 왕 조제프 보나파르트
- **trouble was bound to come** 문제가 발생할 수밖에 없었다
- **canon** [kǽnən] 명 규범, 규율
  - Emperor himself was breaking his own **canon** of the importance of "the unity of command"
  황제 자신이 자신의 대원칙인 "지휘체계의 통일"을 어긴 것이다
- **nominally** [nǽmənl/nɔ́m-] 부 명목상
  - **nominally** leaving Joseph in control of all the troops in Spain
  스페인에 주둔한 모든 군대를 명목상으로는 조제프의 휘하에 두고
- **making the Marshals responsible to himself through the major-general**
  원수들이 소장(베르티에)을 통해 황제 자신에게 책임을 지도록 하는
- **grave** [greiv] 형 중대한, 치명적인
- **He had calculated that Austria could make no forward movement before April 15th**
  오스트리아군이 4월 15일 이전에는 진격하지 않을 것이라고 계산했다

15th, and accordingly he sent Berthier early in March to take temporary command of the Grand Army, with instructions to order Davout to concentrate at Ratisbon and Masséna at Augsburg. His idea was that there would be ample time later to order a concentration on either wing or on the centre. But the Austrians were ready quite a fortnight before he had calculated. The major-general kept him well informed of every movement of the enemy, and pointed out the dangerous isolation of Davout. Still the Emperor did not believe the Austrian preparations were so forward; and a despatch from Paris, written on April 10th, which arrived at headquarters at Donauwörth on the 11th, ordered the major-general to retain Davout at Ratisbon and move his own headquarters there, "and that in spite of anything that may happen." Unfortunately, a semaphore despatch sent a few hours later, when Napoleon had really grasped the situation, went astray and never reached Berthier. The Prince of Neuchâtel understood as clearly as any one the dangerous position of Davout; the Duke of Eckmühl himself thought that the major-general was trying to spoil his career by laying him open to certain defeat; depression spread through all the French corps. But after years of blind devotion to his great chief Berthier could not steel himself to break distinct orders, emphasised as they were by the expression "in spite of whatever may happen," and a great catastrophe was

- **accordingly** [əkɔ́ːrdiŋli] 	✦ 그런 이유로, 그에 따라
- **ample** [ǽmpl] 	✦ 충분한
    - there would be **ample** time later to order a concentration on either wing or on the centre
    나중에 측면이나 중앙으로 집결시키는 명령을 내릴 충분한 시간이 있을 것이다
- **But the Austrians were ready quite a fortnight before he had calculated.**
    그러나 오스트리아군은 그가 예측한 것보다 2주 가까이나 빨리 준비되어 있었다.
- **kept him well informed of every movement of the enemy**
    적의 모든 움직임을 (나폴레옹에게) 정확하게 보고했다
- **isolation** [àisəléiʃən] 	✦ 고립, 분리, 외로운 상태
    - dangerous **isolation** of Davout
    다부 원수의 군대가 위험하게 따로 고립되어 있는 상태
- **Austrian preparations were so forward**
    오스트리아군의 준비가 그렇게 빠르다는 사실을
- **in spite of anything that may happen** 어떤 일이 발생하더라도
- **semaphore** [séməfɔ̀ːr] 	✦ 수기(手旗)신호
- **when Napoleon had really grasped the situation, went astray and never reached Berthier**
    상황을 완전히 파악한 나폴레옹은 베르티에에게 전령을 보냈지만, 도착하지 못했다
- **Duke of Eckmühl himself thought that the major-general was trying to spoil his career by laying him open to certain defeat**
    에크뮐 공작(다부)은 오히려 베르티에가 자신의 경력을 망치기 위해 일부러 패배가 분명한 곳에 배치했다고 생각했다
- **depression** [dipréʃən] 	✦ 우울함, 암울함
- **steel oneself** 마음을 단단히 먹다
    - Berthier could not **steel himself** to break distinct orders
    베르티에는 분명히 주어진 명령과 다른 행동을 할 마음을 먹을 수가 없었다
- **catastrophe** [kətǽstrəfi] 	✦ 재앙, 참사

only just averted by the arrival of Napoleon, who at once ordered Davout to withdraw and Masséna to advance. Berthier himself was visited by the full fury of the Emperor's anger. But the cloud soon passed, for Berthier was as indispensable as ever, and more so when, after the failure at Aspern-Essling, immense efforts had to be made to hurry up troops from every available source. At the end of the campaign the Emperor justly rewarded his lieutenant by creating him Prince of Wagram.

Once again Napoleon left Berthier to arrange for the withdrawal of the army, and it was not till December 1st that the Prince of Wagram regained Paris and took up the threads of the Peninsular campaign. His stay there was short, for by the end of February he was back again in Vienna, this time not as major-general of a victorious army, but as Ambassador Extraordinary to claim the hand of the Archduchess Marie Louise for his master, the Emperor Napoleon, and to escort her to her new home. For the next two years the Prince remained at home at Grosbois or on duty at Fontainebleau, but in spite of great domestic happiness he was much worried by the terrible Spanish war. No one saw more clearly that every effort ought to be made to crush the English, but he was powerless to persuade the Emperor, and he had to endure to the full all the difficulties arising from break-

- **only just** 간신히, 가까스로
- **avert** [əvə́ːrt] 통 방지하다, 피하다
  - a great catastrophe was only just **averted** by the arrival of Napoleon
  나폴레옹이 도착한 덕분에 겨우 대참사는 막을 수 있었다
- **Berthier himself was visited by the full fury of the Emperor's anger**
  베르티에 자신은 대노한 황제에게 호되게 야단을 맞았다
- **indispensable** [ìndispénsəbəl] 형 없어서는 안 될, 필수적인
- **as ~as ever** 변함없이 ~하게
  - for Berthier was **as** indispensable **as ever**
  베르티에는 변함없이 꼭 필요한 존재였기 때문이다
- **immense efforts had to be made to hurry up troops from every available source**
  가능한 수단을 총동원해 군대를 독려하기 위해서는 엄청난 노력이 필요했다
- **thread** [θred] 명 실, 가닥
  - took up the **threads** of the Peninsular campaign
  반도전쟁을 계속해서 이어나갔다
- **not as major-general of a victorious army, but as Ambassador Extraordinary**
  영광스러운 군대의 소장 신분이 아니라 특명 대사의 신분으로
- **to claim the hand of the Archduchess Marie Louise for his master**
  마리 루이즈 공주와 그의 주인의 혼인을 요구하기 위해
- **but in spite of great domestic happiness he was much worried by the terrible Spanish war**
  국내에서 행복한 시간을 보내는 와중에도 끔찍한 스페인 전쟁 때문에 걱정을 많이 했다
- **he had to endure to the full all the difficulties arising from breaking the "unity of command."**
  그는 지휘체계의 통일이 와해된 것 때문에 발생하는 모든 어려움을 감내해야만 했다.

ing the "unity of command." No one understood better what hopeless difficulties would arise when Napoleon ordered him to write, "The King will command the army... The Guard does not form part of the army." To add to these troubles, it became more and more evident that Germany was riddled with secret societies and that war with Russia was inevitable. So it was with a sigh of relief that in January, 1812, he received the order to turn his attention from Spain and resume his functions as major-general of the Grand Army. Not that he desired further active service; like many another of the Emperor's soldiers, he mistrusted the distant expedition to Russia, and feared for the honour and safety of France. Already in his sixtieth year, there was little he could gain personally from war. As he said to Napoleon, "What is the good of having given me an income of sixty thousand pounds a year in order to inflict on me the tortures of Tantalus? I shall die here with all this work. The simplest private is happier than I." The Emperor, knowing the attitude of many of his Marshals, and himself feeling the strain of this immense enterprise, was unusually irritable. Consequently relations at headquarters were often strained, and the Marshals were angry at the severe reprimands to which they were subjected. The controlling leaders being out of gear the machine did not run smoothly: there was nothing but friction and tension. The Marshals were inclined to attribute

- No one understood better what hopeless difficulties would arise when Napoleon ordered him to write
  나폴레옹이 다음과 같은 서신으로 그에게 명령했을 때, 어떤 절망적인 어려움이 발생할지 그보다 더 잘 아는 사람은 없었다
- be riddled with (특히 나쁜 것이) 가득하다, 문제투성이다
- secret societies 비밀결사
- war with Russia was inevitable 러시아와의 전쟁이 불가피했다
- active service (전시의) 현역 복무
  - Not that he desired further **active service**; like many another of the Emperor's soldiers
    황제의 다른 병사들과 마찬가지로 그는 더 이상의 현역 복무를 원하지 않았다
- mistrust [mistrʌst] 동 신뢰하지 않다, 불신하다
- fear for ~을 걱정하다, 염려하다
  - he mistrusted the distant expedition to Russia, and **feared for** the honour and safety of France
    그는 머나먼 러시아 원정을 비관적으로 보았고, 프랑스의 명예와 안전을 걱정했다
- Already in his sixtieth year, there was little he could gain personally from war.
  그는 이미 예순 살이 되었지만, 전쟁을 통해 개인적으로 얻은 것은 거의 없었다.
- inflict [inflíkt] 동 (괴로움 등을) 가하다
- torture [tɔ́ːrtʃər] 명 고문
- Tantalus [tǽntələs] 명 탄탈루스
  (Zeus의 아들; 신들의 비밀을 누설한 벌로 지옥의 물에 턱까지 잠겨 있다가 목이 말라 물을 마시려고 하면 물이 빠졌다고 함)
- himself feeling the strain of this immense enterprise
  그 자신도 이 거대한 원정 때문에 부담을 가지고 있었기 때문에
- irritable [írətəbəl] 형 짜증을 내는, 화가 난
- the Marshals were angry at the severe reprimands to which they were subjected
  원수들은 그들에게 쏟아지는 심한 질책 때문에 화가 나 있었다
- be out of gear 통제할 수 없게 되다
- friction [fríkʃən] 명 마찰
  - there was nothing but **friction** and tension 마찰과 긴장 외에는 아무것도 없었다

their disgrace to the ill-will of Berthier and not to the temper of Napoleon. Particularly was this the case with Davout, who since 1809 had suspected that Berthier desired to ruin his reputation. Accordingly the Prince of Eckmühl set down the succession of reprimands which were hurled at his head to the machinations of the major-general, and not, as was the case, to Napoleon's jealousy of him, because people had prophesied he would become King of Poland. This misunderstanding was most unfortunate, for it prevented Berthier from effecting a reconciliation between Davout and the Emperor. Hence Napoleon was driven more and more to trust to the advice of the rash, unstable King of Naples. The major-general's lot through the campaign was most miserable. Working day and night to supervise the organisation of the huge force of six hundred thousand men; mistrusted by his former comrades; blamed for every mishap by the Emperor, whatever the fault might be, he had to put up with the bitterest insults, and while working as no other man could work, to endure such taunts as, "Not only are you no good, but you are in the way." Everything that went wrong "was the fault of the general staff, which is so organised that it foresees nothing," whether it was the shortcomings of the contractors or the burning of their own magazines by the Russians. But what most moved Napoleon's anger against the chief of the staff was that Berthier, with "the

- **attribute to** ~의 덕분(탓)으로 돌리다
  - **attribute** their disgrace **to** the ill-will of Berthier and not to the temper of Napoleon
    그들의 불명예를 베르티에의 악의 때문이라고 생각하고 나폴레옹의 성격 탓으로 여기지는 않는다
- **Particularly was this the case with Davout**
  특히 다부가 그런 경우에 해당되었다
- **hurl** [həːrl] 동 (욕, 비난, 모욕 등을) 퍼붓다
  - the succession of reprimands which were **hurled** at his head
    그의 머리 위로 계속해서 쏟아지는 질책들
- **machination** [mæ̀kənéiʃən] 명 교묘한 책략, 중상모략
- **prophesy** [práfəsài/prɔ́−] 동 예언하다, 예상하다
- **reconciliation** [rèkənsìliéiʃən] 명 화해, 조화
- **Napoleon was driven more and more to trust to the advice of the rash, unstable King of Naples.**
  나폴레옹은 점차 경솔하고 불안정한 나폴리 왕(뮈라)의 조언에 빠져들고 있었다.
- **mishap** [míshæp, −́−́] 명 작은 사고
- **while working as no other man could work**
  다른 사람들을 도저히 따라올 수 없을 만큼 열심히 일을 하고 있는데도
- **taunt** [tɔːnt, tɑːnt] 명 놀림, 비웃음, 조롱
- **Not only are you no good, but you are in the way.**
  당신은 쓸모없을 뿐만 아니라 방해까지 하고 있어.
- **which is so organised that it foresees nothing**
  너무나도 잘 정리되어 있어서 아무것도 예측할 수 없다(비웃는 의미)
- **whether it was the shortcomings of the contractors or the burning of their own magazines by the Russians**
  물자를 공급할 사람이 부족한 것이나, 러시아군이 자기들 보급창고를 스스로 불태워 버린 것 어느 것이나

parade states" before him, emphasising the enormous wastage of the army, constantly harped on the danger of pressing on to Moscow. So strained became the relations between them, that for the last part of the advance they no longer met at meals. But during the hours of the retreat the old friendship was resumed. Berthier bore no malice, and showed his bravery by himself opposing the enemy with musket and bayonet; and on one occasion, with Bessières, Murat, and Rapp, he saved the Emperor from a sotnia of Cossacks.

When Napoleon quitted the army at Vilna he left the major-general behind to help the King of Naples to withdraw the remnant of the Grand Army. Marching on foot through the deep snow, with fingers and nose frostbitten, the sturdy old veteran of sixty endured the fatigue as well as the hardiest young men in their prime; and in addition to the physical fatigue of marching, had to carry out all the administrative work, and bear the moral responsibility for what remained of the army; for the King of Naples, thinking of nothing but how to save his own crown, when difficulties increased, followed the example of Napoleon and deserted his post. Thereon the major-general took on himself to nominate Prince Eugène as Murat's successor. But in the end his health gave way, and the Emperor himself wrote to Prince

- **the parade states** 행군의 상황
- **wastage** [wéistidʒ] 명 중도 탈락자, 낙오병
- **harp on** (~에 대해 지겹도록) 계속 지껄이다
- **strained** [streind] 형 껄끄러운, 불편한
    - So **strained** became the relations between them, that for the last part of the advance they no longer met at meals.

    그들의 관계는 너무나도 불편해져서 행군의 마지막 즈음에서는 식사 자리에서도 더 이상 만나지 않았다.
- **malice** [mǽlis] 명 악의, 적의
    - bore no **malice**, and showed his bravery by himself

    전혀 악의를 품지 않고 용맹을 보여주었다
- **sotnia** 소트니아(코사크인 기병중대; 약 100명 정도로 구성됨)
- **frostbitten** [frɔ́ːstbìtn] 형 동상에 걸린
- **the sturdy old veteran of sixty endured the fatigue**

    예순 살의 강인한 백전노장(베르티에)은 피로를 견뎌 냈다
- **young men in their prime** 한창때의 젊은이들
- **the moral responsibility for what remained of the army**

    어떻게 병사들을 살릴 것인지에 대한 도덕적 의무
- **for the King of Naples, thinking of nothing but how to save his own crown**

    나폴리 왕이 오직 자신의 왕관을 지킬 방법만 고민하고 있었던 반면
- **followed the example of Napoleon** 나폴레옹의 예에 따랐다

    (본문에서 나온 것처럼 러시아 원정에서 패배한 나폴레옹은 빌나에서 군대를 떠나 프랑스로 탈주했음)
- **Prince Eugène** 외젠 왕자(외젠 드 보아르네, 나폴레옹의 의붓아들로 조제핀 전[前] 황후와 알렉상드르 드 보아르네의 아들)
    - There on the major-general took on himself to nominate **Prince Eugène** as Murat's successor.

    그 후 즉시 소장(베르티에)은 자신이 직접 책임지고 외젠 왕자를 뮈라의 후임자로 임명했다.
- **give way** 무너지다, 못 이기다
    - in the end his health **gave way** 마침내 건강이 악화되고 말았다

Eugène telling him to send the old warrior home.

Berthier reached Paris on February 9th, much broken down in health; but his wonderful physique soon enabled him to regain his strength, and by the end of March he was once again hard at work helping the Emperor to extemporise an army. With his complete knowledge of this force, no one was more astonished than Berthier at the successes of Lützen and Bautzen, and no one more insistent in his advice to the Emperor to accept the terms of the Allies during the armistice; but he advised in vain. Then followed the terrible catastrophe of Leipzig, due undoubtedly to Berthier's dread of acting without the express orders of the Emperor. The engineer officer charged with preparing the line of retreat reported that the one bridge across the Elster was not sufficient. The major-general, knowing that the Emperor desired to hide any signs of retreat from the Allies, replied that he must await the Emperor's orders, so, when, after three days' fighting, the retreat could no longer be postponed, a catastrophe was inevitable.

Yet, in spite of everything, the Emperor refused to acknowledge himself beaten, and by the commencement of 1814 was once again ready to take the field, though by now the Allies had invaded France. Loyal as ever, Berthier worked his hardest; but

- **physique** [fizíːk] 명 (사람의) 체격
- **extemporise(ze)** [ikstémpəràiz] 동 즉석에서 연설하다
- **With his complete knowledge of this force, no one was more astonished than Berthier at the successes of Lützen and Bautzen**
  나폴레옹의 연설이 위력적이라는 것을 잘 알고 있었던 베르티에도 뤼첸과 바우첸에서의 승리에서는 누구보다 놀랐다고 말했다(1813년 나폴레옹은 러시아 원정 패배 후 기회를 보고 공격해 온 프로이센군과 러시아군을 뤼첸과 바우첸에서 격파했음)
- **insistent** [insístənt] 형 고집하는, 우기는
- **armistice** [áːrməstis] 명 휴전, 협정
  - no one more insistent in his advice to the Emperor to accept the terms of the Allies during the **armistice**
  휴전 기간 동안 황제에게 누구보다도 고집스럽게 연합군의 조건을 수용하라고 조언했다
- **the terrible catastrophe of Leipzig**
  라이프치히의 끔찍한 재앙(1813년 10월 16~18일 러시아·프로이센·오스트리아 연합군에게 결정적인 패배를 당한 라이프치히 전투)
- **dread** [dred] 명 (좋지 않은 일이 생길까봐 갖는) 두려움
  - due undoubtedly to Berthier's **dread** of acting without the express orders of the Emperor
  의심할 여지없이 황제의 명령 없이 행동하는 것을 두려워하는 베르티에 때문에
- **The engineer officer charged with preparing the line of retreat**
  퇴각 전선을 준비하는 책임을 지고 있던 공병장교
- **the one bridge across the Elster was not sufficient**
  엘스터 강을 건너기 위한 다리가 하나 부족하다
- **replied that he must await the Emperor's orders**
  황제의 명령을 기다려야 한다고 대답했다
- **acknowledge** [æknálidʒ, ik-/-nɔ́l-] 명 인정하다
- **Loyal as ever** 여전히 충성스러웠던

he once again incurred the Emperor's anger by entreating him to accept the terms offered him at Châtillon. Still, when the end came and Napoleon abdicated, Berthier remained at his side, and it was only when the Emperor had released his Marshals from their allegiance that on April 11th he sent in his adhesion to the new government. When all save Macdonald had deserted the fallen Emperor, Berthier stayed on at Fontainebleau, directing the withdrawal of the remnants of the army, and making arrangements for the guard which was to accompany Napoleon to Elba. But though he remained with him until the day before he started for Elba, Berthier refused to share his exile, and at the time Napoleon was magnanimous enough to see that, owing to his age and the care of his children, he could not expect such a sacrifice.

So far, the Prince had done all that honour and affection could demand of him. But, unfortunately for his fame, instead of withdrawing into private life, he listened to the prayers of his wife, who keenly felt the loss of her title of "Serene Princess." It was at her desire that he continued to frequent the Bourbon court and actually accepted the captaincy of one of the new companies of royal guards. This and the fact that, as senior of the Marshals, Berthier had led his fellow Marshals to meet the King at Compiègne, caused the Prince of Wagram to be regarded as a traitor

- **incur** [inkə́ːr] 동 초래하다, 발생시키다
- **entreat** [entríːt] 동 간청하다
  - he once again incurred the Emperor's anger by **entreating** him to accept the terms offered him at Châtillon 샤티옹에서 황제에게 제시된 협정안을 받아들이자고 간청한 그는 다시 한 번 황제의 노여움을 사게 되었다
- **abdicate** [ǽbdikèit] 동 퇴위하다
- **it was only when** ~하게 된 이후에야 ~하다
- **adhesion** [ædhíːʒən] 명 지지, 참가, 가맹
  - sent in his **adhesion** to the new government 새 정부에 지지를 표명했다
- **allegiance** [əlíːdʒəns] 명 충성
- **Berthier refused to share his exile**
  베르티에는 함께 유배를 떠나는 것은 거절했다
- **magnanimous** [mæɡnǽniməs] 형 도량이 넓은, 관대한
  - at the time Napoleon was **magnanimous** enough to see that, owing to his age and the care of his children 당시 나폴레옹은 베르티에의 나이나 자녀들을 돌보아야 할 책임을 고려해서 그의 행동을 너그럽게 받아들였다
- **he could not expect such a sacrifice** 그는 그런 희생을 기대할 수는 없었다
- **demand of** ~에게 요구하다
  - So far, the Prince had done all that honour and affection could **demand of** him. 여기까지는 공작도 명예와 우정에 부합되는 모든 의무를 다했다.
- **unfortunately for his fame** 그의 명성에는 불행하게도
- **keenly** [kíːnli] 부 날카롭게, 예민하게
  - **keenly** felt the loss of her title of "Serene Princess." '공작비 전하'라는 작위를 잃어버린 것을 예민하게 느낀
- **frequent the Bourbon court** 부르봉 궁정에 자주 드나들다
- **the captaincy of one of the new companies of royal guards**
  새로 조직된 근위부대 중 하나의 대장 직위

by Napoleon and the Imperialists. Moreover, the Prince Marshal now saw in Napoleon the disturber of the peace of Europe, so when the Emperor suddenly returned from Elba he withdrew from France, and retired to Bamberg, in his father-in-law's dominions.

It is commonly supposed that Berthier committed suicide, but the medical evidence shows that his fall was probably the result of giddiness arising from dyspepsia. It was on June 1st that the accident happened. He was watching a division of Russian troops passing through the town, and was much distressed by the sight, and heard to murmur, "My poor country!" Ever interested in soldiers, he got on a chair on the balcony before the nursery windows to get a better view of the troops, and while doing so lost his balance and fell to the ground.

For the moment the tragic death of the Marshal was the talk of Europe, but only for the moment, for the fate of the world was hanging on the issues of the great battle which was imminent in Belgium. If the Prince of Wagram had been there, it is more than conceivable that the scales would have fallen other than they did; for it was the indifferent staff work of Soult and the bad drafting of orders which lost the French the campaign. Of this, Napoleon

- **Imperialist** [impíəriəlist] 명 황제파(나폴레옹의 지지자들)
- **so when the Emperor suddenly returned from Elba he withdrew from France, and retired to Bamberg** 황제가 엘바 섬에서 갑자기 돌아왔을 때, 그는 프랑스에서 떠나 밤베르크로 피신했다
- **It is commonly supposed that Berthier committed suicide**
  일반적으로 베르티에는 자살했다고 알려져 있다
- **his fall** 그가 떨어진 것(베르티에는 발코니에서 떨어져 죽음)
- **giddiness** [gídinis] 명 현기증, 어지럼증
- **dyspepsia** [dispépʃə, -siə] 명 소화불량
- **distressed** [distrést] 형 (심리적으로) 괴로워하는
- **murmur** [mə́ːrmər] 동 속삭이다, 중얼거리다
- **Ever interested in soldiers** 늘 군인에 대해 관심이 많았던 터라
- **nursery** [nə́ːrsəri] 명 (가정집의) 아기방
- **to get a better view of the troops** 군대의 모습을 더 잘 보기 위해
- **while doing so lost his balance and fell to the ground**
  그러다가 중심을 잃고 땅으로 추락하고 말았다
- **For the moment the tragic death of the Marshal was the talk of Europe**
  잠시 동안 베르티에의 비극적인 죽음은 유럽 내에서 가십거리가 되었다
- **issues** [íʃuː/ísjuː] 명 결과
- **imminent** [ímənənt] 형 목전에 닥친, 긴급한
  - great battle which was **imminent** in Belgium 벨기에서 목전에 닥친 대전투 (1815년 워털루 전투)
- **conceivable** [kənsíːvəbl] 형 상상할 수 있는, 가능한
- **the scales would have fallen other than they did**
  운명의 저울이 다른 쪽으로 떨어졌을지도 모른다
- **for it was the indifferent staff work of Soult**
  술트는 참모 업무에 관심이 없었기 때문에
- **bad drafting of orders** 조악한 명령안

was so firmly convinced that he never could efface it from his memory; again and again he was heard saying, "If Berthier had been here I should never have met this misfortune." The Emperor, in spite of the fact that in 1814 he had told Macdonald that Berthier could never return, was convinced that he would, and had told Rapp that he was certain he would come back to him. It was this failure to return which so embittered the fallen Emperor against the Prince of Wagram, and led to those cruel strictures on his character to which he gave vent at St. Helena. Moreover, Napoleon, so great in many things, was so jealous of his own glory that he could be mean beyond words. Even in the early years when he heard people praising Berthier's work in 1796, he told his secretary, Bourrienne, "As for Berthier, since you have been with me, you see what he is—he is a blockhead." At St. Helena, forgetting his old opinions, "Berthier has his talents, activity, courage, character—all in his favour." Forgetting that he himself had taught Berthier to be imperious, he derided his rather pompous manner, saying, "Nothing is so imperious as weakness which feels itself supported by strength. Look at women."

Berthier, with his admirably lucid mind, great physique, methodical powers and ambition, would have made his name in any profession. He undoubtedly chose to be second to Napoleon; he served him with a fidelity that Napoleon himself could not un-

- he never could efface it from his memory
  결코 그의 뇌리에서 지울 수 없었다
- "If Berthier had been here I should never have met this misfortune."
  만약 거기에 베르티에가 있었다면 나는 그런 불운을 겪지 않아도 되었을 것이다.
- The Emperor, in spite of the fact that in 1814 he had told Macdonald that Berthier could never return, was convinced that he would
  1814년 황제는 막도날에게 베르티에는 결코 돌아올 수 없게 되었다고 말했음에도 불구하고(죽었음을 알았음에도), 베르티에가 돌아올 것이라고 확신했다
- **failure** [féiljər] 명 불이행
- **embitter** [imbítər] 동 나쁜 감정을 가지게 만들다
  - It was this failure to return which so **embittered** the fallen Emperor against the Prince of Wagram
  다시 돌아오지 않았다는 사실이 몰락한 황제가 바그람 공작에게 나쁜 감정을 가지도록 만들었다
- **stricture** [stríktʃər] 명 (심한) 비난
- **give vent to** (감정·분통을) 터뜨리다
- **be mean** 심술궂다
- **beyond words** 더 말할 나위 없이
- **imperious** [impíəriəs] 형 오만한, 고압적인
- **deride** [diráid] 동 조롱하다
- **pompous** [pámpəs/pɔ́m-] 형 거만한, 젠체하는
- Nothing is so imperious as weakness which feels itself supported by strength.
  자기 힘으로 산다고 느끼는 미약한 존재만큼 오만한 것은 없다.
- **methodical** [məθádikəl/miθɔ́d-] 형 체계적인, 꼼꼼함
- **would have made his name in any profession**
  어떤 역할도 다 맡을 수 있었을 것이다

derstand, and he won his great commander's love and esteem in spite of the selfishness of the Corsican's nature. "I really cannot understand," said Napoleon to Talleyrand, "how a relation that has the appearance of friendship has established itself between Berthier and me. I do not indulge in useless sentiments, and Berthier is so uninteresting that I do not know why I should care about him at all, and yet when I think of it I really have some liking for him." "It is because he believes in you," said the former bishop and reader of men's souls. It was this belief in Napoleon which in time obsessed the Prince of Wagram's mind, which killed his own initiative and was responsible for his blunders in 1809 and at Leipzig, and turned him into a machine which merely echoed the Emperor's commands. "Monsieur le Maréchal, the Emperor orders." "Monsieur, it is not me, it is the Emperor you ought to thank." These hackneyed phrases typified more than anything else the bounds of the career which the Marshal had deliberately marked out for himself. In Berthier's eyes it was no reproach, but a testimony to his own principles, "that he never gave an order, never wrote a despatch, which did not in some way emanate from Napoleon." It was this which, with some appearance of truth, pointing to his notable failures, allowed Napoleon to say of him at St. Helena, "His character was undecided, not strong enough for a commander-in-chief, but he possessed all the

- **esteem** [istíːm] 명 존경
- **in spite of the selfishness of the Corsican's nature**
  그 코르시카인(나폴레옹)의 이기적인 성격에도
- **how a relation that has the appearance of friendship has established itself between Berthier and me**
  어떻게 나와 베르티에 사이에 우정이 있는 것처럼 보일 수 있는지
- **indulge in** ~에 탐닉하다
  - I do not **indulge in** useless sentiments
    나는 쓸데없는 감정에 사로잡히는 사람이 아니다
- **uninteresting** [ʌníntərəstiŋ] 형 재미없는
- **yet when I think of it I really have some liking for him**
  그를 좋아할 만한 무언가가 진정으로 생긴다 하더라도
- **the former bishop and reader of men's souls**
  전직 주교이자 사람의 마음을 잘 읽는 사람(탈레랑을 뜻함)
- **obsess** [əbsés] 동 사로잡다, ~에게 강박감을 갖게 하다
- **initiative** [iníʃiətiv] 명 결단력, 자주성
- **blunder** [blʌ́ndər] 명 (어리석은) 실수
- **turned him into a machine which merely echoed the Emperor's commands**
  그를 황제의 명령을 그저 반복하기만 하는 기계로 바꿔버렸다
- **hackneyed** [hǽknid] 형 진부한
- **typify** [típəfài] 동 전형적이다, 특징이다
  - These hackneyed phrases **typified** more than anything else
    이 진부한 문장이야말로 그 무엇보다도 ~의 전형적인 특징이다
- **the bounds of the career which the Marshal had deliberately marked out for himself**
  원수(베르티에)가 자기 스스로 부지런히 선을 그은 경력의 한계(스스로 참모로 규정지음)
- **reproach** [rɪˈproʊtʃ] 명 비난, 책망
- **in some way** 어떤 점에서는, 어떤 식으로든
- **emanate** [émənèit] 동 (어떤 느낌·특질 등을) 발하다
- **not strong enough for a commander-in-chief**
  총사령관이 될 만큼 강하지는 않았지만

qualities of a good chief of the staff: a complete mastery of the map, great skill in reconnaissance, minute care in the despatch of orders, magnificent aptitude for presenting with the greatest simplicity the most complicated situation of an army."

- **he possessed all the qualities of a good chief of the staff**
  훌륭한 참모가 되기 위해 필요한 모든 자질을 갖추었다
- **mastery** [mǽstəri, mɑ́ːs-] 명 숙달, 통달
- **reconnaissance** [rikɑ́nəzəns, -səns/-kɔ́n-] 명 정찰
- **aptitude** [ǽptitùːd, -titjùːd] 명 소질, 적성
  - magnificent **aptitude** for presenting with the greatest simplicity the most complicated situation of an army
  군대내의 아무리 복잡한 상황도 아주 간단하게 설명할 수 있는 훌륭한 재능

2. JOACHIM MURAT

MARSHAL, KING OF NAPLES

Stable-boy, seminarist, Marshal, King, Murat holds the unchallenged position of Prince of Gascons: petulant, persevering, ambitious and vain, he surpasses D'Artagnan himself in his overwhelming conceit. The third son of an innkeeper of La Bastide Fortunière in upper Quercy, Joachim Murat was born on March 25, 1767. From his earliest childhood Joachim was a horse-lover and a frequenter of the stables; but his parents had higher aims for their bright, smiling, intelligent darling, and destined him for the priesthood. The young seminarist was highly thought of by the preceptors at the College of Saint Michel at Cahors and the Lazarist Fathers at Toulouse; but neither priest nor mother had truly grasped his dashing character, and one February morning in 1787 Joachim slipped quietly out of the seminary doors and enlisted in the Chasseurs of the Ardennes, who were at the moment billeted in Toulouse. Two years later this promising recruit, having fallen foul of the military authorities, had to leave the

- **stable-boy** 마구간 말 돌보는 남자(소년)
- **seminarist** [ˈseminɛərist] 명 신학교 학생
- **unchallenged** 형 의심의 여지없이 받아들여지는
    - Murat holds the **unchallenged** position of Prince of Gascons
      뮈라는 어느 누구의 반대 없이 가스코뉴 인들의 왕자 자리를 차지하고 있다
- **petulant** [pétʃələnt] 형 성마른, 화를 잘 내는
- **persevering** [pə̀ːrsəvíəriŋ] 형 인내심이 강한, 참을성 있는
- **vain** [vein] 형 자만심이 강한, 허영심이 많은
- **overwhelming conceit** 지나친 자부심
    - he surpasses D'Artagnan himself in his **overwhelming conceit**
      그의 지나친 자부심은 다르타냥의 그것을 능가했다
- **innkeeper** 명 여관주인
- **From his earliest childhood Joachim was a horse-lover and a frequenter of the stables**
  조아생은 어린 시절부터 말을 좋아했고, 마구간에 자주 드나들었다
- **destine for** ~으로 예정해 두다
- **priesthood** [príːsthud] 명 사제직
- **preceptor** [priséptər, príːsep–] 명 교사, 선생
    - was highly thought of by the **preceptors** 교사들에게 높이 평가받았다
- **dashing** 형 씩씩한, 늠름한
- **slipped quietly out of the seminary doors** 조용히 신학교를 빠져나갔다
- **Chasseurs**
  샤쇠르(추격병; 1743년 창설되어 주로 정찰 임무를 수행하는 프랑스의 경기병 및 경보병)
- **billet** [bílit] 동 (전시에 군인을 민간의 임시 숙소에) 보내다
- **fall foul of** ~와 저촉되다, 충돌하다, 문제가 생기다

service under a cloud. A post as draper's assistant was a poor exchange for the young soldier, who found the cavalry service of the royal army scarcely dashing enough, but the Revolution gave an outlet which Murat was quick to seize. For three years the future King harangued village audiences of Quercy on the iniquities of caste and the equality of all men; so that when, in February, 1792, the Assembly called for volunteers for the "Garde Constitutionnelle" of Louis XVI., what better choice could the national guard of Montfaucon make than in nominating Joachim Murat, the handsome ex-sergeant of the Chasseurs of the Ardennes?

In Paris, Joachim soon found that the royal road to success lay in denouncing loudly all superior officers of lack of patriotism. Soon there was no more brazen-voiced accuser than Murat. In the course of a year he worked his way out of the "Garde Constitutionnelle," and by April, 1793, he had attained the rank of captain in the 12th Chasseurs. Meanwhile, he had been selected as aide-de-camp by General d'Ure de Molans. Having seen no service, he owed his appointment largely to his conceit and good looks. Blue-eyed, with an aquiline nose and smiling lips; with long chestnut curls falling over his well-poised head; endowed with great physical strength, shown in his strong, supple arms

- **under a cloud** 의심을 받고, 눈 밖에 나
  - leave the service **under a cloud** 눈 밖에 나 군대를 떠나다
- **draper** [dréipər] 명 직물상
  - A post as **draper's** assistant was a poor exchange for the young soldier
    혈기왕성한 병사에게 직물상의 조수로 일하는 것은 형편없는 경험이었다
- **who found the cavalry service of the royal army scarcely dashing enough**
  왕국 군대에서 기병으로 근무한다는 것은 그다지 멋진 일이 아니라는 것을 알았다
- **outlet** [áutlet, -lit] 명 (어떤 생각 등의)발산 수단, 배출구
  - the Revolution gave an **outlet** which Murat was quick to seize
    혁명이 준 탈출 기회를 뮈라는 재빨리 낚아챘다
- **harangue** [həræŋ] 동 장광설을 늘어놓다, 열변을 토하다
- **iniquity** [iníkwəti] 명 부당성, 부당한 것
- **caste** [kæst, kɑːst] 명 카스트, 계급
  - on the iniquities of **caste** and the equality of all men
    계급제도의 부당성과 만민평등에 대해서
- **call for** 부르다, 요청하다
- **Garde Constitutionnelle** 입헌근위대(1791년 창설된 루이 16세의 친위부대)
- **national guard of Montfaucon** 몽파콩의 국민병
- **make in nominating Joachim Murat** 조아생 뮈라를 지명하다
- **ex-sergeant** 전직 부사관
- **royal road** 쉬운 방법, 지름길, 왕도
- **lay in** (길이) ~에 놓여 있는
- **denounce** [dináuns] 동 맹렬히 비난하다
  - the royal road to success lay in **denouncing** loudly all superior officers of lack of patriotism
    모든 우수한 장교들에 대해 애국심이 부족하다고 강하게 비판하는 것이 곧 출세의 지름길임을 알았다
- **brazen** [bréizən] 형 뻔뻔한, 철면피 같은
  - there was no more **brazen**-voiced accuser than Murat
    뮈라는 가장 뻔뻔한 목소리로 비난을 일삼게 되었다

다음 장에 해설 계속

and in the long flat-thighed legs of a horseman, he appeared the most perfect type of the dare-devil, dashing cavalry soldier. The moderate republican general, d'Ure de Molans, was useful to him for a time, but the young Gascon saw that the days of the extremist were close at hand; accordingly, he allied himself with an adventurer called Landrieux,

JOACHIM MURAT, AFTERWARDS KING OF NAPLES
FROM THE PAINTING BY GÉRARD AT VERSAILLES

- **aide-de-camp** 부관
- **see service** 종군하다, 실전 경험을 얻다
    - Having **seen** no **service**, he owed his appointment largely to his conceit and good looks.

    실전 경험도 없는 그였지만, 허영심과 잘생긴 외모 때문에 발탁된 것이었다.
- **aquiline** [ǽkwəlàin] 휑 매부리코의
- **chestnut** [tʃésnʌt, -nət] 휑 밤색의, 적갈색의
- **curl** [kəːrl] 명 곱슬머리
- **well-poised** 잘 균형 잡힌
- **supple** [sʌ́pəl] 휑 유연한, 탄력 있는
- **dare-devil** 명 저돌적인 사람, 무모한 사람
- **the days of the extremist were close at hand**

    과격주의자들이 권력을 잡을 날이 머지않았다
- **he allied himself with an adventurer called Landrieux**

    랑드리외라는 모험가와 손을 잡았다

who was raising a body of cut-throats whose object was plunder, not fighting. The Convention, which had licensed Landrieux to raise this corps of patriotic defenders of the country, accepted his nomination of Murat as acting lieutenant-colonel. But they soon fell out, for Murat had the audacity to try and make these patriots fight instead of merely seeking plunder. The consequence of this quarrel was that, early in 1794, he found himself accused as a ci-devant noble. Imprisoned at Amiens, and brought before the Committee of Public Safety, in a fit of republican enthusiasm he changed his name to Marat. But this did not save him, and he owed his life to a deputation from his native Quercy, which proved both his humble birth and his high republicanism.

The 13th Vendémiaire was the turning-point in Murat's life, for on that day, for the first time, he came in contact with his future chief, the young General Bonaparte, and gained his attention by the masterly way he saved the guns at Sablons from the hands of the Royalists. The future Emperor ever knew when to reward merit, and on being appointed to command the army in Italy he at once selected him as his aide-de-camp. So far he had seen little or no war service. But the campaign of 1796 proved that Bonaparte's judgment was sound, for by the end of the year there was no longer any necessity for Murat to blow his own trumpet.

- **cut-throat** [kʌ́tθròut] 명 살인자, 암살자
  - was raising a body of **cut-throats** 암살조직을 키우고 있었다
- **plunder** [plʌ́ndər] 명 약탈, 강탈
- **license** [láisəns] 동 (공적으로) 허가하다
- **acting lieutenant-colonel** 중령 대행(代行), 임시 중령
- **fall out** 사이가 틀어지다
  - they soon **fell out** 그들은 곧 사이가 틀어졌다
- **audacity** [ɔːdǽsəti] 명 뻔뻔함, 대담함
  - for Murat had the **audacity** to try and make these patriots fight instead of merely seeking plunder
  뮈라가 대담하게도 이 애국자들을 단지 약탈이 아니라 전투를 위한 조직으로 만들려고 했기 때문이다
- **ci-devant** [sidəvã́] 형 전의, 이전의
- **Committee of Public Safety**
  공안위원회(1793~1795; 프랑스 혁명기간 통치기구로 공포정치를 실시함)
- **in a fit of republican enthusiasm he changed his name to Marat**
  공화주의자로서의 열정을 보여주기 위해 그의 이름을 '마라'로 바꿨다(마라는 프랑스 혁명기의 정치가로, 루이 16세의 처형을 주도함)
- **deputation** [dèpjətéiʃən] 명 대표단
- **proved both his humble birth and his high republicanism**
  그가 미천한 집안 출신이란 것과 열렬한 공화주의자라는 것을 증명해 주었다
- **gained his attention by the masterly way he saved the guns at Sablons from the hands of the Royalists**
  뛰어난 수완으로 왕당파의 수중에서 사블롱 평원의 대포들을 지켜내 나폴레옹의 눈길을 끌었다
- **The future Emperor ever knew when to reward merit**
  미래의 황제는 언제 공적을 보상해야 할지를 늘 알고 있었다
- **sound** [saund] 형 확실한, 탄탄한, 건전한
  - Bonaparte's judgment was **sound** 보나파르트의 판단은 훌륭했다
- **blow one's own trumpet** 자기자랑하다, 자화자찬하다

In the short campaign against the Sardinians he showed his talent as a cavalry leader by his judgment in charges at Dego and Mondovi. He had no cause to grumble that he was not appreciated, for his general selected him to take to Paris the news of this victorious campaign and of the triumphant negotiations of Cherasco. He returned from Paris in May as brigadier-general, in time to take part in the crossing of the Mincio and to rob Kilmaine of some of his honours. The commander-in-chief still kept him attached to the headquarter staff, and constantly employed him on special service. His enterprises were numerous and varied—one week at Genoa on a special diplomatic mission, a week or two later leading a forlorn attack on the great fortress of Mantua, then commanding the right wing of the army covering the siege, he showed himself ever resourceful and daring. But during the autumn of 1796 he fell under the heavy displeasure of his chief, for at Milan and Montebello Josephine had shown too great favour to the young cavalry general. Murat accordingly had no scruples in intriguing with Barras against his chief. But his glorious conduct at Rivoli once again brought him back to favour, and Bonaparte entrusted him with an infantry brigade in the advance on Vienna, and later with a delicate independent mission in the Valtelline. But Murat, unlike Lannes, Marmont, and Duroc, was not yet indispensable to Bonaparte, and accordingly was left with

- **charge** [tʃɑːrdʒ] 명 돌격
    - In the short campaign against the Sardinians he showed his talent as a cavalry leader by his judgment in **charges** at Dego and Mondovi.
    사르데냐군과 싸운 짧은 전쟁 중에 그는 데고와 몬도비의 돌격전에서 기병지휘관으로서 판단력에 대한 재능을 보여주었다.
- **grumble** [grʌmbəl] 동 불평하다, 불만하다
- **triumphant** [traiʌmfənt] 형 승리를 거둔, 의기양양한
- **brigadier-general** 육군준장
- **in time** 머지않아, 조만간
- **His enterprises were numerous and varied**
  그의 공적은 상당히 많았고, 다양했다
- **forlorn** [fərlɔːrn] 형 희망 없는, 절망적인
    - leading a **forlorn** attack on the great fortress of Mantua
    거대한 만토바 요새를 공격하는 어려운 공격
- **he fell under the heavy displeasure of his chief**
  그의 상관(나폴레옹)에게서 커다란 노여움을 사고 말았다
- **Josephine had shown too great favour to the young cavalry general**
  조제핀이 이 젊은 기병 장군에게 지나친 호의를 보인 것이었다
- **scruple** [skrúːpəl] 명 양심의 가책, 주저, 망설임
- **intrigue** [intríːg] 동 음모를 꾸미다, 내통하다
    - had no scruples in **intriguing** with Barras against his chief
    아무런 양심의 가책 없이 바라스와 몰래 내통해 그의 상사에 대해 음모를 꾸몄다
- **entrust** [entrʌst] 동 임명하다, 위임하다
- **in the advance on Vienna** 빈으로 진격하는 중에
- **delicate** [délikət, -kit] 형 미묘한, 신중을 요하는
    - with a **delicate** independent mission in the Valtelline
    발텔린에서 신중을 요하는 개별 임무와 함께
- **indispensable** [ìndispénsəbəl] 형 절대 필요한, 불가결의

the Army of Italy when the general returned in triumph to Paris. It was mainly owing to Masséna's enthusiastic report of his service in the Roman campaign, at the close of 1797, that he was selected as one of the supernumerary officers in the Egyptian expedition.

So far, Murat had not yet been able to distinguish himself above his comrades-in-arms. Masséna, Augereau, Serurier, and Laharpe left him far in the rear, but Egypt was to give him the chance of proving his worth, and showing that he was not only a dashing officer, but a cavalry commander of the first rank. He led the cavalry of the advance guard in the march up the Nile, and was present at the battle of the Pyramids and the taking of Cairo. But so far the campaign, instead of bringing him fresh honours, nearly brought him disgrace; for he joined the party of grumblers, and was one of those who were addressed in the famous reprimand, "I know some generals are mutinous and preach revolt... let them take care. I am as high above a general as above a drummer, and, if necessary, I will as soon have the one shot as the other."

On July 27, 1798, Murat was appointed governor of the province of Kalioub, which lies north of Cairo; to keep order among

- **was left with the Army of Italy when the general returned in triumph to Paris**
  나폴레옹이 파리로 개선하여 돌아갈 때, 이탈리아 군대와 함께 남겨졌다
- **enthusiastic** [enθùːziǽstik] 형 열성적인, 열광적인
  - It was mainly owing to Masséna's **enthusiastic** report of his service in the Roman campaign
  주로 로마 전투에서의 활약에 대한 마세나의 열성적인 보고서 덕분이었다
- **supernumerary** 형 정원 외의, 예비의
  - he was selected as one of the **supernumerary** officers in the Egyptian expedition
  이집트 원정에서 예비 장교 중 하나로 선발되었다
- **So far, Murat had not yet been able to distinguish himself above his comrades-in-arms.**
  지금까지 뮈라는 그의 총사령관의 눈에 확실히 드는 공훈을 세우지 못했다.
- **Masséna, Augereau, Serurier, and Laharpe left him far in the rear**
  마세나, 오주로, 세뤼리에, 라아르프보다도 훨씬 뒤처져 있었다
- **provide his worth** 그의 가치를 입증하다
- **not only a dashing officer, but a cavalry commander of the first rank**
  단지 멋쟁이 장교인 것만이 아니라 최고의 기병 사령관이라는 것을
- **grumbler** 명 불평가, 불만을 말하는 사람
- **was one of those who were addressed in the famous reprimand**
  그 유명한 질책을 들은 사람들 중 하나였다
- **mutinous** [mjúːtənəs] 형 폭동의, 반항적인
- **preach revolt** 반란을 선동하다
- **I am as high above a general as above a drummer**
  내가 바라보는 위치에서는 장군이나 군악대나 별 차이가 없다
- **I will as soon have the one shot as the other**
  군악대를 총살시키는 즉시 장군도 처형시켜버릴 것이다

his turbulent subjects his whole force consisted of a battalion of infantry, twenty-five cavalrymen, and a three-pounder gun. His governorship was only part of the work Bonaparte required of him, for he was constantly away organising and leading light columns by land or river, harrying the Arabs and disbanded Mamelukes, sweeping the country, collecting vast depôts of corn and cattle, remounting the cavalry—proving himself a past master in irregular warfare. So well did he do his work that the commander-in-chief selected him to command the whole of the cavalry in the Syrian expeditionary force. Thanks to his handling of his horsemen, the march through Palestine occasioned the French but little loss. During the siege of Acre he commanded the covering force, and pushed reconnaissances far and wide. So feared was his name that the whole Turkish army fled before him on the banks of the Jordan, and left their camp and immense booty in the hands of the French. But though he had thus destroyed the relieving force, Acre, victualled by the English fleet, still held out, and Bonaparte had to retreat to Egypt.

It was at Aboukir that Murat consolidated his reputation as a great commander. The Turkish general had neglected to rest the right flank of his first line on the sea, and Murat, seizing his opportunity, fell on the unguarded flank with the full weight

- **turbulent** 휑 몹시 거친, 소란스러운
  - his **turbulent** subjects 그의 거친 백성들(이집트인들)
- **a battalion of infantry, twenty-five cavalrymen, and a three-pounder gun**
  1개 보병 대대, 25명의 기병, 3파운드짜리 대포 하나
- **harry** [hǽri] 동 (공격 등의 반복으로) ~을 괴롭히다, 몰아대다
- **disband** [disbǽnd] 동 (군대 등을) 해산시키다
- **remount** [ri:máunt] 동 새로 말을 공급하다
- **past** [pæst, pɑ:st] 형 노련한
  - proving himself a **past** master in irregular warfare
  자신이 비정규 전투에서는 노련한 전문가라는 것을 입증했다
- **So well did he do his work that** 그의 임무를 아주 잘 수행했기 때문에 ~하다
- **occasion** [əkéiʒən] 동 야기하다, 원인이 되다
  - **occasioned** the French but little loss 프랑스군에게 거의 손실을 끼치지 않았다
- **reconnaissance** [rikǽnəzəns, -səns/-kɔ́n-] 명 정찰, 수색
- **bank** [bæŋk] 명 둑, 제방
  - before him on the **banks** of the Jordan
  그가 요르단 강둑에 나타나기도 전에
- **booty** [bú:ti] 명 전리품, 노획물
  - left their camp and immense **booty** in the hands of the French
  엄청난 전리품을 프랑스군에게 넘겨주고는 주둔지를 떠났다
- **relieving force** 구원군
- **victual** [vítl] 동 식량을 공급하다
  - Acre, **victualled** by the English fleet, still held out
  영국 함대에 의해 식량을 공급받고 있던 아크레는 여전히 저항이 완강했다
- **consolidate** [kənsálədèit/-sɔ́l-] 동 굳게 하다, 공고히 하다
- **neglect** [niglékt] 동 무시하다, 소홀히 하다
- **The Turkish general had neglected to rest the right flank of his first line on the sea**
  투르크군 장군은 제1전선의 오른쪽 측면이 바다 쪽에 면해 있어서 크게 신경 쓰지 않았다

of his cavalry, and rolled the unfortunate Turks into the water. Thereafter, by the aid of a battery of artillery, the centre of the second line of the Turkish army was broken, and the French horse dashing into the gap, once again made short work of the enemy, and their leader captured with his own hands the Turkish commander. Bonaparte, in his despatch, did full justice to his subordinate. "The victory is mainly due to General Murat. I ask you to make him general of division: his brigade of cavalry has achieved the impossible." Murat himself was much distressed at being wounded in the face, as he feared it might destroy his good looks; however, he soon had the satisfaction of writing to his father: "The doctors tell me I shall not be in the least disfigured, so tell all the young ladies that even if Murat has lost some of his good looks, they won't find that he has lost any of his bravery in the war of love."

His grumbles forgiven, Murat left Egypt among the chosen band of followers of whose fidelity Napoleon was assured; his special mission was to gain over the cavalry to the side of his chief. He it was who, with Leclerc, on the 18th Brumaire, forced his way into the Orangerie at the head of the grenadiers and hurled out the deputies. The First Consul rewarded him amply, appointing him inspector of the Consular Guard, and, later still,

- fell on the unguarded flank with the full weight of his cavalry
  기병으로 전력을 다해 방어가 부족한 측면을 무너뜨렸다
- roll into 밀어서 넣어버리다
- battery [bǽtəri] 명 포열, 포병중대
- the centre of the second line of the Turkish army was broken
  투르크군의 제2선 중앙이 붕괴되었다
- make short work of ~을 척척 해치우다, ~을 제거하다
- do justice 정당하게 평가하다
- his brigade of cavalry has achieved the impossible
  그의 기병여단은 불가능한 일을 해냈다
- distressed [distrést] 형 비통해하는, 고통스러운
- at being wounded in the face 얼굴을 다친 것에 대해서
- he feared it might destroy his good looks
  그것이 그의 잘생긴 얼굴을 망칠까 두려워했다
- disfigure [disfígjər/-fígər] 동 ~의 모양을 손상하다, 추하게 하다
- not in the least 조금도 ~하지 않은
- they won't find that he has lost any of his bravery in the war of love
  사랑의 전쟁에서 그가 조금도 용기를 잃지 않았다는 것을 알게 될 것이다
- His grumbles forgiven 그의 불만은 용서를 받고
- fidelity [fidéləti, fai-] 명 충실, 충성
- assured 형 보증된, 확실한,
  - chosen band of followers whose fidelity Napoleon was assured
    나폴레옹이 확신하는 충성스러운 부하들로 선발된 무리
- gain over 설득하다, 자기편으로 붙이다
- forced his way into the Orangerie at the head of the grenadiers
  척탄병의 선두에 서서 오랑주리궁으로 진격했다
- hurl 동 내쫓다, 추방하다
- deputy [dépjəti] 명 대리인, 의원
- amply [ǽmpli] 부 충분히
- inspector [inspéktər] 검열관, 감독관

in preference to his rival, Lannes, gave him in marriage his sister Caroline. Murat had met Caroline Bonaparte at Montebello during the Italian campaign of 1796, and had at once been struck by her beauty. Like many another cavalier, he had a flame in every country, or rather, in every town which he visited. But by 1799 the gay Gascon saw that it was time to finish sowing his wild oats, since destiny was offering him a chance which falls to the lot of few mortals. It was by now clear that the First Consul's star was in the ascendant. Already his family were reaping the fruits of his success. Ambition, pride and love were the cords of the net which drew the willing Murat to Caroline. As brother-in-law to the First Consul, Joachim felt secure against his bitter rival, Lannes. To add point to this success, he knew that the victor of Montebello was straining every nerve to gain this very prize. Moreover, Fortune herself favoured his suit. Bonaparte had offered the hand of Caroline to the great General Moreau, but the future victor of Hohenlinden refused to join himself to the Corsican triumph. To cover his confusion the First Consul was glad to give his sister's hand to one of his most gallant officers, especially as by so doing he once and for all removed the haunting fear of an intrigue between him and Josephine. Accordingly, on January 25, 1800, Murat and Caroline were pronounced man and wife in the temple of the canton of Plailly, by the president of

- **in preference to** ~에 우선하여
- **be struck by** ~에 반하다, 끌리다
- **flame** [fleim] 몡 애인, 연인
  - he had a **flame** in every country, or rather, in every town which he visited.
    그는 모든 나라에, 아니 그가 가는 모든 도시에 애인이 하나씩 있었다.
- **gay** [gei] 혱 바람둥이의, 음탕한, 명랑한
- **sow one's wild oats** 젊은 혈기로 난봉부리다
- **mortal** [mɔ́ːrtl] 몡 인간, 죽음을 면할 수 없는 것
  - destiny was offering him a chance which falls to the lot of few mortals
    운명은 그에게 보통 사람들이 만나기 어려운 기회를 주었다
- **the First Consul's star was in the ascendant**
  제1집정관(나폴레옹)의 인기가 한창 상승하고 있었다.
- **were reaping the fruits of his success**
  그의 성공으로 인한 과실을 누리고 있었다
- **willing** [wíliŋ] 혱 열렬한, 적극적인
  - Ambition, pride and love were the cords of the net which drew the **willing** Murat to Caroline
    적극적인 뮈라는 야망과 자부심, 사랑이라는 줄로 짠 그물을 카롤린에게 던졌다
- **secure** [sikjúər] 혱 안전한, 확고한
- **strain every nerve** 모든 노력을 다하다
- **suit** [suːt] 몡 구혼
  - Fortune herself favoured his **suit**.
    운명의 여신 자신도 그의 구혼에 호의적이었다.
- **To cover his confusion** 당황스러움을 감추기 위해
- **give his sister's hand to** 여동생을 ~에게 넘겨주다(결혼시키다)
- **once and for all** 완전히, 최종적으로
- **haunting fear** 뇌리를 떠나지 않는 두려움
- **intrigue between him and Josephine** 그와 조제핀 사이의 내통
- **be pronounced man and wife** (공식적인) 부부로 선언되다
- **canton** [kǽntn, -tɑn, kæntǽn/kǽnton, --́] 몡 (프랑스의)읍, 면

the canton. Though Caroline only brought with her a dot of forty thousand francs, she stood for what was better still, immense possibilities.

Murat's honeymoon was cut short by the Marengo campaign. In April he started, as lieutenant-general in command of the cavalry, to join the Army of the Reserve at Dijon. Once the corps of Lannes had, by the capture of Ivrea, secured the opening into Italy, the cavalry were able to take up their rôle, and with irresistible weight they swept down the plains of Lombardy, forced the river crossings, and on June 2nd entered Milan. Thence the First Consul despatched his horsemen to seize Piacenza, the important bridge across the Po, the key of the Austrian lines of communication. Murat, with a few troops, crossed the river in some twenty small rowing-boats, and, dashing forward, captured the bridge head on the southern bank, and thus secured not only the peaceful crossing of his force, but the capture of the town and the immense Austrian depôts. At Marengo the cavalry acted in separate brigades, and the decisive stroke of the battle fell to the lot of the younger Kellermann, whose brilliant charge decided the day in favour of the French. The despatches only mentioned that "General Murat's clothes were riddled by bullets."

- **dot** [dɑt/dɔt] 명 혼인 지참금
- **stand for** ~을 뜻하다, ~을 나타내다
  - she **stood for** what was better still, immense possibilities
    더욱 안정적이고, 무한한 가능성을 얻었다는 것을 뜻했다
- **was cut short by the Marengo campaign** 마렝고 전투로 중단되었다
- **take up** 계속하다, 재개하다
- **rôle** [roul] 명 역할, 임무
- **irresistible** [ìrizístəbəl] 형 저항할 수 없는, 억제할 수 없는
- **weight** [weit] 명 압박, 중압
  - with irresistible **weight** they swept down the plains of Lombardy
    막강한 힘으로 롬바르디아 평원을 휩쓸었다
- **rowing-boat** 명 노로 젓는 배
- **dash forward** 돌진하다, 돌격하다
- **depôt** [dépou] 명 창고, 보관소
- **secured not only the peaceful crossing of his force, but the capture of the town and the immense Austrian depôts**
  병사들이 순조롭게 강을 건널 수 있었을 뿐만 아니라, 마을과 거대한 오스트리아군의 군수 창고를 점령할 수 있었다
- **acted in separate brigades** 독립된 여단으로 활약했다
- **the decisive stroke of the battle fell to the lot of the younger Kellermann**
  전투의 결정적인 일격은 젊은 켈레르망(켈레르망 원수의 아들 프랑수아 에티엔 켈레르망)의 몫이었다
- **in favor of** ~의 이익이 되도록, ~을 위해
- **General Murat's clothes were riddled by bullets.**
  뮈라 장군의 군복은 총알로 벌집이 되어 있었다.

So far Murat had always held subordinate commands; his great ambition was to become the commander-in-chief of an independent army. His wife, Caroline, and his sister-in-law, Josephine, were constant in their endeavours to gain this distinction for him from the First Consul. But it was not till the end of 1800 that they succeeded; and then only partially, for in December the lieutenant-general was appointed commander of a corps of observation, whose headquarters were at Milan, and whose duty was to overawe Tuscany and the Papal States. His campaign in central Italy is more noticeable for his endeavours to shake himself free from the control of General Brune, the commander-in-chief of the Army of Italy, than for any very brilliant manœuvres. Tuscany and the Papal States were easily conquered, and the King of Naples was only too glad to buy peace at Foligno. Italy lay at the feet of the French general, but what was most gratifying of all, after his successful negotiation with the King of Naples, the First Consul tacitly accepted the title which his brother-in-law had assumed of commander-in-chief of the Army of Naples. Murat had the satisfaction of having under his orders Lieutenant-General Soult, three generals of division and four generals of brigade. For the moment his Gascon vanity was satiated, while his Gascon greed was appeased by substantial bribes from all the conquered countries of the Peninsula. The "commander-in-chief" was

- **subordinate** [səbɔ́:rdənit] 혱 ~아래의, 종속된
  - So far Murat had always held **subordinate** commands
  지금까지 뮈라는 항상 명령을 받는 위치에 있었다
- **endeavour** [endévər] 몡 노력, 시도
- **gain a distinction** 훈장을 받다, 직위를 받다
  - were constant in their endeavours to **gain this distinction** for him from the First Consul
  제1집정관을 설득해 그가 이 직위를 받게 해주기 위해 끊임없이 노력했다
- **it was not till the end of 1800 that they succeeded**
  1800년 말이 되어서야 그들은 성공할 수 있었다
- **and then only partially** 그리하여 비로소 부분적으로나마
- **a corps of observation** 정찰부대
- **overawe** 동 위압하다, 무서워하게 하다
- **noticeable** [nóutisəbəl] 혱 눈에 띄는, 두드러지는
- **shake oneself free from** ~에게서 벗어나다
  - his endeavours to **shake himself free from** the control of General Brune
  브륀 장군의 통제하에서 벗어나려는 시도
- **manœuvre** [mənú:vər] 몡 기동 작전, 작전적 행동
- **the King of Naples was only too glad to buy peace at Foligno**
  나폴리왕은 폴리뇨 조약으로 평화를 얻은 것에 너무 기뻐할 뿐이었다
- **tacitly** 閉 암암리에, 넌지시
- **assume** [əsjú:m] 동 자기 것으로 하다, 사칭하다
  - tacitly accepted the title which his brother-in-law had **assumed** of commander-in-chief of the Army of Naples
  그의 매제(妹弟)가 스스로 나폴리군 총사령관을 사칭한 것을 묵인해주었다
- **have under one's order** ~의 지휘하에 있다
- **satiate** [séiʃièit] 동 물릴 정도로 만족시켜주다
- **appease** [əpí:z] 동 풀다, 채우다
- **substantial** [səbstǽnʃəl] 혱 내용이 풍부한, 상당한, 꽤
- **the Peninsula** 이탈리아 반도를 가리킴

joined at Florence in May, 1801, by his wife, Caroline, and his young son, Achille, born in January, whom he found "charming, already possessed of two teeth." In the capital of Tuscany Murat gravely delivered to the inhabitants a historical lecture on their science, their civilisation, and the splendour of their state under the Medici. He spent the summer in visiting the watering-places of Italy. In August the First Consul raised him to the command of the troops of the Cisalpine Republic, and he retained this post for the next two years, and had his headquarters in Milan, making occasional expeditions to Paris and Rome, and on the whole content with his position, save for occasional quarrels with Melzi, the president of the Italian Republic. Their jurisdictions overlapped and the Gascon would play second fiddle to no one save to his great brother-in-law.

In January, 1804, the First Consul recalled Murat to Paris, nominating him commandant of the troops of the first military division and of the National Guard, and Governor of the city. Bonaparte's object was not so much to please his brother-in-law as to strengthen himself. He was concentrating his own family, clan, and all his most faithful followers in readiness for the great event, the proclamation of the Empire. Men like Lannes, whose views were republican, were discreetly kept out of the way on foreign missions; but Murat, as Bonaparte knew, was a pliant

- **charming, already possessed of two teeth**
  잘 생긴데다가 벌써 이빨이 두 개나 나 있었다
- **capital of Tuscany** 토스카나의 수도, 피렌체(Florence)를 의미
- **gravely** 〔뷔〕 진지하게, 열심히
- **deliver** [dilívər] 〔동〕 전달하다, 연설하다, 말하다
- **a historical lecture on their science, their civilisation, and the splendour of their state under the Medici**
  그들의 과학과 문명, 그리고 메디치가(家) 시절의 화려함에 대한 역사강의
- **watering-place** 〔명〕 해수욕장, 해안가, 온천
- **Cisalpine Republic** 치살피나 공화국(1797~1802, 나폴레옹이 이탈리아 북쪽 지방에 건국한 괴뢰정권, 수도는 밀라노)
- **making occasional expeditions to Paris and Rome**
  이따금 파리와 로마로 여행을 하면서
- **save for** ~을 제외하고
- **jurisdiction** [dʒùərisdíkʃən] 〔명〕 권한, 관할구역, 사법권
- **overlap** [òuvərlǽp] 〔동〕 부분적으로 겹치다
- **play second fiddle to** ~에 대한 보조 역할을 하다
- **not so much A as B** A라기보다는 오히려 B
  - Bonaparte's object was **not so much** to please his brother-in-law **as to** strengthen himself.
  보나파르트의 목적은 매제를 기쁘게 해주려는 것보다는 자신의 세력을 강화시키는 데에 있었다.
- **in readiness for the great event, the proclamation of the Empire**
  대단한 사건, 즉 제국을 선포하는 것을 위한 준비로
- **discreetly** 〔뷔〕 사려 깊게, 신중하게
- **keep out of** ~안에 들이지 않다, ~에서 밀어내다
  - Men like Lannes, whose views were republican, were discreetly **kept out of** the way on foreign missions
  란 같은 공화주의자들은 사려 깊게 외교임무를 빙자해 국외로 보내버렸다
- **pliant** [pláiənt] 〔형〕 (=pliable) 고분고분한, 융통성 있는

tool. As early as 1802 he had hotly favoured the Concordat, and had had his marriage recelebrated by Cardinal Consalvi; and both Caroline and Joachim infinitely preferred being members of the imperial family of the Emperor of the French to being merely relations of the successful general and First Consul of the French Republic. They were willing also to obey the future Emperor's commands, and to aid him socially by entertaining on a lavish scale, and their residence in Paris, the Hotel Thélusson, became the centre of gorgeous entertainments. While Murat strutted about in sky-blue overalls, covered with gold spangles, invented new uniforms, and bought expensive aigrettes for his busby, his wife showed her rococo taste by furnishing her drawing-room in red satin and gold, and her bedroom in rose-coloured satin and old point lace. They had their reward. Five days after the proclamation of the Empire, after a furious scene, Napoleon conceded the title of Imperial Highness to his sister with the bitter words: "To listen to you, people would think that I had robbed you of the heritage of the late King, our father." Meanwhile the Governor of Paris had received his Marshal's bâton, and in the following February was created senator, prince, and Grand Admiral of France.

- he had hotly favoured 열렬히 찬성해왔다
- **Concordat** 명 콘코르다트, 화친조약(교황과 정부 간의 협약, 1801년 교황과 나폴레옹과의 협약)
- had had his marriage recelebrated by Cardinal Consalvi
  콘살비 주교가 그의 혼인식을 다시 거행했었다
- preferred being members of the imperial family of the Emperor of the French to being merely relations of the successful general and First Consul of the French Republic
  단지 성공한 장군과 프랑스 공화국 제1집정관의 관계보다는 프랑스 제국 황실의 일원이 되는 것을 더 선호했다
- **socially** 부 사교상, 사교적으로
- **lavish** [lǽviʃ] 형 아낌없는, 낭비하는
  - to aid him socially by entertaining on a **lavish** scale
    그(황제)가 화려한 규모의 유흥을 즐길 수 있도록 사교적으로 돕는
- **gorgeous** [gɔ́ːrdʒəs] 형 호화로운
- **strut** [strʌt] 동 뽐내면서 걷다, 자랑해보이다
- **overall** [óuvərɔ̀ːl] 명 (장교의) 정장용 통좁은 바지
- **spangle** [spǽŋɡəl] 명 반짝이는 금속조각
- **aigrette** [éiɡret, --́] 명 (모자 등의) 장식 깃털
- **busby** [bʌ́zbi] 명 모피제(毛皮製)의 춤이 높은 모자
- **rococo taste** 로코코 양식에 대한 기호
- **satin** [sǽtən] 명 견수자(絹繻子), 공단, 새틴
- **point lace** 손으로 뜬 레이스
- **concede** [kənsíːd] 동 부여하다, 인정하다, 용인하다
  - **conceded** the title of Imperial Highness to his sister
    그의 여동생에게 황녀의 지위를 수여했다
- To listen to you, people would think that I had robbed you of the heritage of the late King, our father.
  네 말을 듣고 있으면, 왕이었던 우리 아버지로부터 물려받은 네 유산을 내가 가로챘다고 사람들이 생각하겠구나(황녀의 지위가 당연한 것이 아니라는 뜻).

The rupture of the peace of Amiens did not affect the life of the Governor of Paris; for two years he enjoyed this office, with all its opportunities of ostentation and display. But in August, 1805, the approaching war with Austria caused the Emperor to summon his most brilliant cavalry leader to his side. In that month he despatched him, travelling incognito as Colonel Beaumont, to survey the military roads into Germany, and especially to study the converging roads round Würzburg, and the suitability of that town as an advance depôt for an army operating on the Danube. From Würzburg Murat travelled hurriedly through Nuremberg, Ratisbon, and Passau, as far as the river Inn, returning viâMunich, Ulm, the Black Forest, and Strassburg. Immediately on his return the Emperor appointed him "Lieutenant of the Empire, and commandant in his absence" of all the troops cantonned along the Rhine, and of such corps of the Grand Army as reached that river before himself. When war actually broke out Murat's duty was to mask, with his cavalry in the Black Forest, the turning movement of the other corps of the Grand Army which were striking at the Austrian rear. Once the turning movement was completed the Prince was entrusted with the command of the left wing of the army, which included his own cavalry division and the corps of Lannes and Ney. Excellent as he was as cavalry commander in the field, Murat had no head for great

- **rupture** [rʌ́ptʃər] 명 파괴, 결렬, 틀어짐
- **ostentation** [àstentéiʃən/ɔ̀s-] 명 허식, 겉치레, 과장
  - with all its opportunities of **ostentation** and display
  온갖 겉치레와 과시의 기회가 많았기 때문에
- **incognito** [inkǽgnitòu/-kɔ́gni-] 부 잠행으로, 신분을 숨기고
  - travelling **incognito** as Colonel Beaumont
  보몽 대령으로 신분을 숨기고 다니는
- **converge** [kənvə́ːrdʒ] 동 한 점에 모이다
  - especially to study the **converging** roads round Würzburg
  특히 뷔르츠부르크 주변으로 향하는 도로를 조사하는 목적으로
- **advance depôt** 전진기지
- **Lieutenant of the Empire, and commandant in his absence**
  제국의 부관이자 황제의 부재 시 총사령관
- **mask** [mæsk, mɑːsk] 동 엄폐하다, 적의 행동을 방해하다
  - Murat's duty was to **mask**, with his cavalry in the Black Forest, the turning movement of the other corps of the Grand Army which were striking at the Austrian rear.
  뮈라의 임무는 검은 숲 지역에서 대기하고 있던 기병으로 오스트리아군의 후방을 공격하여 대육군의 다른 부대가 선회(旋回)하는 것을 지원해 주는 것이었다.
- **Once the turning movement was completed the Prince was entrusted with the command of the left wing of the army**
  선회가 완전히 끝나자 공작은 군대의 좌익을 지휘하게 되었다
- **have no head for** ~에 약하다
- **combination** [kàmbənéiʃən/kɔ̀m-] 명 조화, 화합, 연합
  - Excellent as he was as cavalry commander in the field, Murat had no head for great **combinations**.
  전장에서 기병 사령관으로는 탁월했던 뮈라였지만, 대규모 연합작전을 수행할 만한 지력이 부족했다.

combinations. Instead of profiting by the advice of those able soldiers, Lannes and Ney, he spent his time quarrelling with them. He accordingly kept his troops on the wrong side of the Danube, with the result that in spite of Ney's brilliant action at Elchingen, two divisions of the Austrians under the Archduke Ferdinand escaped from Ulm. Prince Murat, however, retrieved his error by his brilliant pursuit of the escaped Austrians, and by hard riding and fighting captured quite half of the Archduke's command.

Impetuosity, perseverance, and dash are undoubtedly useful traits in the character of a cavalry commander, and of these he had his fair share. But his jealousy and vanity often led him astray. During the advance down the Danube, in his desire to gain the credit of capturing Vienna, he lost touch completely with the Russians and Austrians, who had retreated across the Danube at Krems, and he involved the Emperor in a dangerous position by leaving the unbeaten Russians on the flank of his line of communications. But the Prince quickly made amends for his rashness. The ruse by which he and Lannes captured the bridge below Vienna was discreditable no doubt from the point of view of morality. It was a direct lie to tell the Austrian commander that an armistice had been arranged and the bridge ceded to the French. But the fact remains that Murat saved the Emperor and

- **Instead of profiting by the advice of those able soldiers, Lannes and Ney, he spent his time quarrelling with them**
  란과 네 같은 유능한 군인들의 조언의 덕을 보기는커녕 그들과 다투느라 시간을 허비했다
- **retrieve** [ritríːv] 图 만회하다, 벌충하다
  - **retrieved** his error by his brilliant pursuit of the escaped Austrians
    탈출한 오스트리아군을 멋지게 추격하여 자신의 실수를 만회했다
- **captured quite half of the Archduke's command**
  (페르디난트) 대공의 병력을 절반 가까이를 사로잡았다
- **perseverance** [pə̀ːrsəvíːrəns] 图 인내심
- **useful traits in the character of a cavalry commander**
  기병 사령관의 성격으로 유리한 장점들
- **of these he had his fair share** 이로 인해 덕을 많이 보았다
- **lead ~astray** ~를 미혹시키다, 타락시키다
- **in his desire to gain the credit of capturing Vienna**
  빈(오스트리아 제국의 수도)을 함락시켜 신임을 얻고 싶다는 욕심에
- **lost touch with** ~와 접촉이 끊기다, 연락이 끊기다
  - he **lost touch** completely **with** the Russians and Austrians
    러시아군과 오스트리아군을 완전히 놓치고 말았다
- **line of commucation** 병참선
  - by leaving the unbeaten Russians on the flank of his **line of communications**
    그의 측면 병참선을 아직 무너지지 않은 러시아군에게 노출되게 함으로써
- **make amends for** ~을 보상하다
- **rashness** 图 분별없음, 경솔함
- **ruse** [ruːz] 图 책략, 계략
- **discreditable** 图 신용을 떨어뜨리는, 불명예스러운
- **direct lie** 노골적인 거짓말
- **an armistice had been arranged and the bridge ceded to the French**
  휴전이 성립되었으니 프랑스군에게 다리를 양도하라
- **the fact remains that** ~한 것은 사실이다

the French army from the difficult and costly operation of crossing the broad Danube in the face of the Allies. A few days later the Prince's vanity postponed for some time the culminating blow, for although he had so successfully bluffed the enemy, he could not realise that they could deceive him, and believing their tales of an armistice, he allowed the Allies to escape from Napoleon's clutches at Hollabrünn. At Austerlitz the Prince Marshal covered himself with glory. In command of the left wing, ably backed by Lannes, he threw the whole weight of his cavalry on the Russians, demonstrating to the full the efficacy of a well-timed succession of charges on broken infantry, and giving a masterly lesson in the art of re-forming disorganised horsemen, by the use he made of the solid ranks of Lannes' infantry, from behind which he issued again and again in restored order, to fall on the shaken ranks of the enemy. At Austerlitz he was at his best. His old quarrel with Lannes was for the moment forgotten; his lieutenants, Nansouty, d'Hautpoul, and Sébastiani, were too far below him to cause him any jealousy. The action on the left was mainly one of cavalry, in which quickness of eye and decision were everything, where a fault could be retrieved by charging in person at the head of the staff, or by a few fierce words to a regiment slightly demoralised. Rapidity of action and a self-confidence which on the battlefield never felt itself beaten were

- **costly** [kɔ́:stli/kɔ́st] 혱 희생이 큰, 타격이 큰
  - **costly** operation of crossing the broad Danube in the face of the Allies
    연합군의 면전에서 넓은 다뉴브 강을 도하하는 위험천만한 작전
- **culminate** [kʌ́lmənèit] 통 정점에 이르다, 최고조에 이르다
- **bluff** [blʌf] 통 허세를 부려 속이다
- **realise** [rí:əlàiz] 통 실감하다, 깨닫다
  - he could not **realise** that they could deceive him
    그는 적들도 자신을 속일 수 있다는 것을 깨닫지 못했다
- **clutch** [klʌtʃ] 명 손아귀, 붙잡음
  - believing their tales of an armistice, he allowed the Allies to escape from Napoleon's **clutches** at Hollabrünn
    그들의 휴전 이야기에 속은 그는 홀라브륀에서 연합군이 나폴레옹의 손아귀에서 벗어날 수 있게 만들었다(뮈라도 러시아의 바르라티온 왕자에게 똑같이 속음)
- **ably backed by Lannes** 란의 훌륭한 지원을 받아
- **effacacy** [éfəkəsi] 명 효험, 효력, 유효
- **well-timed** 혱 때를 잘 맞춘, 시의 적절한
  - a **well-timed** succession of charges on broken infantry
    대열이 흐트러진 보병에게 연이어 시의 적절한 돌격을 감행했다
- **disorganised** 혱 무질서한, 지리멸렬한
  - re-forming **disorganised** horsemen 무질서한 기병의 재정비
- **he issued again and again in restored order**
  몇 번이고 연이어서 대열을 정비해 출격했다
- **fall on** 습격하다, 공격하다
- **in which quickness of eye and decision were everything**
  빠른 눈썰미와 판단이 가장 중요한
- **demoralise** [dimɔ́:rəlàiz, -már-/-mɔ́r] 통 사기를 저하시키다
- **on the battlefield never felt itself beaten**
  전장에서 결코 패배했다고 생각하지 않는

the cause of Murat's success.

It was the fixed policy of Napoleon to secure the Rhine valley, so that never again would it be possible for the Austrians to threaten France. To gain this end he originated the Confederation of the Rhine, grouping all the small Rhineland states in a confederation of which he himself was the Protector, and binding the rulers of the individual states to his dynasty, either by marriage or by rewards. As part of this scheme the Emperor allotted to Murat and Caroline the duchies of Cleves and Berg, welding them into one province under the title of the Grand Duchy of Berg. Thus the Gascon innkeeper's son became in 1806 Joachim, Prince and Grand Admiral of France, and Grand Duke of Berg. He gained this honour not as Murat, the brilliant cavalry general, but as Prince Joachim, the brother-in-law of the Emperor Napoleon. The Grand Duke and the Grand Duchess did not, however, reside long in their capital, Düsseldorf; they infinitely preferred Paris. In their eyes Berg was but a stepping-stone to higher things, a source of profit and a pretext for exalting themselves at the expense of their neighbours. The Grand Duke entrusted the interior management of the Duchy to his old friend Agar, who had served him well in Italy, and who later became Count of Mosburg. Any prosperity which the Grand Duke enjoyed was

- **fixed** [fikst] 휑 고정된, 확고한
- **so that never again would it be possible for the Austrians to threaten France**
  오스트리아군이 다시는 프랑스를 위협하지 못하도록
- **Confederation of the Rhine**
  라인연방[동맹] (1806년 남서 독일의 16개국으로 조직한 프랑스의 속국)
- **binding the rulers of the individual states to his dynasty, either by marriage or by rewards**
  각국의 군주들을 혼인과 보상으로 그의 왕조에 한데 묶는
- **allot** [əlát/əlɔ́t] 동 할당하다, 분배하다, 주다
- **weld** [weld] 동 결합시키다, 합치다
  - **welding** them into one province under the title of the Grand Duchy of Berg
  하나로 묶어 베르크 대공국으로 만듦
- **stepping-stone** 명 디딤돌, 발판
  - Berg was but a **stepping-stone** to higher things
  베르크는 더 높은 것을 위한 발판에 불과했다
- **pretext** [príːtekst] 명 구실, 핑계
- **exalt** [igzɔ́ːlt] 동 (명예·품위 따위를) 높이다,
- **at the expense of** ~의 비용으로, ~에게 폐를 끼치고
- **interior management** 내정
  - The Grand Duke entrusted the **interior management** of the Duchy to his old friend Agar
  대공은 공국의 내정을 오랜 친구인 아가르에게 위임했다
- **prosperity** 명 번영, 번창, 부유
  - Any **prosperity** which the Grand Duke enjoyed was entirely due to the financial ability of Agar.
  대공은 전적으로 아가르의 재정관리 능력 덕택에 부유함을 누릴 수 있었다.

entirely due to the financial ability of Agar. Murat, however, kept foreign affairs in his own hands. As Foreign Minister, by simply taking what he wanted, he added considerably to the extent of his duchy. But, like all Napoleon's satellites, he constantly found his position humiliating, for in spite of his tears and prayers, he had continually to see his duchy sacrificed to France. It was no use to complain that Napoleon had taken away the fortress of Wesel, which had been handed over to the Grand Duchy by special treaty by the King of Prussia, for, as Queen Hortense wisely asked him, "Who had really made that treaty? Who had given him the duchy, the fortress, and everything?"

In September, 1806, Murat's second and last visit to Düsseldorf was brought to an abrupt close by the opening of the Prussian campaign. On the eve of the battle of Jena his cavalry covered forty miles and arrived in time to give the enemy the coup-de-grâce on the following day, driving them in flight into Weimar. Then followed the famous pursuit across Prussia, in which Murat captured first-class fortresses with cavalry regiments, and divisions of infantry with squadrons of horse, and ended by seizing Blücher and the whole of the Prussian artillery on the shore of the Baltic at Lübeck. But though his cavalry had thus wiped the Prussian army out of existence, the war dragged on, for, as

- **kept foreign affairs in his own hands** 외교적인 문제는 직접 처리했다
- **considerably** [kənsídərəbli] 튀 적지 않게, 꽤, 상당히
  - he added **considerably** to the extent of his duchy
    그는 자신의 공국을 상당히 넓게 확장시켰다
- **humiliating** 혱 치욕적인, 굴욕적인
- **he had continually to see his duchy sacrificed to France**
  그는 자신의 공국이 프랑스의 희생양이 되는 것을 계속해서 지켜볼 수밖에 없었다
- **It was no use to complain that** ~라고 불평하는 것은 아무 소용이 없었다
- **which had been handed over to the Grand Duchy by special treaty by the King of Prussia**
  프로이센왕과의 특별조약을 통해 공국에 양도되었던
- **Queen Hortense** 오르탕스 왕비(1783~1837, 오르탕스 드 보아르네, 나폴레옹의 의붓딸로 조제핀 드 보아르네의 딸이며 나폴레옹의 동생 루이와 결혼해 네덜란드 왕비가 됨)
- **"Who had really made that treaty? Who had given him the duchy, the fortress, and everything?"**
  나폴레옹을 말한다
- **abrupt** [əbrʌ́pt] 혱 갑작스러운, 뜻밖의
- **covered forty miles and arrived in time**
  40마일을 달려 정확한 시간에 도착했다
- **coup-de-grâce** 몡 결정적인 한 방
- **squadron** [skwádrən/skwɔ́d-] 몡 기병 대대
- **ended by seizing Blücher and the whole of the Prussian artillery on the shore of the Baltic at Lübeck**
  블뤼허 장군과 뤼벡에 주둔해 있던 발틱 해안의 프로이센 포병 전부를 사로잡으면서 끝이 났다
- **though his cavalry had thus wiped the Prussian army out of existence**
  그의 기병이 이렇게 프로이센군을 소탕했는데도

in 1805, the Russians had entered the field. In November the Emperor despatched his brother-in-law to command the French corps which were massing round Warsaw. The Grand Duke read into this order the idea that he was destined to become the King of a revived Poland; accordingly he made a triumphant entry into Warsaw in a fantastic uniform, red leather boots, tunic of cloth of gold, sword-belt glittering with diamonds, and a huge busby of rich fur bedecked with costly plumes. The Poles greeted him with enthusiasm, and Murat hastened to write to the Emperor that "the Poles desired to become a nation under a foreign King, given them by your Majesty." While the Grand Duke dreamed of his Polish crown, the climate defeated the French troops, and when the Emperor arrived at the front the Prince had to lay aside his royal aspirations. But in spite of his disappointment he was still too much of a Frenchman and a soldier to allow his personal resentment to overcome his duty to his Emperor, and he continued to hope that by his daring and success he might still win his Polish crown. At Eylau he showed his customary bravery and his magnificent talent as a cavalry leader, when he saved the shattered corps of Augereau by a successful charge of over twelve thousand sabres. At the battle of Heilsberg the celebrated light cavalryman, Lasalle, saved his life, but a few minutes later the Grand Duke was able to cry quits by himself rescuing Lasalle

- **the war dragged on, for, as in 1805, the Russians had entered the field**
  1805년 러시아군이 전장에 개입했기 때문에 전쟁은 장기전으로 갔다
- **mass** [mæs] 동 한 덩어리로 만들다, 집결하다
  - French corps which were **massing** round Warsaw
    바르샤바 인근에서 집결하고 있던 프랑스 부대
- **read into** ~의 뜻으로 해석하다(흔히 곡해를 하여)
  - The Grand Duke **read into** this order the idea that he was destined to become the King of a revived Poland
    대공은 이 명령을 자신이 부흥한 폴란드 왕국의 왕으로 임명할 뜻으로 곡해했다(폴란드 왕국은 18세기에 3회에 걸친 오스트리아, 프로이센, 러시아의 분할로 지도상에서 사라졌음)
- **bedeck** [bidék] 동 (화려하게) 꾸미다, 장식하다
- **plume** [pluːm] 명 깃털, 깃털 장식
- **the Poles desired to become a nation under a foreign King, given them by your Majesty.**
  폴란드인들은 폐하께서 임명하시는 외국인 왕을 모시고 왕국을 세우고 싶어 합니다.
- **the climate defeated the French troops** 혹독한 날씨에 프랑스군이 패배했다
- **lay aside** 비켜 두다, 치워 두다
- **aspiration** [æspəréiʃən] 명 열망, 포부
- **he was still too much of a Frenchman and a soldier to allow his personal resentment to overcome his duty to his Emperor**
  그는 여전히 프랑스인이었고 군인의 한 사람이었기 때문에 개인적인 원한으로 황제에 대한 의무를 해태하지는 않았다
- **customary** [kʌ́stəmèri/-məri] 형 습관적인, 늘 그랬던
- **sabre** [séibər] 명 사브르(기병도(刀)), 기병대
- **celebrated** [séləbrèitid] 형 유명한
- **cry quits** 무승부로 하다, 비기다
  - a few minutes later the Grand Duke was able to **cry quits** by himself rescuing Lasalle from the midst of a Russian charge
    몇 분 후 대공은 라살을 러시아군의 돌격 한가운데에서 구해내 빚을 갚을 수 있었다

from the midst of a Russian charge. Unfortunately for Murat, the prospective alliance with Russia once and for all compelled Napoleon to lay aside all thought of reviving the kingdom of Poland, and when the would-be King arrived with a Polish guard of honour and his fantastic uniform, he was met by the biting words of the Emperor: "Go and put on your proper uniform; you look like a clown."

After Tilsit the disappointed Grand Duke returned to Paris, where his equally ambitious wife had been intriguing with Josephine, Talleyrand and Fouché to get her husband nominated Napoleon's successor, in case the accidents of the campaign should remove the Emperor. But Napoleon had no intention of dying without issue. Thanks to his brother-in-law's generosity, Murat was able to neglect his half-million subjects in Berg and spend his revenues right royally in Paris. But early in 1808 his ambition was once again inflamed by the hope of a crown—not a revived kingship in Poland, but the ancient sceptre of Spain. Napoleon had decided that the Pyrenees should no longer exist, and that Portugal and Spain should become French provinces ruled by puppets of his own. Junot already held Portugal; it seemed as if it needed but a vigorous movement to oust the Bourbons from Madrid. Family quarrels had already caused a revolution in Spain. Charles had fled the kingdom, leaving the throne to his

- **prospective** [prəspéktiv] 형 예기되는, 장래의
- **once and for all** 마지막으로 한 번 더, 최종적으로(완전히)
  - the prospective alliance with Russia **once and for all** compelled Napoleon to lay aside all thought of reviving the kingdom of Poland
  러시아와의 최종적인 동맹을 맺을 생각을 했기 때문에 나폴레옹은 폴란드를 부활시킬 모든 생각을 버릴 수밖에 없었다
- **Go and put on your proper uniform; you look like a clown.**
  가서 당신에게 적당한 제복으로 갈아입게. 마치 광대 같아 보이는군.
- **in case the accidents of the campaign should remove the Emperor**
  전장에서 황제가 전사할 경우를 대비해서
- **Napoleon had no intention of dying without issue**
  나폴레옹은 자식 없이 죽을 생각이 없었다
- **generosity** [dʒènərásəti/-rɔ́s-] 명 관대, 아량
- **royally** 부 당당하게
- **revived kingship in Poland** 폴란드의 부활된 왕위
- **sceptre** [séptər] 명 (제왕의) 홀(笏), 왕위
- **Pyrenees should no longer exist**
  (프랑스와 이베리아 반도 사이를 가로막는)피레네 산맥은 더 이상 존재하지 않는다
- **puppet** [pʌ́pit] 명 괴뢰, 꼭두각시
- **vigorous** [vígərəs] 형 강경한, 단호한
- **oust** [aust] 동 내쫓다
  - it seemed as if it needed but a vigorous movement to **oust** the Bourbons from Madrid
  부르봉 가문을 마드리드에서 내쫓기 위해서는 강경한 행동을 할 필요가 있어 보였다
- **Charles had fled the kingdom, leaving the throne to his son Ferdinand.**
  카를로스 국왕은 아들인 페르디난도에게 왕위를 넘겨주고 왕국에서 도망쳤다.

son Ferdinand. Both had appealed to Napoleon; consequently there was a decent pretext for sending a French army into Spain. On February 25th Murat was despatched at a few hours' notice, with orders to take over the supreme command of all the French corps which were concentrating in Spain, to seize the fortresses of Pampeluna and St. Sebastian, and to advance with all speed on Madrid, but he was given no clue as to what the Emperor's ulterior object might be. He was ordered, however, to keep the Emperor daily informed of the state of public opinion in Spain. Prince Joachim very soon perceived that King Charles was rejected by everybody, that the Prime Minister, the Prince of Peace, was extremely unpopular, and that Ferdinand was weak and irresolute: it seemed as if he would follow the example of the King of Portugal, and would flee to the colonies when the French army approached his capital. The only disquieting feature of the situation was the constant annihilation of small parties of French soldiers and the brutal murder of all stragglers. On March 23rd the French army entered Madrid. All was tranquil. Meanwhile the ex-King Charles had retired to Bayonne, and, by the orders of the Emperor, the Prince of Peace was sent there also, whereupon King Ferdinand, fearing that Napoleon might take his father's part, hurried off to France. At Bayonne both the claimants to the Spanish throne surrendered their rights to the Emperor,

- **at a few hours' notice** 불과 몇 시간 전에 통지를 받고
- **to seize the fortresses of Pampeluna and St. Sebastian**
  팜플로나와 산 세바스티안의 요새들을 장악하는 것
- **to advance with all speed on Madrid** 전속력으로 마드리드로 진격하는 것
- **ulterior** [ʌltíəriər] 형 (표면에) 나타나지 않는, 숨은
  - he was given no clue as to what the Emperor's **ulterior** object might be
    황제의 숨은 의도가 무엇인지에 대해서는 들은 바가 전혀 없었다
- **to keep the Emperor daily informed of the state of public opinion in Spain**
  매일 황제에게 스페인의 여론 상황을 전하라고
- **perceive** [pərsíːv] 동 감지하다, 인식하다
- **the Prime Minister, the Prince of Peace**
  마누엘 데 고도이(1762~1851, 스페인의 수상으로 '평화대공'이라는 칭호를 받음)
- **irresolute** [irézəlùːt] 형 결단력이 없는, 우유부단한
- **disquiet** [diskwáiət] 동 불안하게 하다, 걱정시키다
  - The only **disquieting** feature of the situation was~
    현 상황에서 유일하게 걱정되는 측면이 있다면 ~이었다
- **annihilation** 명 전멸, 붕괴
- **straggler** 명 낙오자
  - the brutal murder of all **stragglers** 모든 낙오자에 대한 끔찍한 살해
- **tranquil** [trǽŋkwil] 형 조용한, 평온한
- **take a person's part** ~의 편을 들다
  - fearing that Napoleon might **take his father's part**
    나폴레옹이 그의 아버지의 편을 들까 두려워
- **hurried off to France** 프랑스를 향해 서둘러 떠났다
- **claimant** [kléimənt] 명 요구자, 청구자

while at Madrid, Murat, hoping against hope, played the royal part and kept the inhabitants quiet with bull-fights and magnificent fêtes. So far the Spaniards, though restless, were waiting to see whether the French were friends, as they protested, or in reality stealthy foes. The crisis came on May 2nd, when the French troops were compelled to evacuate Madrid on account of the fury of the populace at the attempted abduction of the little Prince, Don Francisco. Murat showed to the full his indomitable courage, fighting fiercely, not only for his Emperor, but for the crown which he thought was his. Bitter indeed were his feelings when he received a letter dated that fatal day, May 2nd, informing him that Joseph was to be King of Spain, and that he might choose either Portugal or Naples as his kingdom. In floods of tears he accepted Naples, but so cruel was the blow that his health gave way, and instead of hurrying off to his new kingdom he had to spend the summer drinking the waters at Barèges; his sensitive Gascon feelings had completely broken down under the disappointment, and, for the time being, he was physically and morally a wreck.

Murat was in no hurry to commence his reign, and his subjects showed no great anxiety to see their new ruler. But when King Joachim Napoleon, to give him his new title, arrived at Naples he

- **hope against hope** 요행을 바라다, 헛된 바람을 가지다
- **play royal part** 왕 노릇을 하다
- **kept the inhabitants quiet with bull-fights and magnificent fêtes**
  투우와 화려한 축제를 열어 백성들의 동요를 막았다
- **restless** [réstlis] 형 침착치 못한, 들떠 있는
- **whether the French were friends, as they protested,
  or in reality stealthy foes**
  프랑스인들이 그들이 주장하는 것처럼 친구인지, 아니면 속내를 감추고 있는 적인지
- **populace** [pápjələs/pɔ́p-] 명 민중, 서민
- **were compelled to evacuate Madrid** 마드리드에서 철수해야만 했다
- **abduction** [æbdʌ́kt] 명 유괴
  - on account of the fury of the populace at the attempted **abduction** of the little Prince, Don Francisco
  어린 왕자 돈 프란시스코를 유괴하려는 시도에 분노한 시민들 때문에
- **indomitable** [indámətəbəl/-dɔ́m-] 형 굴하지 않는, 불굴의
- **fatal** [féitl] 형 운명의, 숙명의
  - Bitter indeed were his feelings when he received a letter dated that **fatal** day, May 2nd
  5月 2일 그 운명의 날, 한 통의 편지를 받은 그는 말할 수 없는 쓸쓸함을 느꼈다
- **In floods of tears he accepted Naples**
  눈물을 홍수처럼 쏟으며 그는 나폴리 왕국을 받아들였다
- **but so cruel was the blow that his health gave way**
  그 충격이 너무나 커서 건강이 악화되었다
- **drinking the waters at Barèges**
  바레쥬에서 광천수를 마시며 (피레네 산맥에 면한 Barèges는 온천으로 유명함)
- **sensitive** [sénsətiv] 형 민감한, 예민한
- **he was physically and morally a wreck**
  육체적으로나 정신적으로 무너진 상태였다
- **showed no great anxiety to see their new ruler**
  그들의 새 왕을 그리 크게 보고 싶어 하지도 않았다

was received with unexpected warmth. The new monarch, with his striking personality and good looks, at once captivated the hearts of his fickle Southern subjects. Joseph had been prudent and cold, Joachim was ostentatious and fiery. The Neapolitans had never really cared for their Bourbon sovereigns. Some of the noblesse had from interest clung to the old dynasty, but the greater part of the nobility cared little who ruled them so long as their privileges were not interfered with. Among the middle class there was a strong party which had accepted the doctrines of the French Revolution. The lower class were idle and lazy, and willing to serve any sovereign who appealed to them by ostentation. The people who really held the key of the hearts of the mass of the population were the clergy. Joseph, with his liberal ideas, had attempted to free the people from clerical thraldom. Joachim, however, with his Southern instincts, refused to deny himself the use of such a powerful lever, and quickly ingratiated himself with his new subjects. From the moment that he arrived at Naples the new King determined, if not to rule Naples for the Neapolitans, at least, by pretending to do so, to rule Naples for himself and not for Napoleon. It is not, therefore, surprising that before the close of the year 1808 friction arose, which was further increased by the intrigues of Talleyrand and Fouché. These ministers, firmly convinced that Napoleon would never return

- he was received with unexpected warmth 그는 예상치 못한 환대를 받았다
- striking [stráikiŋ] 형 인상적인, 두드러진
- fickle [fíkəl] 형 변덕스러운
    - at once captivated the hearts of his **fickle** Southern subjects
    단번에 변덕스러운 남유럽 신민들의 마음을 사로잡았다
- ostentatious [àstentéiʃəs/ɔ́s-] 형 과시하는, 겉보기를 꾸미는
    - Joseph had been prudent and cold, Joachim was **ostentatious** and fiery
    조제프는 신중하고 냉정했지만, 조아생은 화려하고 열정적이었다
- Neapolitan [niːəpálətən/niːəpɔ́li-] 명 나폴리인
- the greater part of the nobility cared little who ruled them
  대다수의 귀족들은 누가 그들을 통치하느냐는 거의 관심이 없었다
- so long as their privileges were not interfered with
  그들의 특권을 침해당하지 않는 한
- doctrine [dáktrin/dɔ́k-] 명 교의, 교리, 주의
    - a strong party which had accepted the **doctrines** of the French Revolution
    프랑스 혁명의 이념을 받아들인 강력한 세력들
- ostentation [àstentéiʃən/ɔ́s-] 명 허식, 겉치장
- The people who really held the key of the hearts of the mass of the population were the clergy.
  대중의 마음을 움직일 수 있는 진정한 힘을 가진 이들은 성직자였다.
- thraldom [θrɔ́ːldəm] 명 노예의 신분, 속박
- instinct [ínstiŋkt] 명 본능, 천성
- refused to deny himself the use of such a powerful lever
  기꺼이 그런 강력한 수단을 이용했다
- ingratiate [ingréiʃièit] 동 마음에 들도록 하다, 영합하다
- friction arose, which was further increased by the intrigues of Talleyrand and Fouché
  탈레랑과 푸셰의 음모로 인해 훨씬 커진 불화가 발생했다

from the Spanish war, had decided that in the event of his death they would declare Murat his successor rather than establish a regency for the young son of Louis Napoleon, the King of Holland.

In pursuance of the plan of winning his subjects' affections Joachim had at once called to his aid Agar, who had so successfully managed the finances of the Grand Duchy of Berg. The difficulties of finance in Naples were very great, and with Agar the King had to associate the subtle Corsican, Salicetti, who had so powerfully contributed to the rise of Napoleon. Taxation in Naples was heavy, for the Neapolitans had to find the money for the war with their old dynasty, which was threatening them from Sicily, aided by the English fleet. To secure the kingdom against the Sicilians and English, a large Neapolitan army of thirty thousand troops had to be maintained along with an auxiliary force of ten thousand French. Moreover, the Neapolitans had to pay for having a King like Joachim and a Queen Consort like Caroline. The royal household alone required 1,395,000 ducats per annum. To meet this heavy expense the ministers had to devise all sorts of expedients to raise money. Regular taxation, monopolies, mortgages, and loans barely sufficed to provide for the budget. Still the King managed to retain his popularity, and in his own way attempted to ameliorate the lot of his subjects. He introduced the Code Napoleon. He founded a military college, an artillery

- **Napoleon would never return from the Spanish war**
  나폴레옹은 결코 스페인 전쟁에서 돌아올 수 없을 것이라고
- **in the event of his death** 그의 사망 시에
- **establish a regency for the young son of Louis Napoleon, the King of Holland**
  (유력한 왕위계승 후보였던) 네덜란드 왕 루이 나폴레옹의 어린 아들을 위해 섭정을 세우다
- **The difficulties of finance in Naples were very great**
  나폴리 왕국에는 어려운 재정문제가 너무나도 많았다
- **subtle** [sʌtl] 형 교활한, 음흉한
- **Salicetti** 앙투안 크리스토프 살리세티(1757~1810, 바스티아의 국민공회 의원 출신으로 보나파르트가와 친분이 있었음)
- **the war with their old dynasty** 옛 왕실(나폴리의 부르봉 왕가)과의 전쟁
- **threatening them from Sicily, aided by the English fleet**
  영국 함대의 도움을 받아 시칠리아에서 그들을 위협하고 있는
- **pay for having a King like Joachim and a Queen Consort like Caroline**
  조아생과 카롤린 같은 (사치스러운) 사람들을 왕과 왕비로 모시고 있는 대가를 치르다
- **per annum** 매년
- **devise** [diváiz] 동 궁리하다, 고안하다
- **expedient** [ikspíːdiənt] 명 수단, 방편
- **monopoly** [mənápəli/-nɔ́p-] 명 전매, 독점
- **mortgage** [mɔ́ːrgidʒ] 명 저당, 담보
- **suffice** [səfáis, -fáiz] 동 충분하다, 만족시키다
  - Regular taxation, monopolies, mortgages, and loans barely **sufficed** to provide for the budget.
    세금이나 전매수익, 저당, 융자 같은 것으로는 예산을 충족시키기가 어려웠다.
- **Still the King managed to retain his popularity**
  왕은 여전히 자신의 인기를 유지하고 있었다
- **ameliorate** [əmíːljərèit, -liə-] 동 개선하다, 개량하다
- **Code Napoleon** 나폴레옹 법전

and engineer college, a naval college, a civil engineer college and a polytechnic school. He also instituted primary schools in every commune, and started an École Normale for the training of teachers. He expanded the staff of the University and established an Observatory and Botanical Garden at Naples. He attempted to conciliate the Neapolitan noblesse by gradually dismissing his French ministers and officers and appointing Neapolitan nobles in their place. At the same time he abolished feudal dues and customs. He also attempted to develop industries by giving them protection. Above all, by the strict measures of his minister Manhes he established peace in the interior by breaking down the organised system of the freebooters and robbers. As time went on he found that the clergy and monks were too heavy a burden for his kingdom to bear, and, at the expense of his popularity, he had to cut down the numbers of the dioceses and parishes and abolish the religious orders.

From the first the new King grasped the fact that his kingdom would always be heavily taxed, and his throne insecure as long as the Bourbons, backed by the English, held Sicily. His plan of campaign, therefore, was to drive his enemy out of the smaller islands, and thereafter to demand the aid of French troops and make a determined effort against Sicily. In October, 1808, by a

- **polytechnic school** 기술학교
- **for the training of teachers** 유능한 교사들을 길러내기 위해
- **Observatory** [əbzə́ːrvətɔ̀ːri/-tər] 명 나폴리 천문대
- **conciliate** [kənsílièit] 동 달래다, 회유하다
- **by gradually dismissing his French ministers and officers and appointing Neapolitan nobles in their place**
  프랑스인 관리들과 장교들의 수를 점차 줄이고 나폴리인 귀족들로 대신 채움으로써
- **due** [djuː] 명 권리
  - abolished feudal **dues** and customs 봉건적인 권리와 관행을 폐지했다
- **develop industries by giving them protection**
  보호와 지원을 통해 산업을 발전시키다
- **he established peace in the interior** 내정의 평화를 확립시켰다
- **freebooter** 명 해적
  - by breaking down the organised system of the **freebooters** and robbers
  해적과 강도들의 유기적인 조직망을 분쇄시킴으로써
- **the clergy and monks were too heavy a burden for his kingdom to bear**
  성직자와 수도사들은 그의 왕국이 감당하기 어려운 너무나 큰 부담이었다
- **at the expense of his popularity** 인기가 하락하는 것을 감수하고
- **diocese** [dáiəsis, -sìːs] 명 주교관구
- **parish** 명 본당, 교구
- **From the first the new King grasped the fact that**
  왕은 처음으로 ~한 사실을 인지하게 되었다
- **insecure** [ìnsikjúər] 형 불안정한
- **as long as the Bourbons, backed by the English, held Sicily**
  영국의 지원을 업은 부르봉 가문이 시칠리아를 장악하고 있는 한
- **make a determined effort against Sicily**
  시칠리아에 대해 강경한 조치를 취하기로 결정했다

well-planned expedition, he captured the island of Capri, and caused the English commander, Sir Hudson Lowe, to capitulate. It was not till the autumn of 1810, however, that he was ready for the great expedition. Relying on the traditional hatred of the people of Messina for the Bourbons, he collected a strong force on the Straits, and waited till the moment when, after a gale, the English fleet had not yet arrived from the roads of Messina. On the evening of September 17th he sent away his advance guard of two thousand men in eighty small boats. Cavaignac, the commander of this force, secured the important villages of Santo Stefano and Santo Paolo. But at the critical moment the commander of the French division, acting according to the Emperor's orders, refused to allow his troops to cross. Before fresh arrangements could be made the English fleet reappeared on the scene, and Cavaignac and his force were thus sacrificed for no purpose. Joachim, as time showed, never forgave the Emperor for the failure of his cherished plan.

By the commencement of 1812, the coming Russian campaign overshadowed all other questions. Murat, who had earnestly begged to be allowed to share the Austrian campaign of 1809, was delighted to serve in person. But as King of Naples he refused to send a division of ten thousand men to reinforce the

- **capitulate** [kəpítʃəlèit] 동 조건부로 항복하다, 항복하다
  - caused the English commander, Sir Hudson Lowe, to **capitulate**
  영국의 사령관 허드슨 로위 경의 항복을 받아냈다
- It was not till the autumn of 1810, however, that he was ready for the great expedition.
  그러나 대규모 원정은 1810년 가을이 되어서야 착수할 수 있었다.
- traditional hatred of the people of Messina for the Bourbons
  부르봉 가문에 대한 메시나인들의 전통적인 원한
- the Straits 메시나 해협을 의미한다
- **gale** [geil] 명 질풍, 강풍, 폭풍
  - waited till the moment when, after a **gale**, the English fleet had not yet arrived from the roads of Messina
  폭풍이 지나가고 영국 함대가 아직 메시나의 도로에서 도착하지 않았을 때까지 기다렸다
- at the critical moment 결정적인 순간에
- the commander of the French division, acting according to the Emperor's orders, refused to allow his troops to cross
  황제의 명령에 따라 행동하던 프랑스 사단의 사령관은 그의 부대가 강을 건너는 것을 거부했다
- **arrangement** 명 정리, 정돈, 준비
  - Before fresh **arrangements** could be made the English fleet reappeared on the scene
  전열을 새로 정비하기 전에 영국 함대가 전장에 다시 나타났다
- sacrificed for no purpose 아무런 소득 없이 희생당한
- Joachim, as time showed, never forgave the Emperor for the failure of his cherished plan 시간이 흐르면서 드러났지만, 조아생은 황제가 자신의 오랜 계획을 망쳐버린 것을 결코 용서하지 않았다
- **overshadow** 동 빛을 잃게 하다, 그늘을 드리우다
- was delighted to serve in person 직접 출정하는 것을 좋아했다
- he refused to send a division of ten thousand men to reinforce the Grand Army
  대육군을 보강하기 위해서 1만 명 규모의 사단을 파견하는 것을 거부했다

Grand Army, "as a Frenchman and a soldier he declared himself to the core a subject of the Emperor, but as King of Naples he aspired to perfect independence." It was this double attitude which, from the moment Murat became King, clouded the relations between him and Napoleon. But nevertheless, once he rejoined the Emperor at Dantzig, he laid aside all his royal aspirations and became the faithful dashing leader of cavalry.

During the advance on Moscow the cavalry suffered terribly from the difficulties of constant reconnaissances and want of supplies, but in spite of this Murat urged the Emperor not to halt at Smolensk, but to push on, as he believed the Russians were becoming demoralised. Scarce a day passed without some engagement in which the King of Naples showed his audacity and his talent as a leader. Notwithstanding, Napoleon, angry at the constant escape of the Russians, declared that if Murat had only pursued Bagration in Lithuania he would not have escaped. This reproach spurred on the King of Naples to even greater deeds of bravery, and so well was his figure known to the enemy that the Cossacks constantly greeted him with cries of "Hurrah, hurrah, Murat!" At the battle of Moskowa he and Ney completely overthrew the Russians, and if Napoleon had flung the Guard into the action, the Russian army would have been annihilated. In spite

- **aspire** [əspáiər] 통 열망하다, 갈망하다
  - as King of Naples he **aspired** to perfect independence
  나폴리의 왕으로서 그는 완전한 독립을 원하고 있었다
- **double attitude** 양면적 태도, 이중성
- **clouded the relations between him and Napoleon**
  그와 나폴레옹의 관계에 어두운 그림자를 던졌다
- **nevertheless** [nèvərðəlés] 부 그런데도
- **he laid aside all his royal aspirations** 왕위에 대한 열정은 모두 제쳐두었다
- **the difficulties of constant reconnaissances and want of supplies**
  끊임없는 정찰과 보급의 부족으로 인한 어려움
- **not to halt at Smolensk, but to push on**
  스몰렌스크에서 멈추지 말고 계속 밀어붙이자고
- **as he believed the Russians were becoming demoralised**
  러시아군의 사기가 떨어지고 있었다고 믿었기 때문에
- **engagement** [engéidʒmənt] 명 싸움, 교전
  - Scarce a day passed without some **engagement** in which the King of Naples showed his audacity and his talent as a leader
  나폴리 왕이 전투에서 대담하고 용맹한 지휘관의 모습을 보이지 않고 하루가 넘어간 적이 거의 없었다
- **Notwithstanding** 전 그런데도
- **if Murat had only pursued Bagration in Lithuania he would not have escaped**
  뮈라가 리투아니아에서 바그라티온 왕자를 추격하기만 했어도 그는 도망치지 못했을 것이다
- **reproach** [ripróutʃ] 명 비난
- **spur** [spəːr] 명 자극하다, 박차를 가하다
- **so well was his figure known to the enemy**
  그의 활약이 적들에게 너무나도 잘 알려져 있어서
- **overthrow** [òuvərθróu] 통 뒤집어엎다, 무너뜨리다
  - completely **overthrew** the Russians 러시아군을 완전히 괴멸시켰다
- **fling** [fliŋ] 통 던지다, 투입하다
  - if Napoleon had **flung** the Guard into the action, the Russian army would have been annihilated
  나폴레옹이 근위대를 전투에 투입하면 러시아군은 전멸하고 말았다

of the losses during the campaign, when the French evacuated Moscow Murat had still ten thousand mounted troops, but by the time the army had reached the Beresina there remained only eighteen hundred troopers with horses. When the Emperor deserted the Grand Army, he left the King of Naples in command, with orders to rally the army at Vilna. But Murat saw that it was impossible to re-form the army there, and accordingly ordered a retirement across the Niemen, a line which he soon found it was impossible to hold. On January 10, 1813, came the news that the Prussians had actually gone over to the enemy. It seemed as if Napoleon was lost, and Murat thereupon at once deserted the army, and set out in all haste for Italy, thinking only of how to save his crown.

The King arrived in Naples bent on maintaining his crown and on allowing no interference from the Emperor. But in spite of this he could not decide on any definite line of action. He was afraid the English and Russians would invade his country, but on the other hand his old affection for Napoleon, and a sort of sneaking belief in his ultimate success, prevented him from listening to the insidious advice of the Austrian envoy, whom the far-seeing Metternich had at once sent to Naples. If Napoleon had not in his despatch glorified Prince Eugène's conduct to the

- there remained only eighteen hundred troopers with horses
  겨우 1800명의 기병밖에 남지 않게 되었다
- **rally** [rǽli] 동 다시 모으다, 재편성하다
- **retirement** [ritáiərmənt] 명 퇴거, 퇴각, 은퇴
- a line which he soon found it was impossible to hold
  지켜내기가 불가능하다는 것을 즉시 판단한 전선
- **go over to** ~로 전향하다, 옮겨가다
- **at once deserted the army** 즉시 군대를 버렸다
- set out in all haste for Italy, thinking only of how to save his crown
  그의 왕관을 지키겠다는 일념으로 전력을 다해 이탈리아로 달려갔다
- **bend on** ~에 힘을 쓰다, 노력을 기울이다
- he could not decide on any definite line of action
  그는 행동에서 확실한 선을 긋지를 못했다
- but on the other hand his old affection for Napoleon
  그러나 한편으로는 나폴레옹에 대한 옛정 때문에
- **sneaking** 형 비열한, 은밀한
- **insidious** [insídiəs] 형 서서히 퍼지는, 은밀한
  - prevented him from listening to the **insidious** advice of the Austrian envoy
    오스트리아 대사의 은밀한 조언을 받아들이는 것을 가로막고 있었다
- **far-seeing** 형 선견지명이 있는, 앞날을 내다보는
  - whom the **far-seeing** Metternich had at once sent to Naples
    앞날을 내다본 메테르니히가 즉시 나폴리로 보낸
- **glorify** [glɔ́:rəfài] 동 칭찬하다, 영광을 더하다, 명예를 주다

disparagement of the King of Naples, if he had only vouchsafed some reply to the King's persistent letters of inquiry whether he still trusted his old comrade and lieutenant, Murat would have thrown himself heart and soul into the mêlée on the side of his old friend. But in April Napoleon quitted Paris for the army in Germany without sending one line in reply to these imploring letters. Meanwhile on April 23rd came a letter from Colonel Coffin suggesting the possibility of effecting an entente between the English and Neapolitan Governments, or at any rate a commercial convention. Thereupon Murat sent officers to enter into negotiations with Lord William Bentinck, who represented the English Government in Sicily. All through the summer the negotiations were continued, but Murat, in spite of the guarantee of the throne of Naples which the English offered, could not break entirely with his Emperor and benefactor. Still Napoleon, in his blindness, instead of attempting to conciliate his brother-in-law, allowed articles to his disparagement to appear in the Moniteur. Nevertheless Murat at bottom was Napoleon's man. Elated by the Emperor's success at Lützen and Bautzen, although he refused to allow the Neapolitan troops to join the Army of Italy under Prince Eugène, he hurried off in August to join the French army at Dresden. There a reconciliation took place between the brothers-in-law. But after the defeat at Leipzig King Joachim asked

- **disparagement** 몡 비방, 비난
  - If Napoleon had not in his despatch glorified Prince Eugène's conduct to the **disparagement** of the King of Naples

  만약 나폴레옹이 사신을 보내 외젠 왕자가 나폴리 왕을 비난한 행동을 칭찬하지 않았더라면

- **vouchsafe** [vautʃséif] 동 허용해 주다, 주다, 내리다
  - if he had only **vouchsafed** some reply King's persistent letters of inquiry he still trusted his old comrade and lieutenant

  여전히 오랜 전우이자 부관이었던 자신을 신뢰하고 있냐고 묻는 왕(뮈라)의 끊임없는 편지에 조금의 답변만 주었더라면

- **imploring** [implɔ́:riŋ] 형 간절한, 애원하는
  - without sending one line in reply to these **imploring** letters

  이 간절한 편지들에 단 한 줄의 답변도 없이

- **entente** [ɑ:ntá:nt] 몡 (정부 간의) 협정, 협상, 합의

- **at any rate** 적어도

- **commercial convention** 상업(무역) 협정

- **Lord William Bentinck, who represented the English Government in Sicily**

  시칠리아에서 영국 정부 대표로 와 있던 윌리엄 벤팅크 경

- **in spite of the guarantee of the throne of Naples which the English offered**

  나폴리 왕관을 보장해주겠다는 영국의 제안에도

- **benefactor** [bénəfæktər] 몡 후원자, 은인

- **instead of attempting to conciliate his brother-in-law**

  매제와 화해를 시도하는 대신

- **article** [ɑ́:rtikl] 몡 기사, 논설, 고발

- **Nevertheless Murat at bottom was Napoleon's man.**

  그럼에도 불구하고 뮈라는 밑바닥부터 나폴레옹의 사람이었다.

- **elate** [iléit] 동 기운을 돋우다, 의기양양하게 하다

and obtained leave to return to his own dominions.

His presence was needed at home, for in Italy also the war had gone against the French. Prince Eugène had had to fall back on the line of the Adda, and the defection of the Tyrol had opened to the Allies the passes into the Peninsula. Murat, in his hurry, had to leave his coach snowed up in the Simplon Pass and proceed on horseback to Milan, where he halted but a few hours to write a despatch to the Emperor, which practically foretold his desertion. He declared that if he, instead of Eugène, was entrusted with the defence of Italy, he would at once march north from Naples with forty thousand men. He had indeed never forgotten the slight put upon him by the article in the Moniteur, after the Russian campaign, and he was ready to sacrifice even his kingdom if only he could revenge himself on his enemy, Eugène. As Napoleon would not grant him this request, he determined to humiliate Eugène, and, at the same time, to save his crown by negotiating with the enemy. On reaching Naples, he found that his wife, who hitherto had been an unbending partisan of the French, had entirely changed her politics and was now pledged to an Austrian alliance. The King was ever unstable, vanity always governed his conduct: the Queen was always determined, governed solely by a cold, calculating ambition. Negotiations were at once

- **leave** [liːv] 명 허가, 허락
  - Joachim asked and obtained **leave** to return to his own dominions
    조아생은 자신의 왕국으로 돌아갈 것을 요청해 허락을 받았다
- **His presence was needed at home**
  나폴리 왕국에서는 그의 존재가 필요했다
- **go against** ~에 반항하다, 항거하다
- **fall back** 후퇴하다, 뒷걸음치다
- **defection** 명 변절, 이반, 탈당
  - the **defection** of the Tyrol had opened to the Allies the passes into the Peninsula
    티롤의 배신은 연합군이 이탈리아 반도로 진격해 올 수 있는 길을 열어주었다
- **snow** [snou] 동 눈으로 덮다
  - leave his coach **snowed** up in the Simplon Pass and proceed on horseback to Milan
    생플롱 고개의 눈 속에 그의 마차를 내버려두고 말을 타고 밀라노로 달려갔다
- **practically** 부 사실상, 거의 ~나 다름없이
- **foretell** [fɔːrtél] 동 암시하다
- **desertion** [dizə́ːrʃən] 명 탈당, 도망
- **if he, instead of Eugène, was entrusted with the defence of Italy, he would at once march north from Naples with forty thousand men**
  외젠 대신 자신에게 이탈리아의 방어를 맡겨준다면 당장 4만 명의 병력을 이끌고 나폴리에서 북상하겠다
- **if only he could revenge himself on his enemy, Eugène**
  그의 정적인 외젠에게 복수할 수만 있다면
- **humiliate** [hjuːmílièit] 동 굴욕을 주다, 창피를 주다
- **unbending** 형 고집센, 완고한, 꺾이지 않는
  - his wife, who hitherto had been an **unbending** partisan of the French
    지금까지 열정적인 프랑스 제국 지지자였던 그의 아내
- **pledge** [pledʒ] 동 지지를 약속하다
- **unstable** 형 불안정한, 침착하지 않은
- **govern** [gʌ́vərn] 동 좌우하다, 결정하다, 지배하다
  - the Queen was always determined, **governed** solely by a cold, calculating ambition.
    왕비는 항상 자신의 야심을 위해 냉정하고 계산적으로 결정했다.

opened with the Austrians. The King protested "that he desired nothing in the world so much as to make common cause with the allied Powers." He promised that he would join them with thirty thousand troops, on condition that he was guaranteed the throne of Naples, and that he should have the Roman States in exchange for Sicily. Meanwhile he addressed an order of the day to his army, stating that the Neapolitan troops should only be employed in Italy. This of course did not commit him either to Napoleon or the Austrian alliance. Meanwhile the Emperor had despatched Fouché to try to bind his brother-in-law to France, but that distinguished double-dealer merely advised the Neapolitan King to move northwards to the valley of the Po with all his troops, and there to wait and see whether it would be best to help the French, or to enter France with the Allies, and perhaps the Tuileries as Emperor.

Joachim Napoleon quietly occupied Rome and pushed forward his troops towards the Po, using the French magazines and depôts, but still negotiating with the Austrians, and, at the same time, holding out hopes to the purely Italian party. For the national party of the Risorgimento were striving hard to seize this opportunity to unite Italy and drive out the foreigner, and no one seemed more capable of carrying out their policy than the popu-

- **protest** [prətést] 동 항의하다, 주장하다
- **make common cause with** ~와 제휴하다, 협력하다
  - he desired nothing in the world so much as to **make common cause with** the allied Powers
    이 세상에 연합국들과 협력해 가면서는 얻고 싶은 것은 아무것도 없다
- **he should have the Roman States in exchange for Sicily**
  시칠리아 대신 로마 교황령을 그가 가져야 한다
- **the Neapolitan troops should only be employed in Italy**
  나폴리 군대는 이탈리아 안에서만 싸워야 한다
- **commit** [kəmít] 동 입장을 분명히 하다, 관계하다, 말려들다
- **distinguished** [distíŋgwiʃt] 형 유명한
- **double-dealer** 명 이중거래를 하는 사람, 양다리 걸치는 사람(푸셰를 말함)
- **whether it would be best to help the French, or to enter France with the Allies**
  프랑스를 돕는 것이 최선인지, 연합군과 함께 프랑스로 진격하는 것이 최선인지
- **and perhaps the Tuileries as Emperor**
  그리고 어쩌면 황제로 튈르리 궁전에 입성할 수 있을지도 모른다
- **Joachim Napoleon**
  뮈라를 말한다. 뮈라는 나폴리 왕위에 오를 때 '나폴레옹'이라는 이름도 같이 하사받았다.
- **hold out** 제공하다, 약속하다, (희망 따위를) 품게 하다
- **purely Italian party** 토박이 이탈리아인들의 당
- **Risorgimento** [risɔ́ːrdʒiméntou, -zɔ́ːr-] 명 리소르지멘토
  (19세기 이탈리아의 국가 통일 운동)
- **strive** [straiv] 동 노력하다, 애쓰다
- **seize this opportunity to unite Italy and drive out the foreigner**
  이탈리아를 통일하고 외국인을 몰아낼 기회를 잡다
- **no one seemed more capable of carrying out their policy than the popular King of Naples**
  나폴리 왕만큼 그들의 정책을 시행할 만한 능력 있는 사람은 없어보였다

lar King of Naples. The Austrians flattered the hopes of "young Italy" by declaring in their proclamation that they had only entered Italy to free her from the yoke of the stranger, and to aid the King of Naples by creating an independent kingdom of Italy. Still Murat hesitated on the brink. As late as the 27th of December he wrote to the Emperor proposing that Italy should be formed into two kingdoms, that he should govern all the peninsula south of the Po, and that the rest of the country should be left to Eugène. Three days later the Austrian envoy arrived with the proposals of the Allies. But he could not yet make up his mind, and, moreover, the English had not yet guaranteed him Naples. In January, however, these guarantees were given, and against his will he had to sign a treaty. Scarcely was the writing dry when he began to negotiate with Prince Eugène. He used every artifice to prevent a collision between the French and Neapolitan troops. When the campaign opened his troops abandoned their position at the first shot, while he himself took good care not to reach the front until the news of Napoleon's abdication arrived.

But Murat's conduct had alienated everybody. The French loathed him for his duplicity; the Allies suspected him of treachery, and the party of the Risorgimento looked on him as the cause of their subjection to the foreigner; for the Austrian victory

- **yoke** [jouk] 명 멍에, 속박
  - they had only entered Italy to free her from the **yoke** of the stranger
  그들은 단지 외국인들의 속박에서 해방시키기 위해 이탈리아로 진격했다
- **on the brink** (멸망, 죽음 등)에 임하여, 직전에
- **moreover, the English had not yet guaranteed him Naples**
  게다가 영국인들은 아직 그에게 나폴리 왕국을 보장해주지 않았다
- **In January, however, these guarantees were given, and against his will he had to sign a treaty.**
  그러나 1월에 영국이 나폴리 왕국을 보장하자, 그는 자신의 의지에 반해 조약을 체결해야만 했다.
- **Scarcely was the writing dry when he began to negotiate with Prince Eugène.**
  협약서의 잉크가 채 마르기도 전에 그는 외젠 왕자와 교섭을 시작했다.
- **artifice** [ɑ́:rtəfis] 명 교묘한 책략, 술책
- **to prevent a collision between the French and Neapolitan troops**
  프랑스와 나폴리의 군대가 격돌하는 것을 막기 위해
- **abandon** [əbǽndən] 동 버리고 달아나다
- **at the first shot** 단 한 번의 사격에
- **he himself took good care not to reach the front**
  그 자신은 전선에 나아가지 않고 몸조심을 했다
- **alienate** [éiljənèit, -liə-] 동 멀리하다, 소원케 하다
  - Murat's conduct had **alienated** everybody.
  뮈라의 행동에 모두를 적으로 돌렸다.
- **loathe** [louð] 동 몹시 싫어하다, 역겨워하다
- **duplicity** [dju:plísəti] 명 표리부동, 이중성
- **treachery** [trétʃəri] 명 배반, 변절
- **subjection** [səbdʒékʃən] 명 종속, 복종
  - Risorgimento looked on him as the cause of their subjection to the foreigner
  리소르지멘토(이탈리아 부흥운동가)들은 뮈라 때문에 외국인에게 종속되었다고 여겼다

had not brought Italy unity and independence, but had merely established the fetters of the old régime. During the remainder of 1814 the lot of the King of Naples was most unenviable. The restored Bourbons of France and Spain regarded him as the despoiler of the Bourbon house of Sicily. Russia had been no party to the guarantee of his kingdom. England desired nothing so much as his expulsion. Austria alone upheld him, for she had been the chief party to the treaty; but Metternich was waiting for him to make some slip which might serve as a pretext for tearing up that treaty. Even the Pope refused the bribe which the King offered him when he proposed to restore the Marches in return for receiving the papal investiture. In despair Murat once again entered into negotiations with the Italian party. A general rising was planned in Lombardy, but failed, as the Austrians received news of the proposed cession of Milan. With cruel cunning they spread the report that the King of Naples had sold the secret. Henceforward Murat had no further hope. Foreigners, Italians, priests, carbonari and freemasons, all had turned against him.

Such was the situation when on March 8, 1815, the King heard that Napoleon had left Elba. As usual he dealt double. He at once sent a message to England that he would be faithful, while at the same time he sent agents to Sicily to try to stir up a revolt

- **fetter** [fétər] 명 족쇄, 속박
- **unenviable** 형 부러워할 것 없는, 샘나지 않은
  - During the remainder of 1814 the lot of the King of Naples was most **unenviable**.
  1814년의 남은 기간 동안 나폴리왕의 운명은 나락으로 떨어졌다.
- **despoiler** 명 약탈자, 강탈자
- **desire nothing so much as** 매우 ~하고 싶어 하다
- **expulsion** [ikspʌ́lʃən] 명 추방, 배제
- **uphold** [ʌphóuld] 동 지지하다
- **slip** [slip] 명 실수, 과실
  - but Metternich was waiting for him to make some **slip** which might serve as a pretext for tearing up that treaty
  그러나 메테르니히는 그가 조약 파기의 구실이 될 만한 실수를 저지를 때까지 기다리고 있었다
- **papal investiture** 교황의 (왕위) 수여
- **general rising** 민중봉기
- **cession** [séʃən] 명 할양, 양도
- **report** [ripɔ́ːrt] 명 소문
  - With cruel cunning they spread the **report** that the King of Naples had sold the secret.
  너무나도 교활하게 그들은 나폴리 왕이 민중봉기 계획의 기밀을 팔아먹었다는 소문을 퍼뜨렸다.
- **carbonari** [kɑ̀ːrbənɑ́ːri] 명 카르보나리
  (19세기 초 이탈리아 급진 공화주의자의 결사)
- **all had turned against him** 모두 그에게서 등을 돌렸었다
- **Such was the situation when on March 8, 1815, the King heard that Napoleon had left Elba.**
  나폴레옹이 엘바 섬을 탈출했다는 소식을 들은 1815년 3월 8일 당시의 상황이 이와 같았다.
- **stir up a revolt** 반란을 선동하다

against the Bourbons. As soon as the news of Napoleon's reception in France arrived, he set out at the head of forty thousand troops, thinking that all Italy would rise for him. But the Italians mistrusted the fickle King; the Austrian troops were already mobilised, and accordingly, early in May, the Neapolitan army fled homewards before its enemies. King Joachim's popularity was gone. A grant of a constitution roused no enthusiasm among the people. City after city opened its gates to the enemy. Resistance was hopeless, so on the night of May 19th the King of Naples, with a few hundred thousand francs and his diamonds, accompanied by a handful of personal friends, fled by sea to Cannes. But the Emperor refused to receive the turncoat, though at St. Helena he bitterly repented this action, lamenting "that at Waterloo Murat might have given us the victory. For what did we need? To break three or four English squares. Murat was just the man for the job." After Waterloo the poor King fled before the White Terror, and for some time lay hid in Corsica. There he was given a safe conduct by the Allies and permission to settle in Austria. But the deposed monarch could not overcome his vanity. He still believed himself indispensable to Naples. Some four hundred Corsicans promised to follow him thither. The filibustering expedition set out in three small ships on the 28th of September. A

- **reception** [risépʃən] 명 받아들임, 응접, 환영회, 입회
  - soon as the news of Napoleon's **reception** in France
    나폴레옹이 프랑스에 환영받았다는 소식을 듣자마자
- **he set out at the head of forty thousand troops**
  4만 명의 병력을 이끌고 출발했다
- **all Italy would rise for him** 이탈리아 전체가 자신을 위해 일어나 줄 것이다
- **mistrust** 동 신용하지 않다, 의심하다
- **fickle** [fíkəl] 형 변덕스러운, 변하기 쉬운
- **mobilise** [móubəlàiz] 동 (군사·함대)를 동원하다
- **Neapolitan army fled homewards before its enemies**
  나폴리 군대는 적에게 패해 고향으로 도망치고 말았다
- **grant** [grænt, grɑːnt] 명 허가, 승인
- **constitution** [kɑ̀nstətjúːʃən/kɔ̀n-] 명 헌법
  - A grant of a **constitution** roused no enthusiasm among the people.
    헌법을 승인해 준 것 가지고는 사람들 사이에 아무런 열의도 불러일으키지 못했다.
- **turncoat** 명 배반자, 변절자
- **repent** [ripént] 동 후회하다, 유감으로 생각하다
  - though at St. Helena he bitterly **repented** this action
    비록 (후일) 세인트헬레나에서 그는 (뮈라를 거부한) 이 행동을 몹시 후회했지만
- **lament** [ləmént] 동 슬퍼하다, 비탄하다
- **at Waterloo Murat might have given us the victory**
  워털루에서 뮈라만 있었더라면 우리가 이길 수 있었을 텐데
- **square** [skwɛər] 명 (옛 군대의) 방진
- **White Terror** 백색 테러(프랑스 혁명기에 혁명파에 가한 왕당파의 보복)
- **the deposed monarch could not overcome his vanity**
  폐위된 군주(뮈라)는 자신의 허영심을 이겨내지 못했다
- **Some four hundred Corsicans promised to follow him thither.**
  거기에서 4백 명 가량의 코르시카인들이 그를 따르기로 약속했다.
- **filibuster** 동 약탈하다, 해적질하다, 외국 영토에 침입하다

storm arose and scattered the armada, but in spite of this, on October 7th, the ex-King decided to land at Pizzo. Dressed in full uniform, amid cries of "Long live our King Joachim," the unfortunate man landed with twenty-six followers. He was at once arrested, and on October 13th tried by court martial, condemned to death, and executed a few hours later.

Joachim Murat met his death like a soldier. As he wrote to his wife, his only regret was that he died far off, without seeing his children. Death was what he courted when landing at Pizzo, for he must have known how impossible it was for him to conquer a kingdom with twenty-six men. Still, he preferred to die in the attempt to regain his crown rather than to spend an ignoble old age, a pensioner on the bounty of his enemies. Murat died as he had lived, brave but vain, with his last words calling out, "Soldiers, do your duty: fire at my heart, but spare my face."

The King of Naples owed his elevation entirely to his fortunate marriage with the Emperor's sister; otherwise it is certain he would never have reached such exalted rank, for Napoleon really did not like him or trust him, and had a true knowledge of his ability. "He was a Paladin," said the Emperor at St.
Helena, "in the field, but in the Cabinet destitute of either deci-

- **armada** [ɑːrmɑ́ːdə, -méi-] 명 함대
  - A storm arose and scattered the **armada**
    태풍이 불어와 함대를 뿔뿔이 흩어버렸다
- **the ex-King decided to land at Pizzo**
  이 옛날의 왕은 피초에 상륙하기로 결심했다
- **He was at once arrested** 그는 즉시 체포되었다
- **court martial** 군사 법정
- **condemned to death, and executed a few hours later**
  사형을 언도받고 몇 시간 후에 처형되었다
- **met his death like a soldier** 군인답게 죽음을 맞이했다
- **that he died far off, without seeing his children**
  머나먼 땅에서 아이들도 보지 못하고 죽는다는 것을
- **court** [kɔːrt] 동 (화를) 자초하다
  - Death was what he **courted** when landing at Pizzo
    죽음은 그가 피초에 상륙했을 때부터 자초한 것이었다
- **ignoble** [ignóubəl] 형 비천한, 비열한
- **pensioner** 명 연금 수령자
- **bounty** [báunti] 명 관대함, 보상금, 하사품
  - rather than to spend an ignoble old age, a pensioner on the **bounty** of his enemies
    적들이 주는 연금이나 받아먹으면서 비굴한 늙은이로 살아가기보다는
- **Soldiers, do your duty: fire at my heart, but spare my face**
  병사들이여, 그대들의 임무를 수행하라. 내 심장을 정확하게 쏘아라. 그러나 얼굴만은 쏘지 말게
- **elevation** [èləvéiʃən] 명 승진, 출세
- **exalted** [igzɔ́ːltid] 형 고귀한, (신분이) 높은
- **had a true knowledge of his ability** 그의 능력을 정확히 간파하고 있었다
- **destitute** [déstətjùːt] 형 빈곤한, ~이 결핍된
  - He was a Paladin in the field, but in the Cabinet **destitute** of either decision or judgment.
    그는 전장에서는 위대한 전사였지만, 내각에서는 결단력이나 판단력이 부족했다.

sion or judgment. He loved, I may rather say, adored me; he was my right arm; but without me he was nothing. In battle he was perhaps the bravest man in the world; left to himself, he was an imbecile without judgment." Murat was a cavalry leader pure and simple. His love of horses, his intuitive knowledge of exactly how much he could ask from his horsemen, his reckless bravery, his fine swordsmanship, his dashing manners, captivated the French cavalry and enabled him to "achieve the impossible." Contrary to accepted opinion Napoleon believed "that cavalry, if led by equally brave and resolute men, must always break infantry." Consequently we find that at Austerlitz, Jena, and Eylau, the decisive stroke of the day was in each case given by immense bodies of some twenty thousand men under the command of Murat, whose genius lay in his ability to manœuvre these huge bodies of cavalry on the field of battle, and in the tenacity with which he clung to and pursued a beaten enemy. But this was the sum total of his military ability. He had no conception of the use of the other arms of the service, and never gained even the most elementary knowledge of strategy. When trusted with anything like the command of a mixed body of troops he proved an utter failure. Before Ulm he nearly ruined Napoleon's combination by failing to get in contact with the enemy. In the later half of the campaign of 1806 he hopelessly failed to make any headway

- **He loved, I may rather say, adored me**
  그는 나를 사랑했다, 아니 숭배했다는 것이 맞을 것이다
- **left to himself** 혼자 내버려두면
- **imbecile** [ímbəsil, -sàil/-sìːl] 명 저능아, 바보
- **intuitive** [intjúːitiv] 형 직관적인, 직관력 있는
- **exactly how much he could ask from his horsemen**
  그의 기병에게 정확히 얼마만큼 능력을 끌어낼 수 있는지
- **reckless** [réklis] 형 분별없는, 무모한
- **swordsmanship** 명 군인정신, 상무(尚武)정신
- **captivate** [kǽptəvèit] 동 ~의 넋을 빼앗다, 매혹시키다
- **Contrary to accepted opinion** 일반적인 견해와는 달리
- **cavalry, if led by equally brave and resolute men, must always break infantry**
  똑같은 용맹과 단호함을 가진 지휘관이 이끈다고 가정할 때, 기병은 반드시 보병을 이기게 되어 있다
- **consequently** 부접 따라서, 그 결과로
- **genius lay in his ability to manœuvre these huge bodies of cavalry**
  대규모의 기병 군단을 자유자재로 지휘하는 천부적인 재능이 있다
- **tenacity** [tənǽsəti] 명 고집, 끈기, 불굴
- **he clung to and pursued a beaten enemy**
  패주하는 적에게 끝까지 달려들며 추격했다
- **But this was the sum total of his military ability.**
  그러나 이것이 그의 군사적 재능의 전부였다.
- **other arms of the service** 군사(軍事)의 다른 부문
- **When trusted with anything like the command of a mixed body of troops**
  (기병 외에) 혼재된 군대의 지휘 같은 것을 맡기면
- **utter** [ʌ́tər] 형 전적인, 완전한
- **headway** 명 전진, 진행

against the Russians east of the Vistula. In the retreat across the Niemen he proved himself absolutely incapable of reorganising a beaten force. As a king, Murat was full of good intentions towards his people, but his extravagance, his vanity, his indecision cost him his crown. As a man he was generous and extraordinarily brave. In the Russian campaign he used to challenge the Cossacks to single combat, and when he had beaten them he sent them away with some medal or souvenir of himself. He was a good husband, and lived at peace and amity with his wife, and was exceedingly fond of his children. His faults were numerous; he was by nature intensely jealous, especially of those who came between him and Napoleon, and he stooped to anything whereby he might injure his rivals, Lannes and Prince Eugène. His hot Southern blood led him into numerous quarrels. Although extremely arrogant, at bottom he was a moral coward, and before the Emperor's reproaches he scarcely dared to open his mouth. But his great fault, through which he gained and lost his crown, was his vanity. Vanity, working on ambition and an unstable character, is the key to all his career. His blatant Jacobinism, his intrigue with Josephine, his overtures to the Directors, his underhand treatment of his fellow Marshals, his discontent with his Grand Duchy, his subtle dealings in Spain, his system of government in Naples, his opposition to Napoleon's schemes, his dis-

- he proved himself absolutely incapable of reorganising a beaten force
  패한 병사들을 수습하는 데에 전혀 능력이 없다는 것을 보여주었다
- **extravagance** [ikstrǽvəgəns] 몡 사치, 낭비, 무절제함
- **indecision** [ìndisíʒən] 몡 우유부단, 주저
- **cost him his crown** 그가 왕관을 잃게 했다
- he used to challenge the Cossacks to single combat
  그는 자주 코사크인들에게 일대일 전투로 도전하곤 했다
- **souvenir** [sùːvəníər] 몡 기념품, 선물
- **amity** [ǽməti] 몡 친목, 친선, 우호
- **exceedingly** [iksíːdiŋli] 튀 대단히, 몹시
  - was **exceedingly** fond of his children
    자녀들을 대단히 사랑했다
- **intensely** 튀 격렬하게, 심하게
- especially of those who came between him and Napoleon
  특히 누군가 자신과 나폴레옹 사이에 끼어드는 것을
- **stoop** [stuːp] 동 수치를 무릅쓰고 ~하다
- anything whereby he might injure his rivals
  그의 경쟁자들을 해칠 수 있는 있다면 어떤 것이라도
- **arrogant** [ǽrəgənt] 형 거만한, 오만한
- **moral** [mɔ́(ː)rəl, már-] 형 양심적인, 순진한
  - at bottom he was a **moral** coward
    実제로는 순진한 겁쟁이였다
- before the Emperor's reproaches he scarcely dared to open his mouth
  황제가 질책할 때면 그는 감히 입도 떼지 못했었다
- **the key to all his career** 모든 그의 삶을 설명해주는 열쇠
- **blatant** [bléitənt] 형 소란스러운, 뻔뻔스러운
- **overture** [óuvərtʃər, -tʃùər] 몡 신청, 제안
- **underhand** 형 음험한, 비열한
- **discontent** [dìskəntént] 몡 (욕구) 불만(의 근원), 불평
- **subtle** [sʌ́tl] 형 미묘한, 교활한

simulation and desertion, his almost theatrical bravery, and his very death were due to nothing save extravagant vanity.

- **dissimulation** [disímjəlèit] 명 시치미 뗌, 위선
- **theatrical** [θiǽtrikəl] 형 연극 같은, 과장된
- **extravagant** [ikstrǽvəgənt] 형 터무니없는, 지나친
- **save** [seiv] 전 ~을 제외하고
    - his very death were due to nothing **save** extravagant vanity
    그가 그렇게 죽은 것은 바로 그 터무니없는 허영심이 유일한 이유였다

3. ANDRÉ MASSÉNA

*MARSHAL, DUKE OF RIVOLI,
PRINCE OF ESSLING*

André Masséna, "the wiliest of Italians," was born at Nice on May 6, 1758, where his father and mother carried on a considerable business as tanners and soap manufacturers. On his father's death, when André was still but a small boy, his mother at once married again. Thereon André and two of his sisters were adopted by their uncle Augustine, who proposed to give his nephew a place in his business. But André's restless, fiery nature could not brook the idea of a perpetual monotonous existence in the tanyard and soap factory, so at the age of thirteen he ran away from home and shipped as a cabin boy; as such he made several voyages in the Mediterranean, and on one occasion crossed the Atlantic to Cayenne. But, in spite of his love of adventure, the life of a sailor soon began to pall, and on August 18, 1775, at the age of seventeen, he enlisted in the Royal Italian regiment in the French service. There he came under the influence of his uncle Marcel,

- **willy** [wáili] 휑 교활한, 약삭빠른
  - the **wiliest** of Italians
    이탈리아인들 중 가장 교활한 자(마세나의 고향인 니스는 전통적으로 사보이공국의 영토로 이탈리아의 일부분으로 간주되어 왔다. 여러 차례 소유자가 바뀌다가 1860년 사르데냐 왕국이 최종적으로 프랑스의 나폴레옹 3세에게 양도했다. 니스는 마세나 외에 이탈리아 통일의 주역인 주세페 가리발디의 고향이기도 하다)
- **tanner** [tǽnər] 명 무두장이, 제혁(製革)업자
  - carried on a considerable business as **tanners** and soap manufacturers
    아주 큰 규모의 가죽과 비누를 제조하는 공장을 운영하고 있었다
- **when André was still but a small boy** 앙드레가 아직 어린 소년에 불과했을 때
- **were adopted by their uncle Augustine** 삼촌 오귀스틴의 양자가 되었다
- **restless** [réstlis] 휑 침착하지 못한, 활동적인
- **brook** [bruk] 동 참다, 견디다
- **perpetual** [pərpétʃuəl] 휑 부단한, 끊임없는
- **monotonous** [mənátənəs/-nɔ́t-] 휑 단조로운, 지루한
- **tanyard** 명 무두질 공장, 가죽제조 공장
- **cabin boy** 선실 보이(1·2등 선객 및 고급 선원의 시중을 듦)
  - ran away from home and shipped as a **cabin boy**
    집에서 도망쳐 나와 선실 보이로 배를 탔다
- **on one occasion** 이따금, 때때로
  - **on one occasion** crossed the Atlantic to Cayenne
    이따금 대서양을 건너 카옌으로 가기도 했다(카옌은 남아메리카 북동부의 프랑스 식민지이며 현재도 프랑스령 기아나의 수도임)
- **pall** [pɔːl] 동 시시해지다, 흥미를 잃다
- **he enlisted in the Royal Italian regiment in the French service**
  프랑스군 내에 있는 왕실 이탈리아 연대에 입대했다

who was sergeant-major of the regiment; thanks to his advice and care he made rapid strides in his profession, and received a fair education in the regimental school. In later years the Marshal used to say that no step cost him so much trouble or gave him such pleasure as his promotion to corporal; be that as it may, promotion came rapidly, and with less than two years' service he became sergeant on April 15, 1777. For fourteen years Masséna served in the Royal Italians, but at last he retired in disgust. Under the regulations a commission was unattainable for those who were not of noble birth, and the officers of the regiment had taken a strong dislike to the sergeant, whom the colonel constantly held up as an example, telling them, "Your ignorance of drill is shameful; your inferiors, Masséna, for example, can manœuvre the battalion far better than any of you." On his retirement Masséna lived at Nice. To occupy his time and earn a living he joined his cousin Bavastro, and carried on a large smuggling business both by sea and land; he thus gained that intimate knowledge of the defiles and passes of the Maritime Alps which stood him in such good stead in the numerous campaigns of the revolutionary wars, while the necessity for keeping a watch on the preventive men and thus concealing his own movements developed to a great extent his activity, resource, and daring. So successful were his operations that he soon found himself in the position to

- **stride** [straid] 명 (보통 pl.) 진보, 발달, 전진
  - he made rapid **strides** in his profession 군인으로서 장족의 발전을 하다
- **received a fair education in the regimental school**
  연대의 학교에서 훌륭한 교육을 받았다
- **cost** [kɔːst/kɔst] 동 (좋지 않은 일을) 겪게 만들다
  - no step **cost** him so much trouble 그를 승진시켜주어도 아무런 문제가 없다
- **corporal** [kɔ́ːrpərəl] 명 상등병, 상병
  - gave him such pleasure as his promotion to **corporal**
  상병으로 진급시켜 그를 기쁘게 해주었다
- **be that as it may** 어쨌든, 그것이 어떻든
- **sergeant** [sáːrdʒənt] 명 병장
- **in disgust** 싫어져서, 정이 떨어져서
- **regulation** [règjəléiʃən] 명 규칙, 규정
- **commission** [kəmíʃən] 명 (장교의) 임관
- **unattainable** 형 얻기 어려운, 도달하기 어려운
  - Under the regulations a commission was **unattainable** for those who were not of noble birth
  규정상 귀족출신이 아니면 장교가 되는 것은 불가능했다
- **hold up as an example** 예시로 거론하다
- **drill** [dril] 명 훈련
- **occupy one's time** ~의 시간을 보내다, 차지하다
- **earn a living** 생계를 꾸리다
- **smuggle** [smʌ́gəl] 동 밀수하다
- **defile** [difáil] 명 (종대가 지나갈 정도의) 애로(隘路), 좁은 골짜기
- **Maritime Alps** 마리팀 알프스(프랑스의 동남부와 이탈리아의 서북부)
- **stood him in such good stead** 그에게 큰 도움이 되어주었다
- **preventive men** 밀수 단속관들
- **conceal** [kənsíːl] 동 숨기다, 숨다
- **to a great extent** 대부분은, 크게

demand the hand of Mademoiselle Lamarre, daughter of a surgeon, possessed of a considerable dowry. When the revolutionary wars broke out the Massénas were established at Antibes, where they did a fair trade in olive oil and dried fruits; but a respectable humdrum existence could not satisfy the restless nature of the ex-sergeant, and in 1791 he applied for a sub-lieutenancy in the gendarmerie, and it is to be presumed that, on the principle of setting a thief to catch a thief, he would have made an excellent policeman. It was at this moment that the invasion of France by the monarchs of Europe caused all patriotic Frenchmen to obey the summons to arms. Masséna gladly left his shop to serve as adjutant of the volunteers of the Var. His military knowledge, his erect and proud bearing, his keen incisive speech, and absolute self-confidence in all difficulties soon dominated his comrades, and it was as lieutenant-colonel commanding the second battalion that he marched to the frontier to meet the enemy. Lean and spare, below middle height, with a highly expressive Italian face, a good mouth, an aquiline nose, and black sparkling eyes, from the very first Masséna inspired confidence in all who met him; but it was not till he was seen in action that the greatness of his qualities could best be appreciated.

As Napoleon said of him at St. Helena, "Masséna was at his best and most brilliant in the middle of the fire and disorder of

- **surgeon** [sə́:rdʒən] 명 외과의사, 군의관
- **dowry** [dáuəri] 명 신부의 지참금
- **When the revolutionary wars broke out the Massénas were established at Antibes.** 혁명이 일어났을 때, 마세나 부부는 앙티브에 정착하고 있었다.
- **humdrum** 형 평범한, 단조로운, 지루한
- **sub-lieutenancy** 소위 직책
- **gendarmerie** [ʒɑ:ndá:rməri] 명 (프랑스의) 헌병대
- **presume** [prizú:m] 동 추정하다, 상상하다, 생각하다
    - it is to be **presumed** that, on the principle of setting a thief to catch a thief, he would have made an excellent policeman.
    도둑으로 도둑을 잡게 한다는 원칙에 근거해서 생각해 봤을 때, 그는 뛰어난 경찰이 되었을 것이다(마세나가 밀수업의 경험을 가지고 있었기 때문에 하는 말).
- **summons** [sʌ́mənz] 명 소환, 소집
    - caused all patriotic Frenchmen to obey the **summons** to arms
    모든 애국심 있는 프랑스인들이 군대의 소집명령에 따르도록 만들었다
- **adjutant** [ǽdʒətənt] 명 부관, 조수
- **bearing** [bɛ́əriŋ] 명 태도, 행동거지
- **incisive** [insáisiv] 형 날카로운, 예리한
- **dominated his comrades** 그의 동료들을 능가했다
- **lean** [li:n] 형 야윈, 깡마른
- **spare** [spɛər] 형 여윈, 마른
- **a highly expressive Italian face**
    매우 표정이 풍부한 전형적인 이탈리아인의 얼굴
- **but it was not till he was seen in action that the greatness of his qualities could best be appreciated**
    그러나 그의 탁월한 자질은 실전에 투입되었을 때 비로소 최고로 인정받을 수 있었다
- **brilliant** [bríljənt] 형 훌륭한, 화려한
    - Masséna was at his best and most **brilliant** in the middle of the fire and disorder of battle
    마세나는 전투의 총격과 혼란의 한 가운데에서 최고로 훌륭한 모습을 보여주었다

battle; the roar of the cannon used to clear his ideas, give him insight, penetration, and gaiety... In the middle of the dead and dying, among the hail of bullets which swept down all around him, Masséna was always himself giving his orders and making his dispositions with the greatest calmness and good judgment. There you see the true nobility of blood." In the saddle from morning till night, absolutely insensible to fatigue, ready at any moment to take the responsibility of his actions, he returned from the first campaign in the Riviera as major-general. During the siege of Toulon he commanded the "Camp de milles fourches," which included the company of artillery commanded by Bonaparte, and distinguished himself by taking the forts of Lartigues and St. Catharine, thus earning his step as lieutenant-general while his future commander was still a major in the artillery. In the campaign of 1794 it was Masséna who conceived and carried out the turning movement which drove the Sardinians from the Col de Tenda, while Bonaparte's share in the action merely consisted of commanding the artillery. As the trusted counsellor of Dumerbion, Kellermann, and Schérer, for the next two years, the lieutenant-general was the inspirer of the successive commanders of the Army of Italy. He it was who, amid the snow and storms, planned and carried out the combinations which gained for Schérer the great winter victory at Loano, and thus

- **roar** [rɔːr] 몡 포효
- **insight** [ínsàit] 몡 간파, 통찰, 통찰력
- **penetration** 몡 간파, 통찰, 통찰력
- **gaiety** [géiəti] 몡 유쾌, 쾌활, 명랑
- **sweep** [swiːp] 동 스쳐 지나가다
  - among the hail of bullets which **swept** down all around him
    그의 주위로 온통 쏟아져 내리는 총탄 세례의 와중에
- **make one's dispositions** 만반의 준비를 하다
- **insensible** [insénsəbəl] 혱 무감각한, 느끼지 못하는
- **distinguished himself by taking the forts of Lartigues and St. Catharine**
  라르티그 요새와 생 카타린 요새를 함락시켜 이름을 떨쳤다
- **earning his step as lieutenant-general** 중장까지 승진했다
- **while his future commander was still a major in the artillery**
  그의 미래의 사령관(나폴레옹)은 아직 포병 소령에 불과했던 반면
- **conceive** [kənsíːv] 동 고안하다, 착상하다
  - it was Masséna who **conceived** and carried out the turning movement which drove the Sardinians from the Col de Tenda
    콜 드 탕드에서 사르데냐인들을 몰아내는 우회 작전을 고안하고 실행한 것이 바로 마세나이다
- **inspirer** 몡 고무(격려)하는 사람, 영감을 주는 사람
- **successive** [səksésiv] 혱 잇따른, 계속되는
- **the lieutenant-general was the inspirer of the successive commanders of the Army of Italy**
  이탈리아군에 잇따라 부임하는 지휘관들에게 고무적인 존재가 되었다
- **combination** [kὰmbənéiʃən/kɔ̀m-] 몡 조합, 연합
- **which gained for Schérer the great winter victory at Loano**
  로아노의 겨울 전투에서 사단장 쉐레(1747~1804)에게 큰 승리를 안겨 주었다

first taught the French the secret, which the English had grasped on the sea and Napoleon was to perfect on land, of breaking the enemy's centre and falling on one wing with overwhelming force. The campaign of 1796 for the time being altered the current of Masséna's military life. Before the young Corsican's eagle gaze even the impetuous Italian quailed, and from being the brain of the officer commanding the army he had to revert to the position of the right arm and faithful interpreter of orders. Two things, however, compensated Masséna for the change of rôle, for Bonaparte gave his subordinate fighting and glory with a lavish hand, and above all winked at, nay, rather encouraged, the amassing of booty; and wealth more even than glory was the desire of Masséna's soul.

At the very commencement of the campaign Masséna committed a fault which almost ruined his career. After defeating the enemy's advance guard near Cairo, hearing by chance that the Austrian officers had left an excellent dinner in a neighbouring inn, he and some of his staff left his division on the top of a high hill and set off to enjoy the good things prepared for the enemy. At daybreak the enemy attempted a surprise on the French position on the hill, and the troops, without their general and staff, were in great danger. Fortunately, Masséna had time to make his

- **secret** [síːkrit] 명 비결, 비법
  - the **secret**, which the English had grasped on the sea and Napoleon was to perfect on land

  영국이 바다를 장악해왔고, 나폴레옹이 육지에서 무적이 될 그 비결
- **fall on** ~에게 덤벼들다, 달려들다
  - of breaking the enemy's centre and **falling on** one wing with overwhelming force

  압도적인 병력으로 적의 중앙을 격파하고 한쪽 날개에 달려드는
- **impetuous** [impétʃuəs] 형 충동적인, 맹렬한, 격렬한
- **quail** [kweil] 동 기가 죽다, 주춤하다
  - Before the young Corsican's eagle gaze even the impetuous Italian **quailed**

  그 젊은 코르시카인의 날카로운 시선 앞에서 이 격정적인 이탈리아인도 한 풀 기가 꺾였다
- **from being the brain of the officer commanding the army**

  군대를 지휘하는 장군들의 두뇌 역할에서
- **revert** [rivə́ːrt] 동 본래 상태로 되돌아가다, 복귀하다
  - he had to **revert** to the position of the right arm and faithful interpreter of orders

  그는 심복이자 명령의 충실한 이행자로 되돌아가야만 했다
- **with a lavish hand** 아낌없이
- **wink at** 눈감아주다
  - above all **winked at**, nay, rather encouraged, the amassing of booty

  무엇보다도 전리품을 긁어모으는 것을 눈감아줄 뿐만 아니라 오히려 장려해주기까지 했다
- **wealth more even than glory was the desire of Masséna's soul**

  영예보다는 오히려 부의 축적이 진정으로 마세나가 바라는 것이었다
- **After defeating the enemy's advance guard near Cairo**

  카이로 인근에서 적의 전위대를 격파한 뒤(여기에서 Cairo는 이탈리아에 있는 현재의 Cairo Montenotte를 말함)
- **the Austrian officers had left an excellent dinner in a neighbouring inn**

  인근 여관에서 오스트리아 장교들이 성대한 만찬을 할 예정이었다
- **set off to enjoy the good things prepared for the enemy**

  적을 위해 준비한 멋진 선물을 선사하려고 출발했다(가서 공격하겠다는 뜻)

다음 장에 해설 계속

way through the Austrian skirmishers and resume his command. He was greeted by hoots and jeers, but with absolute imperturbability he reorganised his forces and checked the enemy.

ANDRÉ MASSÉNA, PRINCE OF ESSLING

But one battalion was isolated on a spur, from which there

- **daybreak** [déibrèik] 명 새벽녘, 동틀 녘
  - At **daybreak** the enemy attempted a surprise on the French position on the hill, and the troops, without their general and staff, were in great danger.
  새벽녘에 적들은 언덕의 프랑스군 주둔지에 기습공격을 가했고, 장군과 참모들이 없던 프랑스군은 큰 위험에 빠지고 말았다(거짓 정보에 마세나가 완전히 속음).
- **skirmishers** 명 전위, 전초 척후병
- **hoot** [hu:t] 명 야유소리, 올빼미 울음소리
- **jeer** [dʒiər] 명 조롱, 야유
- **imperturbability** [ìmpəːrtərbəbíləti] 명 침착, 냉정
- **check the enemy** 적을 저지하다
- **spur** 명 (산·언덕의) 돌출부, (산맥의) 지맥
- **scorch** [skɔːrtʃ] 동 ~을 누렇게 하다, 그슬리다
- **flank fire** 측방사격
  - But one battalion was isolated on a spur, from which there seemed no way of escape save under a scorching **flank fire**.
  그러나 부대 하나가 언덕의 돌출부에서 고립되어, 적의 측방사격을 뚫지 않고서는 탈출할 방법이 전혀 없어보였다.

seemed no way of escape save under a scorching flank fire. Masséna made his way alone to this detached post, scrambling up the steep slope on his hands and knees, and, when he at last reached the troops, remembering his old smuggling expedients, he showed them how to glissade down the steep part of the hill, and brought them all safely back without a single casualty. This escapade came to Bonaparte's ears, and it was only Masséna's great share in the victory of Montenotte which saved him from a court-martial.

Bonaparte, at the commencement of the campaign, had ended a letter of instructions to his lieutenant with the words "Watchfulness and bluff, that is the card," and well Masséna learned his lesson. Montenotte, the bridge of Lodi, the long struggle at Castiglione, the two fights at Rivoli and the marshes of Arcola proved beyond doubt that of all the young conqueror of Italy's lieutenants, none had the insight, activity, and endurance of Masséna. But empty flattery did not satisfy him, for as early as Lonato, greedy for renown, he considered his success had not been fully recognised. In bitter anger he wrote to Bonaparte: "I complain of your reports of Lonato and Roveredo, in which you do not render me the justice that I merit. This forgetfulness tears my heart and throws discouragement on my soul. I will recall the fact under

- **scramble up** (손을 집어가며 힘들게) 기어오르다
- **steep** [stiːp] 형 가파른, 깎아지른 듯한
- **slope** [sloup] 명 경사면, 비탈
- **expedient** [ikspíːdiənt] 명 수단, 방편
  - remembering his old smuggling **expedients**
    그가 밀수하던 시절의 방법을 기억해내
- **glissade** [glisάːd, -séid] 통 글리사드로 내려가다, 활강하다
  - how to **glissade** down the steep part of the hill
    언덕의 가파른 부분을 어떻게 내려가는지
- **brought them all safely back without a single casualty**
  단 한 명의 부상자도 없이 안전하게 그들을 데리고 돌아왔다
- **escapade** [éskəpèid] 명 멋대로 구는 짓, 모험행위
- **it was only Masséna's great share in the victory of Montenotte which saved him from a court-martial**
  이것이 몽테노트의 승리에서 마세나가 보여준 유일하게 훌륭한 공적이었고, 덕분에 그는 군법재판소를 모면할 수 있었다
- **watchfulness** 명 신중, 경계
- **bluff** [blʌf] 명 허세
- **beyond doubt** 의심의 여지 없이
- **of all the young conqueror of Italy's lieutenants, none had the insight, activity, and endurance of Masséna**
  이 젊은 이탈리아 정복자의 부관들 중에 어느 누구도 마세나 만큼 통찰력과 활동력, 인내력을 가지지 못했다
- **flattery** [flǽtəri] 명 아첨, 치렛말
- **renown** [rináun] 명 명성
- **merit it** [mérit] 통 ~할 만하다
  - you do not render me the justice that I **merit**
    당신은 내가 응당 받아야만 하는 공정한 평가를 받지 못하게 했다
- **forgetfulness** 명 부주의, 태만

compulsion that the victory of Saintes Georges was due to my dispositions, to my activity, to my sangfroid, and to my prevision." This frank republican letter greatly displeased Bonaparte, who, since Lodi, had cherished visions of a crown, and to realise this desire had begun to issue his praise and rewards irrespective of merit, and to appeal to the private soldier while visiting his displeasure on the officers. But Masséna's brilliant conduct at the second battle of Rivoli, for the moment, blotted out all rancour, for it was Masséna who had saved the day, who had rushed up to the commander of the shaken regiment, bitterly upbraiding him and his officers, showering blows on them with the flat of his sword, and had then galloped off and brought up two tried regiments of his own invincible division and driven back the assailants; from that moment Bonaparte confirmed him in the title of "the spoilt child of victory." In 1797 Bonaparte gave his lieutenant a more substantial reward when he chose him to carry the despatches to Paris which reported the preliminary treaty of Leoben; thus it was as the right-hand man of the most distinguished general in Europe that the Italian saw for the first time the capital of his adopted country.

In choosing Masséna to carry to Paris the tidings of peace, it was not only his prestige and renown which influenced Bonaparte. For Paris was in a state of half suppressed excitement, and

- **under compulsion** 강요되어, 부득이
  - I will recall the fact **under compulsion** that
    ~나는 부득이하게 ~라는 사실을 상기시킬 수밖에 없다
- **sangfroid** [sɑːŋfrwáː, sæŋ-] 몡 냉정, 침착
- **This frank republican letter greatly displeased Bonaparte**
  이 솔직한 공화주의자의 편지는 보나파르트를 대단히 불쾌하게 만들었다
- **cherish** [tʃériʃ] 통 (소원 등을) 품다
  - who, since Lodi, had **cherished** visions of a crown
    로디 전투에서부터 왕관을 쓸 생각을 품어왔던 그
- **irrespective** [ìrispéktiv] 혱 관계없는, 상관없는
  - had begun to issue his praise and rewards **irrespective** of merit
    공적에 관계없이 칭찬과 보상을 주고 있었다
- **blot out** 지우다, 없애다
- **rancour** [ræŋkər] 몡 깊은 원한, 증오
- **shaken** 몡 충격을 받은, 겁먹은, 동요하는
  - who had rushed up to the commander of the **shaken** regiment
    동요하는 연대 지휘관을 다그쳤다
- **upbraid** [ʌpbréid] 통 신랄하게 비판하다, 비난하다
- **shower blows on a person** 사람에게 주먹다짐을 하다
- **the flat of a sword** 칼의 몸체(넓적한 부분)
- **tried** 혱 믿을 만한, 시련을 견디는
- **invincible** [invínsəbəl] 혱 무적의, 극복할 수 없는
- **the spoilt child of victory** 승리의 여신이 가장 아끼는 아들
- **preliminary** [prilímənèri/-nəri] 혱 예비의, 준비의, 임시의
- **the Italian saw for the first time the capital of his adopted country**
  그 이탈리아인은 처음으로 자신이 선택한 국가의 수도(파리)를 보게 되었다
- **tidings** [táidiŋz] 몡 통지, 소식
- **it was not only his prestige and renown which influenced Bonaparte**
  보나파르트의 결정에 영향을 준 것은 그의 위신과 명성 때문만은 아니었다
- **suppress** [səprés] 통 억누르다, 가라앉히다, 진압하다

signs were only too evident that the Directory was unstable; accordingly the wily Corsican, while despatching secret agents to advance his cause, was careful to send as the bearer of the good news a man who was well known to care for no political rewards, and who would be sure to turn a deaf ear to the insidious schemes of those who were plotting to restore the monarchy, or to set up a dictatorship, and were searching for a sovereign or a Cæsar as their political views suggested. It was for these reasons and because he was tired of Masséna's greed and avarice that Bonaparte refused to admit him among those chosen to accompany him to Egypt. Masséna saw clearly all the secret intrigue of the capital, and found little pleasure in his newly gained dignity of a seat among the Ancients, for he was extremely afraid of a royalist restoration, in which case he feared "our honourable wounds will become the titles for our proscription."

Tired of Paris, in 1798, he was glad to accept the command of the French corps occupying Rome when its former commander, Berthier, was called away to join the Egyptian expedition. On his arrival at Rome, to take over his new command, he found himself face to face with a mutiny. The troops were in rags and badly fed, their pay was months in arrear, and meanwhile the civil servants of the Directory were amassing fortunes at the ex-

- **only too** 아주, 매우
  - For Paris was in a state of half suppressed excitement, and signs were **only too** evident that the Directory was unstable

  파리는 겨우 소동을 억누르고 있는 상황이었으며, 총재정부가 불안정하다는 징후는 아주 명백했다
- **advance** [ædvǽns, -váːns, əd-] 동 진척시키다, 촉진시키다
- **cause** [kɔːz] 명 주장, 대의, 큰 목적
- **who was well known to care for no political rewards**

  정치적 보상에는 아무런 관심이 없는 것으로 잘 알려진
- **turn a deaf ear to** ~에 귀를 기울이지 않다
- **insidious** [insídiəs] 형 틈을 엿보는, 교활한
  - to turn a deaf ear to the **insidious** schemes those who were plotting to restore the monarchy, or to set up a dictatorship

  군주제를 부활시킨다든가 독재체제를 구축하려는 음모를 꾸미는 사람의 교활한 계획 같은 것에는 귀를 기울이지 않는
- **avarice** [ǽvəris] 명 탐욕, 허욕
- **all the secret intrigue of the capital** 수도에서 벌어지고 있는 모든 비밀 음모
- **the Ancients** 총재정부시대의 원로원(Council of Ancients)
- **proscription** [prouskrípʃən] 명 인권박탈, 추방, 금지
  - our honourable wounds will become the titles for our **proscription**

  (왕당파가 복귀한다면) 우리의 영광스러운 상처는 우리를 추방하는 명분이 될 것이다
- **called away** 다른 일로 불러내다
- **face to face** 정면으로 대하여, 직면하여
- **mutiny** [mjúːtəni] 명 폭동, 반란, 하극상
- **The troops were in rags and badly fed**

  군대는 누더기를 입으면서 거의 굶주리고 있었다
- **months in arrear** 수개월이나 지체된

pense of the Pope, the Cardinals, and the Princes of Rome. Discontent was so widespread that the new general at once ordered all troops, save some three thousand, to leave the capital. Unfortunately Masséna's record was not such as to inspire confidence in the purity of his intentions. Instead of obeying, the officers and men held a mass meeting to draft their remonstrance to the Directory. In this document they accused, first of all, the agents who had disgraced the name of France, and ended by saying, "The final cause of all the discontent is the arrival of General Masséna. The soldiers have not forgotten the extortions and robberies he has committed wherever he has been invested with the command. The Venetian territory, and above all Padua, is a district teeming with proofs of his immorality." In the face of such public feeling Masséna found nothing for it but to demand a successor and throw up his command.

But with Bonaparte in Egypt and a ring of enemies threatening France from all sides, the Directors, whose hands were as soiled as Masséna's, could ill spare the "spoilt child of victory." Accordingly, early in 1799 the general found himself invested with the important command of the Army of Switzerland. This was a task worthy of his genius and he eagerly accepted the post, but refused to abide by the stipulations the Directors desired to enforce

- **record** [rékərd/-kɔːrd] 몡 이력, 전과, 경력
  - Masséna's **record** was not such as to inspire confidence in the purity of his intentions
  (탐욕을 많이 부렸던) 마세나의 이력 때문에 사람들은 그의 순수한 의도를 믿지 못했다
- **save some three thousand** 3천여 명만 남기고
- **leave the Capital** 수도를 떠나다(Capital은 로마를 의미)
- **remonstrance** [rimánstrəns/-mɔ́n-] 몡 항의, 진정서
- **The final cause of all the discontent is the arrival of General Masséna.**
  모든 불만의 근본적인 원인은 마세나가 장군으로 부임했기 때문이다.
- **invest with** ~에게 주다, 서임하다, 임명하다
  - wherever he has been **invested with** the command 그가 지휘관으로 임명되는 곳 어디에서나
- **teem** [tiːm] 통 풍부하다, 많이 있다
- **immorality** [ìmərǽləti] 몡 부도덕, 패행
- **In the face of such public feeling** 그런 공연한 감정 앞에서
- **throw up** 사직하다
  - Masséna found nothing for it but to demand a successor and **throw up** his command
  마세나는 후임자를 요구하고 지휘관을 사직하는 것밖에 다른 수가 없었다
- **with Bonaparte in Egypt** 보나파르트는 이집트에 가 있고
- **a ring of enemies** 적들의 연합
- **soild** [sɔil] 통 더럽히다, 타락시키다
  - the Directors, whose hands were as **soiled** as Masséna's
  마세나만큼이나 부도덕한 짓을 많이 한 총재정부
- **can ill spare** ~을 내놓기가 아깝다, 꼭 필요한 인재이다
- **worthy** [wə́ːrði] 형 ~에 어울리는
  - This was a task **worthy** of his genius
  이것은 그의 천재적인 재능에 어울리는 임무였다
- **abide by** (약속·규칙 등을) 지키다, (협정·결정 따위를) 따르다
- **stipulation** 몡 약속, 조항, 조건

on him, as, according to their plan, the Army of Switzerland was to form part of the Army of the Rhine commanded by Joubert. Masséna had obeyed Bonaparte, but he had no intention of playing second fiddle to any other commander, and, after some stormy interviews and letters, he at last had his way. As the year advanced it became more and more evident that on the Army of Switzerland would fall the full brunt of the attack of the coalition, for Joubert was defeated by the Archduke Charles at Stockach and thrown back on the Rhine, Schérer was defeated in Italy at Magnano, and by June the Russians and Austrians had begun to close in on Switzerland. It was clear that, if the French army were driven out of Switzerland, both the Rhine and the Maritime Alps would be turned, and the enemy would be in a strong position from which to invade France. On Masséna, therefore, hung all the hopes of the Directory. Fortunately for France, the general was admirably versed in mountain warfare. Well aware of the difficulty of keeping up communication between the different parts of his line of defence, Masséna skilfully withdrew his outposts, as the enemy pressed on, with the intention of concentrating his troops round Zurich, thereby covering all the possible lines of advance. But early in the summer his difficulties were further increased by the rising of the Swiss peasantry; luckily, however, the Archduke Charles advanced most cautiously, while

- **was to form part of the Army of the Rhine commanded by Joubert**
  주베르가 지휘하는 라인군의 일부가 될 예정인
- **play secone fiddle to** ~밑에 종속되다
- **stormy** [stɔ́ːrmi] 〚형〛 격렬한, 격정적인
- **have one's way** ~마음대로 하다
- **brunt** [brʌnt] 〚명〛 공격의 예봉, 주력
- **fall on** (몸에) 닥치다, ~을 습격하다
  - **on** the Army of Switzerland would **fall** the full brunt of the attack of the coalition
    스위스군은 연합군의 가장 강력한 주력부대의 공격 앞에 놓여 있었다는
- **close in** 포위하다, 밀려오다
  - Russians and Austrians had begun to **close in** on Switzerland
    러시아군과 오스트리아군이 스위스를 향해 밀려오기 시작했다
- **both the Rhine and the Maritime Alps would be turned**
  라인과 마리팀 알프스(프랑스의 동남부와 이탈리아의 서북부)가 모두 적의 편으로 등을 돌리게 될 것이다
- **On Masséna, therefore, hung all the hopes of the Directory.**
  마세나에게 총재정부의 모든 희망이 달려있었다.
- **admirably** 〚부〛 감탄할만하게, 훌륭하게
- **versed in mountain warfare** 산악전에 정통한
- **Well aware of the difficulty of keeping up communication between the different parts of his line of defence**
  방어선의 각 부분끼리의 연락망을 유지하는 것이 어렵다는 것을 잘 알고는
- **skilfully** 〚부〛 능숙하게, 능란하게
- **outpost** 〚명〛 전초부대, 전진기지
- **as the enemy pressed on** 적이 밀려들어오자
- **covering all the possible lines of advance** 진격이 가능한 모든 길을 방어하는

the Aulic Council at Vienna, unable to grasp the vital point of the problem, stupidly sent its reserve army to Italy to reinforce the Russians under Suvaroff. By June 5th the Archduke had driven in all the outlying French columns, and was in a position to attack the lines of Zurich with his entire force. Thanks, however, to Masséna's courage and presence of mind, the attack was driven off, but so overwhelming were the numbers of the enemy that during the night the French army evacuated Zurich, though only to fall back on a strong position on Mount Albis, a rocky ridge at the north end of the lake, covered on one flank by the lake and on the other by the river Aar. The two armies for the time being lay opposite to each other, too exhausted after the struggle to recommence operations. The Archduke Charles awaited the arrival from Italy of Suvaroff, who was to debouch on the French right by the St. Gothard Pass. But fortune, or rather the Aulic Council at Vienna, once again intervened and saved France. The Archduke Charles was ordered to leave fifty-five thousand Russians under Korsakoff before Zurich and to march northwards and across the Rhine. Protests were useless; the Court of Vienna merely ordered the Archduke to "perform the immediate execution of its will without further objections." But even yet disaster threatened the French, for Suvaroff was commencing his advance by the St. Gothard. But Masséna at once grasped the opportunity

- **Aulic Council** (신성 로마 황제의) 자문 회의
- **vital** [váitl] 형 치명적인, 지극히 중요한
  - unable to grasp the **vital** point of the problem
    문제의 가장 중요한 핵심을 파악할 능력이 없었던
- **outlying** 형 외진, 동떨어진
- **the attack was driven off** 공격은 격퇴되었다
- **but so overwhelming were the numbers of the enemy that during the night the French army evacuated Zurich**
  적의 수가 너무 많았기 때문에 프랑스군은 밤중에 취리히를 버리고 떠났다
- **only to do** 그 결과는 ~뿐, 단지 ~하기 위해
- **fall back** ~에 기대다, 의지하다
- **covered on one flank by the lake and on the other by the river Aar**
  한쪽 측면은 호수가, 다른 한쪽 측면은 아르 강이 감싸고 있는
- **for the time being lay opposite to each other** 한동안 서로 대치하고 있었다
- **debouch** [dibúːʃ, -báutʃ] 동 진출하다, 흘러나오다
  - who was to **debouch** on the French right by the St. Gothard Pass
    생 고타르 고개를 넘어 프랑스군의 우측을 공격하기로 예정된
- **intervene** [ìntərvíːn] 동 사이에 끼다, 개입하다, 방해하다
- **to leave fifty-five thousand Russians under Korsakoff before Zurich**
  코르사코프 장군 휘하 5만 5천 명의 러시아군을 취리히 앞에 남겨두고
- **to march northwards and across the Rhine** 북상해서 라인 강을 건너라고
- **Protests were useless** 항의해보았자 소용이 없었다
- **perform the immediate execution of its will without further objections**
  더 이상 항명하지 말고, 자문 회의의 뜻을 즉시 이행하라

fortune had placed in his power by opposing him to a commander like Korsakoff, who was so impressed by his own pride that he considered a Russian company equal to an Austrian battalion. On September 26th, by a masterly series of manœuvres, the main French force surprised Korsakoff and drove him in rout out of Zurich. Suvaroff arrived just in time to find Masséna in victorious array thrust in between himself and his countrymen, and was forced to save himself by a hurried retreat through the most difficult passes of the Alps.

The campaign of Zurich will always be studied as a masterpiece in defensive warfare. The skilful use the French general made of the mountain passes, the methods he employed to check the Archduke's advance on Zurich, the care with which he kept up communications between his different columns, the skilful choice of the positions of Zurich and Mount Albis, his return to the initiative on every opportunity, and his masterly interposition between Korsakoff and Suvaroff, alone entitle him to a high place among the great commanders of history, and Masséna was rightly thanked by the legislature and hailed as the saviour of the country.

- at once grasped the opportunity fortune had placed in his power by opposing him to a commander like Korsakoff

  코르사코프 같은 지휘관을 상대하게 된, 이 운명이 그에게 쥐어준 기회를 곧바로 활용했다
- **company** [kʌ́mpəni] 명 중대
  - a Russian **company** equal to an Austrian battalion

    러시아군 1개 중대는 오스트리아군 1개 대대와 맞먹는다
- **rout** [raut] 명 참패, 패주
  - drove him in **rout** out of Zurich

    그를 취리히 밖으로 패퇴시켰다
- **thrust in** 밀어젖히고 나아가다, 헤치고 들어가다
  - to find Masséna in victorious array **thrust in** between himself and his countrymen

    기세등등한 마세나의 군대가 자신과 다른 러시아군들 사이를 밀고 들어오는 것을 보았다
- was forced to save himself by a hurried retreat through the most difficult passes of the Alps

  알프스의 가장 험준한 길을 따라 급히 퇴각해서야 겨우 자신의 목숨을 구할 수 있었다
- **masterpiece** [mǽstərpìːs, mάːs-] 명 걸작, 명작
  - The campaign of Zurich will always be studied as a **masterpiece** in defensive warfare.

    취리히 전투는 방어전의 걸작으로 여겨져 늘 중요한 연구대상이 될 것이다.
- **employ** [emplɔ́i] 동 (물건·수단을) 쓰다, 사용하다
- **check** [tʃek] 동 저지하다, 방해하다
  - the methods he employed to **check** the Archduke's advance on Zurich

    (카를) 대공이 취리히로 진격하는 것을 저지하기 위해 그가 사용한 방법
- **initiative** [iníʃiətiv] 명 주도권, 창의
  - his return to the **initiative** on every opportunity

    모든 기회마다 주도권을 회복했다
- **interposition** [ìntərpəzíʃən] 명 간섭, 방해
- **entitle him to a high place** 그에게 높은 위치에 설 자격을 주었다
- **legislature** [lédʒislèitʃər] 명 입법부, 입법기관, 의회

Six weeks after the victory of Zurich came the 18th Brumaire, and Napoleon's accession to the consulate. Masséna, a staunch republican, was conscious of the defects of the Directory, but could not give his hearty consent to the coup d'état, for he feared for the liberty of his country. Still, he said, if France desired to entrust her independence and glory to one man she could choose none better than Bonaparte. The latter, on his side, was anxious to retain Masséna's affections, and at once offered him the command of the Army of Italy. But the conqueror of Zurich foresaw that everything was to be sacrificed to the glory of the First Consul, and it was only after great persuasion, profuse promises, and appeals to his patriotism that he undertook the command, with the stipulation that "I will not take command of an army condemned to rest on the defensive. My former services and successes do not permit me to change the rôle that I have heretofore played in the wars of the Republic." The First Consul replied by giving Masséna carte blanche to requisition whatever he wanted, and promised him that the Army of Italy should be his first care. But when Masséna arrived at Genoa he discovered, as he had suspected, that Bonaparte's promises were only made to be broken; for he found the troops entrusted to his care the mere shadow of an army, the hospitals full, bands of soldiers, even whole battalions, quitting their posts and trying to escape

- **accession** [ækséʃən] 명 취임, 즉위
- **staunch** [stɑːntʃ, stɔːntʃ] 형 철두철미한, 완고한
- **conscious** [kɑ́nʃəs/kɔ́n–] 형 의식하고 있는, 알고 있는
  - Masséna, a staunch republican, was **conscious** of the defects of the Directory
    철두철미한 공화주의자였던 마세나는 총재정부의 약점을 알고 있었다
- **consent** [kənsént] 명 동의, 승낙
  - but could not give his hearty **consent** to the coup d'état
    그러나 쿠데타에 진심으로 동의할 수는 없었다
- **still** 부 그런데도, 하지만, 그러나
- **if France desired to entrust her independence and glory to one man she could choose none better than Bonaparte**
  만약 프랑스가 그 자유와 영광을 단 한 사람에게 맡기길 원한다면 보나파르트 외에는 달리 선택할 사람이 없을 것이다
- **The latter** 후자(後者, 보나파르트를 말함)
- **everything was to be sacrificed to the glory of the First Consul**
  제1집정관의 영광을 위해서 모든 것을 희생해야만 했다
- **profuse** [prəfjúːs] 형 아낌없이, 마음이 후한
- **it was only after great persuasion, profuse promises, and appeals to his patriotism that**
  거듭된 설득과 함께 후한 보상을 약속하고 애국심에 호소를 한 뒤에야
- **with the stipulation that** ~라는 조건을 붙여서
- **condemn** [kəndém] 동 운명지우다; 폐기처분하다
  - an army **condemned** to rest on the defensive 방어를 위해 (후방에) 배치된 군대
- **carte blanche** [káːrtblάːntʃ] 명 백지 위임장
- **requisition** [rèkwəzíʃən] 동 요구하다, 강제 사용하다, 소집하다
- **Bonaparte's promises were only made to be broken**
  보나파르트는 처음부터 약속을 지킬 생각이 없었다
- **the mere shadow of an army, the hospitals full**
  병원에 부상병으로 가득 찬 단지 이름뿐인 군대

into France, and the officers and generals absolutely unable to contend with the mass of misery and want. In spite of his able lieutenants, Soult and Suchet, he could make no head against the Austrians in the field, and after some gallant engagements was driven back into Genoa, where, for two months, he held out against famine and the assaults of the enemy. While the wretched inhabitants starved, the troops were fed on "a miserable ration of a quarter of a pound of horse-flesh and a quarter of a pound of what was called bread—a horrible compound of damaged flour, sawdust, starch, hair-powder, oatmeal, linseed, rancid nuts, and other nasty substances, to which a little solidity was given by the admixture of a small portion of cocoa. Each loaf, moreover, was held together by little bits of wood, without which it would have fallen to powder." A revolt, threatened by the inhabitants, was checked by Masséna's order that an assemblage of over five persons should be fired on, and the approaches to the principal streets were commanded by guns. Still he refused to surrender, as every day he expected to hear the cannon of the First Consul's army thundering on the Austrian rear. One day the hopes of all were aroused by a distant roar in the mountains, only to be dashed by finding it to be thunder. It was simply the ascendancy of Masséna's personality which prolonged the agony and upheld his authority, and in bitter earnestness the soldiers used to say,

- **bands of soldiers, even whole battalions, quitting their posts and trying to escape into France**
  병사들 무리, 심지어는 대대 전체가 주둔지를 떠나 프랑스로 달아나려고 시도하기도 했다
- **unable to contend with the mass of misery and want**
  비참하고 결핍된 수많은 상황과 씨름을 벌이기에는 역량이 부족한
- **make head against** ~에 맞서다, 대항하다
- **gallant** [gǽlənt] 형 씩씩한, 용감한
- **engagement** [engéidʒmənt] 명 싸움, 전투
  - and after some gallant **engagements** was driven back into Genoa
  몇 번의 용감한 전투를 치렀는데도 제노바로 쫓겨났다
- **hold out against** 마지막까지 견디다, 계속 저항하다
- **ration** [rǽʃən, réi-] 명 배급, 할당, 식량
- **sawdust** 명 톱밥
- **starch** [stɑːrtʃ] 명 녹말, 전분, 풀
- **hair-powder** 명 머리에 바르는 분
- **inseed** [línsìːd] 명 아마인(亞麻仁) (아마(flax)의 씨)
- **rancid** [rǽnsid] 형 고약한 냄새가 나는, 불쾌한
- **admixture** [ædmíkstʃər, əd-] 명 혼합물, 첨가제
- **Each loaf, moreover, was held together by little bits of wood, without which it would have fallen to powder**
  게다가 빵은 분말 대신 나무 부스러기를 넣어서 반죽한 것이었다
- **assemblage** [əsémblidʒ] 명 회중, 집합, 모임
- **be fired on** 총살당하다
- **the approaches to the principal streets were commanded by guns**
  주(主) 대로로 접근하는 길은 포병들이 통제했다
- **be dashed** (희망 등이) 물거품이 되다, 부서지다
- **ascendancy** [əséndənsi] 우월, 우세, 지배권
- **prolong** [prouló:ŋ, -láŋ] 동 오래 끌다, 연기하다
- **agony** [ǽgəni] 명 고통, 괴로움
- **earnestness** 명 진지함, 열심

"He will make us eat his boots before he will surrender." At last the accumulated horrors shook even his firm spirit, and on June 4th a capitulation was agreed on. The terms were most favourable to the French; but, as Lord Keith, the English admiral, said, "General, your defence has been so heroic that we can refuse you nothing." However, the sufferings of Genoa were not in vain, for Masséna had played his part and held the main Austrian force in check for ten days longer than had been demanded of him; thus the First Consul had time to fall on the enemies' line of communication, and it may be truly said that without the siege of Genoa there could have been no Marengo. Masséna had once again demonstrated the importance of the individual in war; as Bonaparte wrote to him during the siege, "In such a situation as you are, a man like you is worth twenty thousand men." In spite of this, at St. Helena, the Emperor, ever jealous of his own glory, affected to despise Masséna's generalship and endurance at Genoa, and blamed him for not taking the offensive in the field, forgetting the state of his army and the paucity of his troops. But at the moment he showed his appreciation of his services by giving him the command of the army when he himself retired to Paris after the victory of Marengo. Unfortunately Masséna's avarice and greed were unable to withstand the temptations of the position, and the First Consul had very soon to recall him from Italy

- **accumulated** 형 누적된, 축적된
- **shook even his firm spirit** 그의 완고한 생각마저 흔들었다
- **capitulation** 명 조건부 항복
- **General, your defence has been so heroic that we can refuse you nothing.**
  장군, 당신의 방어가 너무나도 영웅적이었기 때문에 우리는 당신의 요청을 어떤 것도 거절하지 못하겠소.
- **hold in check** 억제하다, 저지하다
- **without the siege of Genoa there could have been no Marengo**
  제노바 포위전이 없었더라면 마렝고 전투도 없었을 것이다
- **blamed him for not taking the offensive in the field**
  전장에서 공격적인 자세를 취하지 않았다고
- **paucity** [pɔ́:səti] 명 소수, 소량, 결핍
- **at the moment** 바로 그 때는
- **he showed his appreciation of his services by giving him the command of the army when he himself retired to Paris after the victory of Marengo**
  나폴레옹은 마세나의 공훈에 대한 감사를 표하는 의미에서 자신이 마렝고 전투의 승리 후 파리로 돌아가게 되었을 때 군대의 지휘권을 그에게 수여했다
- **avarice** [ǽvəris] 명 탐욕, 허욕
- **withstand** [wiðstǽnd, wiθ-] 동 저항하다, 잘 견디다
- **temptation** [temptéiʃən] 명 유혹
  - Unfortunately Masséna's avarice and greed were unable to withstand the **temptations** of the position
  불행하게도 마세나는 자신의 탐욕 때문에 그 지위에서 오는 유혹을 이겨낼 수가 없었다
- **recall** [rikɔ́:l] 동 소환하다

and mark his displeasure by placing him on half-pay.

For two years the disgraced general brooded over his wrongs in retirement, and showed his attitude of mind by voting against the Consulate for life and the establishment of the Empire. The gift of a Marshal's bâton did little to reconcile him to the Emperor, for, as he scoffingly replied to Thiebault's congratulations, "Oh, there are fourteen of us." So uncertain was the Emperor of his Marshal's disposition that, on the outbreak of the war with Austria, Masséna alone of all the greater Marshals held no command. But with the prospect of heavy fighting in Italy the Emperor could not afford to entrust the Italian divisions to a blunderer, and he once again posted Masséna to his old command. The Austrians had occupied the strong position of Caldiero, near the marshes of Arcola, and the French in vain attempted to force them from it, but the success of the Emperor on the Danube at last compelled the Archduke John to fall back on Austria. The Marshal at once commenced a spirited pursuit, and ultimately joined hands with the Grand Army, south of the Danube.

After the treaty of Pressburg Napoleon despatched Masséna to conquer Naples, which he had given as a kingdom to his brother Joseph. With fifty thousand men the Marshal swept through Italy.

- **half-pay** 반급(半給), (육·해군 장교의) 휴직급
  - mark his displeasure by placing him on **half-pay**
    그를 휴직 처분하여 자신의 불쾌감을 표했다
- **brood** [bruːd] 동 곰곰이 생각하다, 마음을 앓다
  - **brooded** over his wrongs in retirement
    자신을 퇴직시킨 처사에 대한 부당함 때문에 속을 앓았다
- **vote against** ~에 반대투표를 하다
- **for life** 죽을 때까지, 평생, 필사적으로
- **by voting against the Consulate for life and the establishment of the Empire**
  필사적으로 집정정부와 제국의 성립을 반대함으로써
- **The gift of a Marshal's bâton did little to reconcile him to the Emperor**
  원수의 지위도 그와 황제를 화해시키는 데 별 도움이 되지 않았다
- **scoffingly** 부 냉소적으로
- **there are fourteen of us** 우리 중에 14명이나 있군요
- **disposition** [dìspəzíʃən] 명 성질, 기질, 의향
  - So uncertain was the Emperor of his Marshal's **disposition**
    황제는 자신의 원수(마세나)가 어떤 생각을 지녔는지 확신할 수 없었기 때문에
- **Masséna alone of all the greater Marshals held no command**
  모든 위대한 원수들 중에서 마세나 혼자만 지휘권을 갖지 못했다
- **with the prospect of heavy fighting in Italy**
  이탈리아에서 격렬한 전투가 있을 것이라고 예상하여
- **blunderer** [blʌ́ndərər] 명 실수하는 자, 얼간이
  - could not afford to entrust the Italian divisions to a **blunderer**
    이탈리아 사단을 얼간이들에게 맡길 여유가 없었다
- **marsh** [mɑːrʃ] 명 습지, 늪
- **spirited** [spíritid] 형 기운찬, 혼신을 다한
- **join hands with** ~와 제휴하다, 손잡다, 연합하다
- **which he had given as a kingdom to his brother Joseph**
  그리고 그 왕국(나폴리)을 그의 형 조제프에게 주었다

In vain the gallant Queen Caroline armed the lazzaroni; Capua opened its gates, Gaeta fell after twelve days' bombardment, and Joseph entered Naples in triumph. Calabria alone offered a stern resistance, and this resistance the French brought upon themselves by their cruelty to the peasantry, whom they treated as brigands. Unfortunately his success in Naples was once again tarnished by his greed, for the Marshal, by selling licences to merchants and conniving at their escape from the custom-house dues, amassed, within a few months of his entering Naples, a sum of three million francs. Napoleon heard of this from his spies, and, writing to him, demanded a loan of a million francs. The Duke of Rivoli replied that he was the poorest of the Marshals, and had a numerous family to maintain and was heavily in debt, so he regretted that he could send him nothing. Unfortunately, the Emperor knew where he banked in Leghorn, and as he refused to disgorge a third of his illicit profits, the Emperor sent the inspector of the French Treasury and a police commissary to the bank, and demanded that the three millions, which lay at his account there, should be handed over. The seizure was made in legal form; the banker, who lost nothing, was bound to comply with it. Masséna, on hearing of this misfortune, was so furious that he fell ill, but he did not dare to remonstrate, knowing that he was in the wrong, but he never forgave the Emperor: his titles

- **lazzarone** [læzəróuni] 명 (pl. -ni) (나폴리의) 부랑자, 거지
- **bombardment** 명 포격, 폭격
- **and this resistance the French brought upon themselves by their cruelty to the peasantry**
  그리고 이 저항은 프랑스군이 농민들을 잔혹하게 대하게 된 원인이 되었다
- **brigand** [brígənd] 명 산적, 도적
- **tarnish** [tá:rniʃ] 통 흐리게 하다, 녹슬게 하다, 더럽히다
- **selling licences to merchants** 상인들에게 허가증을 판매함
- **connive** [kənáiv] 통 눈감아주다, 묵인하다
- **custom-house dues** 세관 수수료
- **amassed, within a few months of his entering Naples, a sum of three million francs**
  나폴리에 입성한 지 몇 달이 채 안 되어 3백만 프랑이나 돈을 긁어모았다
- **demanded a loan of a million francs** 백만 프랑을 빌려줄 것을 요구했다
- **regret** [rigrét] 통 유감으로 생각하다, 안타깝게 여기다
  - so he regretted that he could send him nothing
    그래서 그(나폴레옹)에게 아무것도 보낼 수 없는 것을 안타깝게 생각한다
- **disgorge** [disgɔ́:rdʒ] 통 토해내다, (부당이득을) 게워내다
- **illicit** [ilísit] 형 불법의 부정한
- **police commissary** (프랑스의) 총경(總警)
- **and demanded that the three millions, which lay at his account there, should be handed over**
  그 은행의 계좌에 있던 3백만 프랑을 양도하라고 요구했다
- **seizure** [sí:ʒər] 명 압류, 압수, 몰수
  - The **seizure** was made in legal form
    몰수는 적법한 절차에 따라 이루어졌다
- **the banker, who lost nothing, was bound to comply with it**
  아무것도 잃을 것이 없는 은행업자는 그에 동의할 수밖에 없었다
- **remonstrate** [rimánstreit, rémənstrèit/rimɔ́nstreit] 통 이의를 제기하다, 항의하다
  - but he did not dare to **remonstrate**, knowing that he was in the wrong
    자신이 잘못했다는 것을 알았기 때문에 감히 항의하지 못했다

and a pension never consoled him for what he lost at Leghorn, and, in spite of his cautious habits, he was sometimes heard to say, "I was fighting in his service and he was cruel enough to take away my little savings which I had invested at Leghorn."

From what he called a military promenade in Italy the Marshal was summoned early in 1807 to the Grand Army in Poland, and was present in command of one of the army corps at Pultusk, Ostralenka, and Friedland. In 1808 he received his title of Duke of Rivoli and a pension of three hundred thousand francs per annum, but in spite of this he absented himself from the court. When Joseph was given the crown of Spain he requested his brother to send Masséna to aid him in his new sphere, but the Emperor, full of mistrust, refused, while the Marshal himself had no great desire to serve in Spain. When it was clear that Austria was going to seize the occasion of the Spanish War once again to fight France, Napoleon hastened to send the veteran Duke of Rivoli to the army on the Danube. At Abensberg and Eckmühl, for the first time since 1797, he fought under the eye of Napoleon himself. "Activité, activité, vitesse," wrote the Emperor, and well his lieutenant carried out his orders. Following up the Five Days' Fighting, Masséna led the advance guard to Vienna, and commanded the left wing at Aspern-Essling. Standing in the church-

- **console** [kənsóul] 동 위로하다, 위문하다
- **in spite of his cautious habits, he was sometimes heard to say**
  그의 조심스러운 성격에도 이따금 ~라는 말을 하는 것이 들렸다
- **he was cruel enough to take away my little savings**
  그는 나의 약간의 저축을 빼앗아 갈 정도로 잔인했다
- **promenade** [pràmənéid, -ná:d/prɔ́m-] 명 행진, 행렬
  - From what he called a military **promenade** in Italy
    이탈리아에서 군대행진을 지휘하던 것에서부터
- **his title of Duke of Rivoli and a pension of three hundred thousand francs per annum** 리볼리 공작의 작위와 연간 30만 프랑의 연금
- **but in spite of this he absented himself from the court**
  그러나 이런 상황에서도 그는 궁정에 나타나지 않았다
- **sphere** [sfiər] 명 지위, 신분 계급
  - he requested his brother to send Masséna to aid him in his new **sphere**
    그의 새로운 지위(국왕)를 도울 수 있도록 마세나를 보내달라고 동생에게 부탁했다
- **full of mistrust, refused** 믿을 수 없었기 때문에 거절했다
- **had no great desire to serve in Spain**
  스페인에서 그다지 복무하고 싶은 생각이 없었다
- **seize the occasion of** ~의 기회를 잡다
- **under the eye of Napoleon himself** 나폴레옹 자신이 지켜보는 아래에서
- **Activité, activité, vitesse** 활기 넘치고, 또 활기 넘친다. 그리고 빠르다

나폴레옹의 원수들 213

yard at Aspern, with the boughs swept down by grapeshot crashing round him, he was in his element; never had his tenacity, his resource, and skill been seen to such advantage. But in spite of his skill and the courage of his troops, at the end of the first day's fighting his shattered forces were driven out of the heap of smoking ruins which marked all that remained of Aspern. On the morning of the second day he had regained half of the village when news came that the bridge was broken, and that he was to hold off the Austrians while communication with the Isle of Lobau was being established. The enemy, invigorated by the news of the success of their plan for breaking the bridges, strained every nerve to annihilate the French force on the left bank of the river, but Masséna, Lannes, and Napoleon worked marvels with their exhausted troops. The Duke of Rivoli seemed ubiquitous: at one moment on horseback and at another on foot with drawn sword, wherever the enemy pressed he was there animating his troops, directing their fire, hurrying up supports; thus, thanks to his exertions, the Austrians were held off, the cavalry and the artillery safely crossed the bridge, and the veteran Marshal at midnight brought the last of the rear-guard safely to the Isle of Lobau, where, exhausted by fatigue, the troops fell asleep in their ranks.

- **churchyard** [tʃə́ːrtʃjàːrd] 명 교회 부속 뜰, 교회 경내
- **grapeshot** 명 포도탄
- **sweep** [swiːp] 동 스쳐 지나가다, 휙 지나가다
- **be in one's element** 물 만난 물고기 같다,
- **tenacity** [tənǽsəti] 명 고집, 끈기, 완강
- **to advantage** 돋보이게, 유리하게
  - never had his tenacity, his resource, and skill been seen **to** such **advantage**.
    그의 끈기와 기지, 그리고 노련함이 그만큼 돋보인 적이 없었다.
- **heap** [hiːp] 명 쌓아올린 것, 퇴적, 더미, 덩어리
  - were driven out of the **heap** of smoking ruins
    연기가 자욱한 폐허 더미로 쫓겨났다
- **hold off** 저지하다
- **while communication with the Isle of Lobau was being established**
  로바우 섬과 연락이 취해지는 동안
- **invigorate** [invígərèit] 동 원기를 돋우다, 북돋다
- **strain every nerve** 모든 노력을 다하다
- **marvel** [máːrvəl] 명 놀라운 일, 경이
  - worked **marvels** with their exhausted troops
    그들의 지친 군대로 놀라운 일을 해냈다
- **ubiquitous** [juːbíkwətəs] 형 도처에 있는, 여기저기에 나타나는
- **with drawn sword** 칼을 빼어들고
- **animate** [ǽnəmèit] 동 생기를 주다, 활기차게 하다
  - wherever the enemy pressed he was there **animating** his troops
    적들이 공격하는 곳이면 어디서든 나타나 그의 군대에 생기를 불어넣어주었다
- **exertion** [igzə́ːrʃən] 명 노력, 분발
- **and the veteran Marshal at midnight brought the last of the rear-guard safely to the Isle of Lobau**
  그리고 노련한 원수는 한밤중에 후위대의 마지막까지 안전하게 로바우 섬으로 이끌고 왔다
- **fell asleep in their ranks** 열을 지은 채 곯아떨어져 버렸다

The death of Lannes threw Napoleon back on the Duke of Rivoli, who for the time became his confidant and right-hand man. It was Masséna who commanded at Lobau and made all the arrangements for the crossing before Wagram. The Emperor and his lieutenant were indefatigable in the care with which they made their preparations. On one occasion, wishing to inspect the Austrian position, dressed in sergeants' greatcoats, attended by a single aide-de-camp in the kit of a private, they went alone up the north bank of the island and took their coats off as if they wanted to bathe. The Austrian sentinels, seeing, as they thought, two French soldiers enjoying a wash, took no notice of them, and thus the Emperor and the Marshal were able to determine the exact spot for launching the bridges. On another occasion, while they were riding round the island, the Marshal's horse put its foot into a hole and fell, and injured the rider's leg so that he could not mount again. This unfortunate accident happened a few days before the battle of Wagram, so the Duke of Rivoli went into battle lying in a light calèche, drawn by four white horses, with his doctor beside him changing the compresses on his injured leg every two hours. During the battle Masséna's corps formed the left of the line. While Davout was carrying out his great turning movement, it was the Duke of Rivoli who had to endure the full fury of the Austrians' attack. In the pursuit after the battle he

- **throw a person back on** (부득이하게) ~을 의지하게 하다
  - The death of Lannes **threw** Napoleon **back on** the Duke of Rivoli
    란의 죽음으로 인해 나폴레옹은 어쩔 수 없이 리볼리 공작에게 의지해야만 했다
- **indefatigable** [ìndifǽtigəbəl] 형 지칠 줄 모르는, 끈기 있는
  - were **indefatigable** in the care with which they made their preparations
    지치지 않고 만반의 준비를 갖추기 위한 노력을 다했다
- **greatcoat** 명 (군인들이 입는) 두꺼운 외투
- **attended by** ~를 데리고
- **kit** [kit] 명 배낭, 장구, 연장통
  - dressed in sergeants' greatcoats, attended by a single aide-de-camp in the **kit** of a private
    자신은 두꺼운 부사관용 외투를 걸치고, 대동한 부관(마세나)에게는 사병용 배낭을 메게 하고는
- **sentinel** [séntənl] 명 보초, 파수
- **thus the Emperor and the Marshal were able to determine the exact spot for launching the bridges**
  이렇게 해서 황제와 원수는 다리를 설치할 만한 위치들을 정확하게 결정할 수 있었다
- **the Marshal's horse put its foot into a hole and fell and injured the rider's leg so that he could not mount again.**
  원수가 타던 말의 다리가 구멍에 빠져 넘어지고 말았다. 말에 타고 있던 그는 다리가 다쳐 다시 말을 타지 못하게 되었다.
- **calèche** [kəléʃ] 명 2륜 마차
- **compress** [kámpres/kɔ́m-] 명 압박붕대
  - with his doctor beside him changing the **compresses** on his injured leg every two hours
    곁에서 그의 의사가 두 시간마다 다친 다리의 압박붕대를 새 것으로 갈아주며
- **it was the Duke of Rivoli who had to endure the full fury of the Austrians' attack**
  오스트리아군의 맹렬한 공격을 견디어 내는 것은 리볼리 공작의 몫이었다

pressed the enemy with his wonted activity. At the last encounter at Znaim he had a narrow escape, for hardly had he got out of his carriage when a cannon-ball struck it, and a moment later another shot killed one of the horses.

After the treaty of Vienna the Marshal, newly created Prince of Essling, retired to rest at his country house at Rueil, but the Emperor could not spare him long. In April, 1810, within eight months, he was once again hurried off on active service, this time to Spain, where Soult had been driven out of Portugal by Sir Arthur Wellesley, and Jourdan and Joseph defeated at Talavera. The Emperor promised the Prince of Essling ninety thousand troops for the invasion of Portugal, and placed under his command Junot and Ney. The Marshal did his best to refuse the post; he knew the difficult character of Ney and the jealousy of Junot, and he pointed out that it would be better to reorganise the army of Portugal under generals appointed by himself. Berthier replied that "the orders of the Emperor were positive, and left no point in dispute. When the Emperor delegated his authority obedience became a duty; however great might be the pride of the Dukes of Elchingen and Abrantès, they had enough justice to understand that their swords were not in the same line as the sword of the conqueror of Zurich." Still, the Prince foresaw the future, and

- **wonted** [wɔːntid, wountid, wʌntid] 휑 버릇처럼 된, 일상의
- **he had a narrow escape** 그는 간신히 탈출했다
- **hardly ~when** ~하기가 무섭게, ~하자마자
  - for **hardly** had he got out of his carriage **when** a cannon-ball struck it
    그가 마차에서 빠져나오자마자 포탄이 마차에 떨어졌기 때문이었다
- **newly created Prince of Essling** 새로 에슬링 공작에 임명되었다
- **but the Emperor could not spare him long**
  그러나 황제는 그를 오랫동안 쉬게 놔둘 수가 없었다
- **where Soult had been driven out of Portugal by Sir Arthur Wellesley**
  술트는 아더 웰즐리 경(훗날 웰링턴 공작)의 공격을 받아 포르투갈에서 쫓겨났었다
- **and placed under his command Junot and Ney**
  그리고 그의 휘하에 쥐노와 네를 배치하려고 했다
- **point out** 지적하다
  - he **pointed out** that it would be better to reorganise the army of Portugal under generals appointed by himself
    그는 자신이 직접 선택한 장군들의 지휘 아래 군대를 재정비하는 것이 더 낫다고 지적했다
- **positive** [pázətiv/pɔ́z-] 휑 확신하는, 확실한, 단호한
  - the orders of the Emperor were **positive**, and left no point in dispute
    황제의 명령들은 단호하기 때문에 이론의 여지가 없다
- **When the Emperor delegated his authority obedience became a duty**
  황제가 그의 권한을 위임하면 무조선 복종해야 한다
- **however great might be the pride of the Dukes of Elchingen and Abrantès**
  엘힝엔 공작(네)과 아브란테스 공작(쥐노)의 자부심이 아무리 크다고 해도
- **their swords were not in the same line as the sword of the conqueror of Zurich**
  그들의 무훈이 취리히의 정복자(마세나)와 같은 선상에 설 수는 없다

appealed to the Emperor himself, but the Emperor was obdurate. "You are out of humour to-day, my dear Masséna. You see everything black, yourself and your surroundings. To listen to you one would think you were half dead. Your age? A good reason! How much older are you now than at Essling? Your health? Does not imagination play a great part in your weakness? Are you worse than at Wagram? It is rheumatism that is troubling you. The climate of Portugal is as warm and healthy as Italy, and will put you on your legs... Set out then with confidence. Be prudent and firm, and the obstacles you fear will fade away; you have surmounted many worse." Unfortunately for the Marshal, his forebodings were truer than the Emperor's optimism. On arriving at Salamanca his troubles began. Delays were inevitable before he could bring into order his unruly team. Junot and Ney were openly contemptuous, Regnier hung back, and was three weeks late in his arrangements. Meanwhile, all that Masséna saw of the enemy, whom the Emperor had in past years stigmatised as the "slow and clumsy English," confirmed him in his opinion that the campaign was going to prove the most arduous he had ever undertaken.

- **obdurate** [ábdjurit/ɔ́b-] 휑 완고한, 고집센
- **out of humour** 기분이 언짢은
- **You see everything black, yourself and your surroundings**
  그대는 그대 자신과 주변에 있는 것 모두를 부정적으로만 보는군
- **To listen to you** 그대의 말을 듣고 있으면
- **imagination** [imædʒənéiʃən] 몡 상상(력), 임기응변의 지혜
  - Does not **imagination** play a great part in your weakness?
    그대의 지략으로 몸 약한 것 정도는 충분히 대신할 수 있지 않은가?
- **Are you worse than at Wagram?** 바그람 전투 때보다 몸이 안 좋은가?
- **and will put you on your legs** 그대의 다리에 좋을 걸세
- **surmount** [sərmáunt] 동 극복하다, 이겨내다
- **foreboding** 몡 불길한 예감, 전조
- **Delays were inevitable before he could bring into order his unruly team.**
  제멋대로인 그의 팀이 명령을 수행하기 위해서는 불가피하게 시간이 지체될 수밖에 없었다.
- **contemptuous** [kəntémptʃuəs] 휑 모욕적인, 경멸하는
- **hang back** 주춤거리다, 꽁무니 빼다
- **and was three weeks late in his arrangements**
  준비하는 데 3주나 더 늦어버렸다
- **Meanwhile, all that Masséna saw of the enemy**
  그러나 마세나는 오직 적들에게만 신경 썼다
- **stigmatise** [stígmətàiz] 동 오명을 씌우다, 비난하다
- **clumsy** [klʌ́mzi] 휑 솜씨 없는, 서투른
- **the campaign was going to prove the most arduous he had ever undertaken**
  이번 전쟁은 그가 지금까지 해왔던 어떤 것보다도 어려운 전쟁임이 드러날 것이라고

In spite of everything, operations opened brilliantly for the French. Ciudad Rodrigo and Almeida fell without the English commander making any apparent effort to relieve them. On September 16th the invasion of Portugal commenced. But losses, disease, and garrison duty had already reduced his troops to some seventy thousand men, and the French found "an enemy behind every stone"; while, as the Prince of Essling wrote, "We are marching across a desert; women, children, and old men have all fled; in fact, no guide is to be found anywhere." Still the English fell back before him, and he was under the impression that they were going to evacuate Portugal without a blow, although he grasped the fact that it was the immense superiority of the French cavalry which had prevented the "sepoy general" making any effort to relieve the fortresses. But on September 26th Masséna found that the English had stayed their retreat, and were waiting to fight him on the rocky ridge of Busaco. Unfortunately for his reputation, he made no reconnaissance of the position, and, trusting entirely to the reports of Ney, Regnier, and Junot, who asserted the position was much less formidable than it looked, sustained a heavy reverse. After the battle his lieutenants urged him to abandon the invasion of Portugal; but the veteran refused such timorous advice, and, rousing himself, soon showed the energy which had made his name so famous at

- **brilliantly** 튄 훌륭히, 휘황찬란하게
- **any apparent effort to relieve them**
  그들을 구원하려는 어떤 외견상의 노력도
- **garrison duty** 요새의 수비병력으로 남겨두는 것
- **reduced his troops to some seventy thousand men**
- **in fact, no guide is to be found anywhere**
  사실 어디에서도 길 안내해 줄 사람을 찾지 못했다
- **Still the English fell back before him**
  여전히 영국군은 그의 앞에서 후퇴하고만 있었다
- **be under the impression** ~라고 생각하고 있다
  - he **was under the impression** that they were going to evacuate Portugal without a blow
  그는 전투 한 번 없이 포르투갈을 점령하게 될 것이라고 생각하고 있었다
- **grasp** [græsp, grɑːsp] 튄 납득하다, 이해하다
- **which had prevented the "sepoy general" making any effort to relieve the fortresses**
  '세포이 장군'이 요새를 탈환하려는 시도를 저지한('세포이 장군'은 웰링턴을 말하는데 스페인 전쟁에 참전하기 전까지 웰링턴이 인도에서 복무했었기 때문임)
- **reconnaissance** [rikánəzəns, -səns/-kɔ́n-] 튄 정찰, 수색
  - he made no **reconnaissance** of the position
    적의 위치에 대한 정찰을 전혀 하지 않았다
- **assert** [əsə́ːrt] 튄 단언하다, 강력히 주장하다
- **the position was much less formidable than it looked**
  저들의 진형은 보이는 것만큼 그리 훌륭한 것이 아니다
- **sustain** [səstéin] 튄 확증하다, 입증하다
- **reverse** [rivə́ːrs] 튄 역, 반대
  - sustained a heavy **reverse** 크게 오판했다는 것이 드러났다
- **to abandon the invasion of Portugal** 포르투갈 원정을 포기하자고
- **but the veteran refused such timorous advice**
  그러나 그 노장(마세나)은 그런 소심한 제안을 거절했다

Zurich and Rivoli. Turning the position, the French swept down on Portugal, while the English hurriedly fell back before them. What caused Masséna most anxiety was the ominous desertion of the countryside. He was well aware of the bitter hatred of the Portuguese, and knew that his soldiers tortured and hung the wretched inhabitants to force them to reveal hidden stores of provisions, but it was not until October 10th, when the French had arrived within a few miles of the lines of Torres Vedras, that he learned of the vast entrenched camp which the English commander had so secretly prepared for his army and the inhabitants of Portugal. Masséna was furious, and covered with accusations the Portuguese officers on his staff. "Que diable," he cried, "Wellington n'a pas construit des montagnes." But there had been no treachery, only so well had the secret been kept that hardly even an officer in the English army knew of the existence of the work, and as Wellington wrote to the minister at Lisbon on October 6th, "I believe that you and the Government do not know where the lines are." For six weeks the indomitable Marshal lay in front of the position, hoping to tempt the English to attack his army, now reduced to sixty thousand men. But Wellington, who had planned this victorious reply to the axiom that war ought to feed war, grimly sat behind his lines, while the English army, well fed from the sea, watched the French writhe in the toils of hunger.

- **Turning the position** 형세가 전환되자
- **anxiety** [æŋzáiəti] 명 근심, 불안
- **ominous** [ámənəs/ɔ́m—] 형 불길한, 나쁜 징조의
- **desertion** [dizə́ːrʃən] 명 버림, 유기(遺棄), 도망
- **countryside** [kʌ́ntrisàid] 명 시골, 지방, 지방민
  - What caused Masséna most anxiety was the ominous desertion of the **countryside**.
  마세나가 가장 우려한 것은 불길하게도 농민들이 농촌지역을 그냥 버려두고 달아나는 현상이었다.
- **bitter hatred of the Portuguese** 포르투갈인들의 극심한 증오
- **wretched** [rétʃid] 형 가엾은, 불쌍한
- **to force them to reveal hidden stores of provisions**
  보급창고가 어디에 숨겨져 있는지 실토하도록 만들기 위해서
- **the lines of Torres Vedras** 토레스 베드라스 방어선
- **entrench** [entréntʃ] 동 참호로 에워싸다
  - the vast **entrenched** camp
    참호로 방비된 거대한 주둔지
- **covered with accusations the Portuguese officers on his staff**
  포르투갈 장교 출신의 참모들에게 비난을 쏟아부었다
- **Que diable, Wellington n'a pas construit des montagnes.**
  (프랑스어) 이런 제길, 웰링턴이 산을 쌓아 놓았지 않은가!
- **there had been no treachery**
  (포르투갈 참모들이) 배신한 것이 아니었다
- **only so well had the secret been kept that**
  단지 비밀이 너무 잘 지켜져서 ~할 정도였던 것이다
- **hardly even an officer in the English army knew of the existence of the work**
  영국군의 장교들조차 그 작업(참호)의 존재를 알지 못했었다
- **and as Wellington wrote to the minister at Lisbon on October 6th,**
  "I believe that you and the Government do not know where the lines are."
  웰링턴은 10월 6일 리스본에 있는 공사(公使)에게 이렇게 쓸 정도였다. "나는 그대와 내각도 방어선이 어디에 있는지 모를 거라고 확신하고 있소."

다음 장에 해설 계속

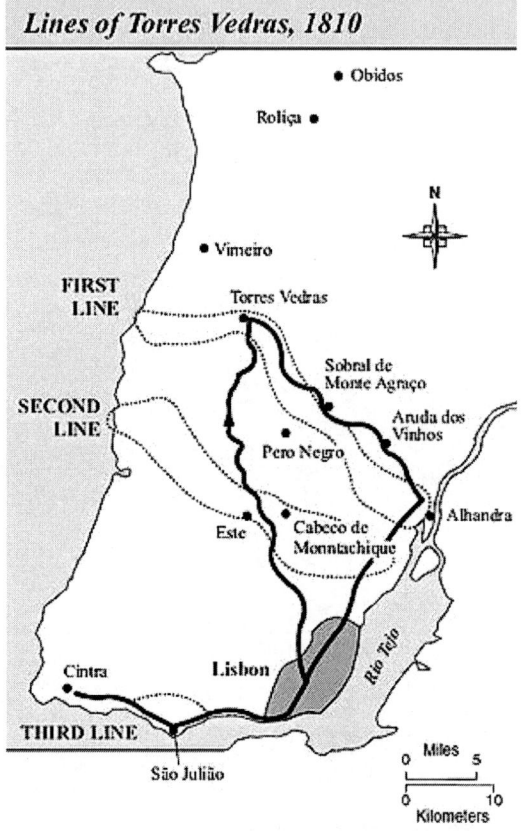

토레스 베드라스 방어선(출처: en.wikipedia.org)

※ 웰링턴의 지시로 쌓은 이 방어선 때문에 마세나 원수는 결국 포르투갈에서 퇴각해야만 했다

- **indomitable** [indámətəbəl/-dɔ́m-] 형 불굴의, 완강한
  - For six weeks the **indomitable** Marshal lay in front of the position
  6주 동안 원수는 완강하게 적의 진지 앞에서 대치하고 있었다
- **tempt** [tempt] 동 유혹하다, 꾀다
  - hoping to **tempt** the English to attack his army
  영국군이 유혹에 넘어가 그의 군대를 공격하기를 기대하면서
- **axiom** [ǽksiəm] 명 자명한 이치, 격언, 금언
  - who had planned this victorious reply to the axiom that war ought to feed war
  '전쟁으로 전쟁을 먹여 살려라'는 격언에 대해 이 필승의 작전으로 대응하기로 생각한(보급이 부족한 프랑스군에게 지구전으로 대응함)
- **grimly sat behind his lines** 잔인하게도 방어선 뒤에 앉아서
- **writhe** [raið] 동 몸부림치며 괴로워하다
  - watched the French **writhe** in the toils of hunger
  프랑스군이 굶주림에 괴로워하는 모습을 지켜보았다

Masséna was now roused, and as his opponent wrote, "It is certainly astonishing that the enemy have been able to remain in this country so long... It is an extraordinary instance of what a French army can do." At last even Masséna had to confess himself beaten and fall back on Santarem. The winter passed in a fruitless endeavour on the part of the Emperor and the Marshal to force Soult, d'Erlon, and Regnier to co-operate for an advance on Lisbon by the left bank of the Tagus. Meanwhile, in spite of every effort, the French army dwindled owing to disease, desertion, and unending fatigue. So dangerous was the country that a despatch could not be sent along the lines of communication without an escort of three hundred men. The whole countryside had been so swept bare of provisions that a Portuguese spy wrote to Wellington saying, "Heaven forgive me if I wrong them in believing they have eaten my cat."

By March, 1811, it became clear that the French could no longer maintain themselves at Santarem; but so skilful were Masséna's dispositions that it was three days before Wellington realised that at last the enemy had commenced their retreat. Never had the genius of the Marshal stood higher than in this difficult retirement from Portugal. With his army decimated by hunger and disease, with the victorious enemy always hanging on his heels,

- **extraordinary** [ikstrɔ́ːrdənèri, èkstrəɔ́ːr-/-dənər] 형 놀라운, 대단한
- **instance** [ínstəns] 명 실례, 사례
  - It is an extraordinary **instance** of what a French army can do.
    프랑스 군대가 얼마나 대단한지 보여주는 사례이다.
- **confess himself beaten** 졌다는 것을 인정하다
- **in a fruitless endeavour on the part of the Emperor and the Marshal to force Soult, d'Erlon, and Regnier to co-operate for an advance on Lisbon by the left bank of the Tagus**
  황제와 원수는 술트, 데를롱, 레그니에에게 연합하여 타호강의 좌안을 통해 리스본으로 진격하도록 했지만 헛수고로
- **dwindle** [dwíndl] 동 줄어들다, 쇠퇴하다
- **So dangerous was the country that** 그 나라는 너무 위험해서
- **without an escort of three hundred men** 300명의 호위병력 없이는
- **bare** [bɛər] 형 벌거벗은, 텅 빈
  - The whole countryside had been so swept **bare** of provisions that
    모든 농촌이 먹을 것 하나 없이 텅 비어 있어
- **Heaven forgive me if I wrong them in believing they have eaten my cat.**
  제가 그들(프랑스군)이 제 고양이까지 잡아먹었을 거라고 생각할 정도로 궁지에 몰아넣었지만, 주님께서는 저를 용서해 주실 겁니다.
- **it was three days before Wellington realised that at last the enemy had commenced their retreat**
  웰링턴은 프랑스군이 후퇴하기 시작한 후 3일이 지나서야 알아챌 수 있었다
- **Never had the genius of the Marshal stood higher than in this difficult retirement from Portugal.**
  원수의 천재성은 포르투갈에서 후퇴하는 이 어려움 속에서 무엇보다 높이 발휘되었다.
- **decimate** [désəmèit] 동 많은 사람을 죽이다
- **with the victorious enemy always hanging on his heels**
  승리한 적들이 끊임없이 그의 바로 뒤에서 바짝 추격하는

with his subordinates in open revolt, and a Marshal of France refusing to obey orders in the face of the enemy, he lost not a single gun, baggage-wagon or invalid. Still, the morale of his army was greatly shaken; as he himself wrote, "It is sufficient for the enemy to show the heads of a few columns in order to intimidate the officers and make them loudly declare that the whole of Wellington's army is in sight." When the Marshal at last placed his wearied troops behind the fortress of Ciudad Rodrigo and Almeida, he found his difficulties by no means at an end. The Emperor, who "judged men only by results," wrote him a letter full of thinly-veiled criticism of his operations, while he found that the country round the fortresses was now included in the command of the northern army under Bessières. Accordingly he had to apply to that Marshal for leave to revictual and equip his troops. Meanwhile Wellington proceeded to besiege Almeida.

By the end of April, after a vigorous correspondence with Bessières, Masséna had at last reorganised his army and was once again ready to take the field against the English. Reinforced by fifteen hundred cavalry of the Guard under Bessières, at Fuentes d'Onoro he surprised the English forces covering the siege of Almeida; after a careful reconnaissance at dawn on May 5th he attacked and defeated the English right, and had it not been for the

- **a Marshal of France refusing to obey orders in the face of the enemy**
  프랑스의 원수 하나는 적의 면전에서 명령에 불복하고 있었다
- **he lost not a single gun, baggage-wagon or invalid**
  그는 대포 하나나 짐마차 하나도 잃거나 망가지게 놔두지 않았다
- **intimidate** [intímədèit] 동 겁을 주다, 위협하다
  -It is sufficient for the enemy to show the heads of a few columns in order to **intimidate** the officers and make them loudly declare that the whole of Wellington's army is in sight.
  소수의 적 대열 중 선두만 보여도 장교들은 겁을 먹고 웰링턴의 군대 전체가 보인다며 큰 소리로 외쳤다.
- **wearied** [wíərid] 형 피곤한, 지친
- **he found his difficulties by no means at an end**
  아직 고난이 끝난 것이 절대 아니라는 것을 알았다
- **The Emperor, who "judged men only by results,"**
  사람을 결과로만 판단하는 황제
- **thinly-veiled** 얄팍한, 애써 숨기지 않은
- **was now included in the command of the northern army under Bessières** 이제 베시에르의 북부군 관할에 속해 있었다
- **leave** [liːv] 명 허락, 허가
- **revictual** 동 ~에게 다시 식량을 공급하다
- **Meanwhile Wellington proceeded to besiege Almeida.**
  그동안 웰링턴은 계속해서 알메이다를 포위 공격하고 있었다.
- **vigorous** [vígərəs] 형 활발한, 원기 왕성한
  - after a **vigorous** correspondence with Bessières
  베시에르의 적극적인 협조 덕택에
- **he surprised the English forces covering the siege of Almeida**
  그는 알메이다를 포위하고 있던 영국군을 기습 공격했다

action of Bessières, who spoiled his combination by refusing to allow the Guard to charge save by his orders, the English would have been totally defeated. Masséna wished at all hazards to continue the fight on the morrow, but his principal officers were strongly opposed to it. Overborne by their counsels, after lying in front of the position for three days he withdrew to Ciudad Rodrigo. It was through no fault of his that he was beaten at Fuentes d'Onoro; Wellington himself confessed how closely he had been pressed when he wrote: "Lord Liverpool was quite right not to move thanks for the battle of Fuentes, though it was the most difficult I was ever concerned in and against the greatest odds. We had nearly three to one against us engaged: above four to one of cavalry: and moreover our cavalry had not a gallop in them, while some of that of the enemy were quite fresh and in excellent order. If Bony had been there we should have been beaten."

Soon after the battle Masséna was superseded by Marmont, and retired to Paris. The meeting with the Emperor was stormy. "Well, Prince of Essling," said Napoleon, "are you no longer Masséna?" Explanations followed, and the Emperor at last promised that once again he should have an opportunity of regaining his glory in Spain. But Fate willed otherwise. After Salamanca, when Marmont was recalled, Masséna set out again for Spain,

- **had it not been for the action of Bessières** 베시에르의 행동만 아니었으면
- **who spoiled his combination by refusing to allow the Guard to charge save by his orders**
  자신의 명령 없이는 근위사단이 돌격하는 것을 허락하지 않아 마세나의 연합작전을 망쳐버렸던
- **at all hazards** 어려움을 무릅쓰고, 꼭
- **but his principal officers were strongly opposed to it**
  그러나 그의 주요 장교들은 그 생각에 강하게 반대했다
- **overbear** 동 위압하다, 압박하다
  - **Overborne** by their counsels 억지로 그들의 조언을 받아들인
- **It was through no fault of his that he was beaten at Fuentes d'Onoro**
  푸엔테스 데 오노로 전투에서 패배한 것은 그의 잘못이 아니었다
- **Lord Liverpool was quite right not to move thanks for the battle of Fuentes**
  리버풀 백작이 푸엔테스 전투의 결과에 대해 감사의 뜻을 표하지 않은 것은 충분히 일리가 있다(리버풀 백작 로버트 젱킨슨은 1812~1827년까지 영국의 수상을 역임했음)
- **against the greatest odds** 가장 큰 어려움에 맞서서
- **We had nearly three to one against us engaged**
  우리를 공격해온 적의 병력은 거의 3배 가까이나 되었다
- **above four to one of cavalry** 기병의 경우에는 4배가 넘었다
- **gallop** [gǽləp] 명 전속력으로 말을 몰기, 질주
  - moreover our cavalry had not a **gallop** in them
    게다가 우리 기병들은 적들 사이에서 전속력으로 달리지도 못했다
- **If Bony had been there we should have been beaten.**
  '보니'가 거기에 있었더라면 우리는 분명히 패배했을 것이다(보니는 보나파르트의 애칭, 즉 나폴레옹을 말함).
- **supersede** [sùːpərsíːd] 동 ~에 대신하다, 경질시키다
- **stormy** [stɔ́ːrmi] 형 격렬한, 험악한
- **explanation** [èksplənéiʃən] 명 설명, 변명
- **Fate willed otherwise** 운명은 다른 방향으로 흘러갔다
- **After Salamanca** 살라망카 전투의 패배 이후

only to fall ill at Bayonne and to return home and try to restore his shattered health at Nice. In 1813 and 1814 he commanded the eighth military district, composed of the Rhône Valley, but he was getting too old to take strenuous measures and was glad to make submission to the Bourbons.

Very cruelly the new Government placed an affront on the Marshal by refusing to create him a peer of France under the plea that he was an Italian and a foreigner, but in spite of this the Prince remained faithful during the first part of the Hundred Days, and only went over to Napoleon when he found that the capital and army had recognised the Emperor. At Paris the Emperor greeted him with "Well, Masséna, did you wish to serve as lieutenant to the Duke of Angoulême and fight me... would you have hurled me back into the sea if I had given you time to assemble your forces?" The old warrior replied: "Yes, Sire, inasmuch as I believed that you were not recalled by the majority of Frenchmen." Ill-health prevented the Marshal from actively serving the Emperor. But during the interval between Napoleon's abdication and the second restoration it fell to the Marshal's lot to keep order in Paris as Governor and Commander of the National Guard. The new Government, to punish him for the aid he had given to the Emperor, nominated him one of the judges

- **only to fall ill at Bayonne** 바욘에서 병에 걸리고 말았다
- **shattered** (건강 상태가) 엉망인, 기진맥진한
- **strenuous** [strénjuəs] 형 정력적인, 열심인
- **submission** [səbmíʃən] 명 복종, 항복
  - but he was getting too old to take strenuous measures and was glad to make **submission** to the Bourbons

  그러나 그는 열정적인 활약을 보여주기에는 너무 노쇠해가고 있었고, 부르봉가가 돌아오자 기꺼이 복종했다
- **affront** [əfrʌ́nt] 명 (공공연한·의도적인) 무례, 모욕
- **peer** [piər] 명 동료, 동등한 사람
  - by refusing to create him a **peer** of France under the plea that he was an Italian and a foreigner

  그가 이탈리아 출신이라는 것을 구실로 동등한 프랑스인으로 대우해 주지 않는
- **remained faithful during the first part of the Hundred Days**

  백일천하의 초기에는 (새 정부에) 충실한 상태로 있었다
- **only went over to Napoleon when he found that the capital and army had recognised the Emperor**

  수도와 군대가 나폴레옹을 황제로 인정한다는 사실을 알았을 때야 그의 편으로 넘어갔다
- **did you wish to serve as lieutenant to the Duke of Angoulême and fight me**

  앙굴렘 공작 휘하의 부관이 되어 나와 싸우길 원했다지?
- **hurl** [həːrl] 동 집어던지다
  - would you have **hurled** me back into the sea if I had given you time to assemble your forces

  만약 자네가 군대를 조직할 시간만 충분했었다면 나를 바다 속으로 다시 처넣고 말았겠지?
- **inasmuch as** ~인 까닭에, ~때문에
  - **inasmuch as** I believed that you were not recalled by themajority of Frenchmen

  대다수의 프랑스인들이 당신이 돌아오는 것을 원하지 않았다고 믿었기 때문에
- **keep order** 질서를 유지하다
- **nominated him one of the judges of Marshal Ney**

  그를 네 원수를 재판하는 법관 중 하나로 임명했다

of Marshal Ney. This was the last occasion the Prince of Essling appeared in public. Suspected as a traitor by the authorities, weighed down by the horror of Ney's death and the assassination of his old friend Brune, and racked by disease, after a lingering painful illness the conqueror of Zurich breathed his last at the age of fifty-nine on April 4, 1817. Even then the ultra royalists could not conceal their hatred of him. The War Minister, Clarke, Duke of Feltre, his old comrade, now turned furious legitimist, had hitherto withheld the Marshal's new bâton, and it was only the threat of Masséna's son-in-law, Reille, to place on the coffin the bâton the Marshal had received from the Emperor which at last forced the Government to send the emblem.

Great soldier as he was, Masséna's escutcheon was stained by many a blot. His avarice was disgusting beyond words, and with avarice went a tendency to underhand dealing, harshness, and malice. During the Wagram campaign the Marshal's coachman and footman drove him day by day in a carriage through all the heat of the fighting. The Emperor complimented these brave men and said that of all the hundred and thirty thousand men engaged they were the bravest. Masséna, after this, felt bound to give them some reward, and said to one of his staff that he was going to give them each four hundred francs. The staff officer replied

- **This was the last occasion the Prince of Essling appeared in public.**
  이것이 에슬링 공작이 공식적으로 역사에 나타나는 마지막 사건이었다.
- **weigh down** 압박하다, 억압하다, 침울케 하다
  - **weighed down** by the horror of Ney's death and the assassination of his old friend Brune
    네 원수의 죽음과 오랜 친구인 브륀의 암살로 인해 침울해져
- **racked by disease** 병으로 고통받는
- **linger** [líŋgər] 통 (병 등이) 오래 끌다
- **legitimist** [lidʒítəmìst] 명 정통주의자(부르봉 왕가의 지지자)
- **withhold** [wiðhóuld, wiθ-] 통 (승낙 등을) 보류하다
- **coffin** [kɔ́:fin, káf-] 명 관
  - to place on the **coffin** the bâton the Marshal had received from the Emperor
    황제(나폴레옹)에게서 받은 원수의 지휘봉을 관 위에 올려놓는 것
- **escutcheon** [iskʌ́tʃən, es-] 명 가문(家紋)이 붙은 방패
  - Great soldier as he was, Masséna's **escutcheon** was stained by many a blot
    뛰어난 군인이었음에도 마세나는 많은 오명으로 얼룩져 있었다
- **disgusting** [disgʌ́stiŋ] 형 구역질 나는, 역겨운
- **underhand** 형 뒤가 구린, 비열한
- **harshness** 명 가혹함, 모질게 함
- **Marshal's coachman and footman drove him day by day in a carriage through all the heat of the fighting**
  원수의 마부와 종복은 매일같이 그가 탄 마차를 몰고 격렬한 전장을 모두 누볐다
- **compliment** [kámpləmənt/kɔ́m-] 통 칭찬하다
- **of all the hundred and thirty thousand men engaged**
  전장에서 싸우는 13만 명의 병사들 중
- **felt bound to give them some reward**
  그들에게 보상을 해야한다는 생각이 들었다

that a pension of four hundred francs would save them from want in their old age. The Marshal, in a fury, turned on his aide-de-camp, exclaiming, "Wretch, do you want to ruin me? What, an annuity of four hundred francs! No, no, no, four hundred francs once and for all"; adding to his staff, "I would sooner see you all shot and get a bullet through my arm than bind myself to give an annuity of four hundred francs to any one." The Marshal never forgave the aide-de-camp who had thus urged him to spend his money. His harshness was also well known, and the excesses of the French troops in Switzerland, Naples, and Portugal were greatly owing to his callousness; in the campaign in Portugal he actually allowed detachments of soldiers to set out with the express intention of capturing all girls between twelve and twenty for the use of his men. But while oblivious to the sufferings of others, as a father he was affectionate and indulgent. As he said after Wagram of his son Prosper, "That young scamp has given me more trouble than a whole army corps;" so careful was he of his safety that he refused during the second day of the battle to allow him to take his turn among the other aides-de-camp; but the young Masséna was too spirited to endure this, and Napoleon, hearing of the occurrence, severely reprimanded the Marshal. Staunch republican by profession, blustering and outspoken at times, he was at bottom a true Italian, and knew well how to

- **a pension of four hundred francs would save them from want in their old age**
  4백 프랑의 연금이라면 그들의 노년에 궁핍하지 않게 살 수 있을 것이다
- **Wretch, do you want to ruin me?** 이 멍청아, 나를 파산시키려고 하느냐?
- **annuity** [ənjúːəti] 명 연금
- **four hundred francs once and for all** 4백 프랑 단 한 번, 그걸로 끝이야
- **excess** [iksés, ékses] 명 부절제, 난폭한 행위
- **callousness** 명 무정, 냉담
  - the excesses of the French troops in Switzerland, Naples, and Portugal were greatly owing to his **callousness**
    스위스와 나폴리, 포르투갈에서 프랑스군이 난폭하게 굴었던 것은 그의 무정함이 주된 원인이었다
- **detachments of soldiers** 병사들의 이탈
- **with the express intention of capturing all girls between twelve and twenty for the use of his men**
  노리개로 삼기 위해서 12살에서 20살의 모든 여자애들을 잡아오려는 분명한 의도로
- **oblivious** [əblíviəs] 형 염두에 없는, 안중에 없는
- **indulgent** [indʌ́ldʒənt] 형 관대한, 멋대로 하게 하는
  - But while **oblivious** to the sufferings of others, as a father he was affectionate and **indulgent**.
    그러나 남들의 고통에는 무감각하면서도 아버지로서 자기 자녀들에게는 애정이 넘치고 관대한 사람이었다.
- **scamp** [skæmp] 명 개구쟁이, 장난꾸러기
- **so careful was he of his safety that**
  그는 아들의 안전에 매우 신경 썼기 때문에
- **take one's turn** 교대하다, 자기 순서를 맞다
- **the young Masséna** 마세나의 아들 프로스페(Prosper)
- **too spirited to endure this** (이런 지나친 보살핌)을 견디기에는 기백이 넘치는
- **occurrence** [əkə́ːrəns, əkʌ́r−] 명 사건, 일
- **staunch** [stɑːntʃ, stɔːntʃ] 형 완고한, 충실한
- **blustering** 형 사납게 불어대는, 고함치는
- **outspoken** 형 거리낌 없는, 솔직한

use the delicate art of flattery. Writing in 1805 to the Minister of War, he thus ends a despatch: "I made my first campaign with His Majesty, and it was under his orders that I learned what I know of the trade of arms. We were together in the Army of Italy." Again, when at Fontainebleau he had the misfortune to lose an eye when out pheasant shooting, he attacked Berthier as the culprit, although he knew full well that the Emperor was the only person who had fired a shot.

But in spite of all this meanness and his many defects, he must always be remembered as one of the great soldiers of France, a name at all times to conjure with. Both Napoleon and Wellington have paid their tribute to his talents. At St. Helena the fallen Emperor said that of all his generals the Prince of Essling "was the first," and the Duke, speaking to Lord Ros of the French commanders, said, "Masséna gave me more trouble than any of them, because when I expected to find him weak, he generally contrived somehow that I should find him strong." The Marshal was a born soldier. War was with him an inspiration; being all but illiterate, he never studied it theoretically, but, as one of his detractors admits, "He was a born general: his courage and tenacity did the rest. In the best days of his military career he saw accurately, decided promptly, and never let himself be cast down

- **delicate** [délikət, -kit] 형 섬세한, 우아한, 미묘한
  - how to use the **delicate** art of flattery
    어떻게 하면 우아하게 아첨을 할 수 있는지
- **pheasant** [fézənt] 명 꿩
  - he had the misfortune to lose an eye when out **pheasant** shooting
    야외에서 꿩사냥을 하다가 총에 한쪽 눈을 잃는 불운한 사고를 당했다
- **culprit** [kʌ́lprit] 명 죄인, 범죄자, 피고인
- **meanness** 명 비열함, 야비함
- **conjure** [kándʒər, kʌ́n-] 동 그려내다, 생각하다, (마물·영혼 등을) 불러내다
  - a name at all times to **conjure** with 항상 떠올리는 이름
- **Both Napoleon and Wellington have paid their tribute to his talents.**
  나폴레옹과 웰링턴 모두 그의 재능을 칭찬했다.
- **of all his generals the Prince of Essling "was the first,"**
  그의 장군들 중 에슬링 공작(마세나)이 가장 뛰어났다
- **contrive** [kəntráiv] 동 용케 ~하다, 그럭저럭 ~을 해내다
- **somehow** [sʌ́mhàu] 부 어떻게 하여서든, 여하튼
  - when I expected to find him weak, he generally contrived **somehow** that I should find him strong
    내가 그의 약점을 찾아내려고 기대할 때면, 그는 늘 자신의 강점만 보이도록 만들었다
- **illiterate** [ilítərit] 형 문맹의, 무식한, 교양이 없는
- **theoretically** 부 이론상으로, 이론적으로
- **detractor** [ditrǽktər] 명 비방하는 사람
  - but, as one of his **detractors** admits
    그러나 그를 비방하는 사람 중 하나도 ~는 인정했다
- **tenacity** [tənǽsəti] 명 고집, 끈기
  - He was a born general: his courage and **tenacity** did the rest.
    그는 타고난 장군이었다. 그리고 그의 용기와 끈기가 다른 부분을 채웠다.
- **be cast down** 낙담하다

by reverses." It was owing to this obstinacy combined with clear vision that his great successes were gained, and the dogged determination he showed at Zurich, Loano, Rivoli and Genoa was no whit impaired by success or by old age, as he proved at Essling, Wagram, and before the lines of Torres Vedras. Like his great commander, none knew better than the Prince of Essling that fortune must be wooed, and, as Napoleon wrote to him, "It is not to you, my dear general, that I need to recommend the employment of audacity." In spite of his ill success in his last campaign, to the end the Prince of Essling worthily upheld his title of "The spoilt child of victory."

- **reverse** [rivə́ːrs] 명 불운, 실패, 패배
- **dogged** 형 완강한, 끈질긴, 집요한
- **no whit** 조금도 ~아니다
- **impaired** 형 정상적으로 제 구실을 하지 않는, 망가진, 고장 난
  - the dogged determination he showed at Zurich, Loano, Rivoli and Genoa was no whit **impaired** by success or by old age

  나이도 들고 출세도 했지만, 그가 취리히와 로아노, 리볼리, 제노바에서 보여준 완강한 결단력에는 조금도 손색이 없었다
- **as he proved at Essling, Wagram, and before the lines of Torres Vedras**

  (그 완강한 결단력을) 에슬링과 바그람, 그리고 토레스 베드라스 전선 앞에서 증명했다
- **woo** [wuː] 동 (명예·행운·재산 따위를) 추구하다
  - none knew better than the Prince of Essling that fortune must be **wooed**

  행운은 구하는 자에게만 찾아온다는 사실을 에슬링 대공은 누구보다 잘 알고 있었다
- **It is not to you, my dear general, that I need to recommend the employment of audacity.**

  친애하는 마세나 장군, 다른 사람에게는 모르겠지만 그대에게는 더 대담해지라는 충고가 필요가 없을 것 같구려.
- **uphold** [ʌphóuld] 동 유지하다, 확인하다

4. JEAN BAPTISTE JULES BERNADOTTE

MARSHAL, PRINCE OF PONTE CORVO, KING OF SWEDEN

Gascony has ever been the mother of ambitious men, and many a ruler has she supplied to France. But in 1789 few Gascons even would have believed that ere twenty years had passed one Gascon would be sitting on the Bourbon throne of Naples and a second would be Crown Prince of Sweden, the adopted son of the House of Vasa.

Jean Baptiste Bernadotte, the son of a petty lawyer, was born at Pau on January 26, 1763. At the age of seventeen he enlisted in the Royal Marine regiment and passed the next nine years of his life in garrison towns in Corsica, Dauphiné and Provence. His first notable exploit occurred in 1788, when, as sergeant, he commanded a section of the Marines whose duty it was to maintain order at Grenoble during the troubles which preceded the outbreak of the Revolution. The story goes that Bernadotte was responsible for the first shedding of blood. One day, when the mob

- **Gascony has ever been the mother of ambitious men**
  가스코뉴는 늘 야심 있는 사내들의 고향이었다
- **few Gascons even would have believed that**
  ~라고 믿는 가스코뉴인들은 거의 없었다
- **ere** [εər] 젭 ~하기 전에
  - **ere** twenty years had passed 20년도 지나지 않아
- **one Gascon would be sitting on the Bourbon throne of Naples**
  한 명의 가스코뉴인은 부르봉 왕가를 대신해 나폴리의 왕좌에 앉고(뮈라를 말함)
- **adopt** [ədápt/ədɔ́pt] 동 양자로 삼다
  - a second would be Crown Prince of Sweden, the **adopted** son of the House of Vasa
  다른 한 명은 바사 가문의 양자가 되어 스웨덴의 왕세자가 된다는(베르나도트를 말함)
- **petty** [péti] 형 대단찮은, 하찮은
- **Royal Marine regiment** 왕실 해병 연대
- **garrison** [gǽrəsən] 명 요새, 주둔지
- **exploit** [éksplɔit, iksplɔ́it] 명 공훈, 업적
  - His first notable **exploit** occurred in 1788
  그의 주목할 만한 업적은 1788년에 있었다
- **section** [sékʃən] 명 분대(分隊)
- **maintain order** 치안을 유지하다
- **precede** [prisíːd] 동 ~에 선행하다, 먼저 일어나다
  - the troubles which **preceded** the outbreak of the Revolution
  대혁명이 일어나기 이전에 발생한 민란
- **shed blood** 피를 흘리다, 사람을 죽이다
- **the story goes that** ~라는 이야기다
  - **The story goes that** Bernadotte was responsible for the first shedding of blood.
  처음으로 피를 보게 된 데에는 베르나도트에게 책임이 있다는 이야기다.

was threatening to get out of hand, a woman rushed out of the crowd and caught the sergeant a cuff on the face, whereon the fiery Gascon ordered his men to open fire. In a moment the answer came in a shower of bricks. Blood had been shed, and from that moment the people of France declared war to the death on the old régime. Impetuous, generous, warm-hearted and ambitious, for the next three years Jean Baptiste pursued a policy which is typical of his whole career. Ready when at white heat of passion to take the most extreme measures, even to fire on the crowd, in calmer moments full of enthusiasm for the Rights of Man and the well-being of his fellows; spending long hours haranguing his comrades on the iniquity of kingship and the necessity of taking up arms against all of noble birth, yet standing firm by his colonel, because in former days he had done him a kindness, and saving his officers from the mutineers who were threatening to hang them; watching every opportunity to push his own fortunes, Bernadotte pursued his way towards success. Promotion came rapidly: colonel in 1792, the next year general of brigade, and a few months later general of division, he owed his advancement to the way in which he handled his men. Naturally great neither as tactician or as strategist, he could carry out the orders of others and above all impart his fiery nature to his troops; his success on the battlefield was due to his personal magnetism, whereby he in-

- **threaten** [θrétn] 동 ~에 임박하다, 상황에 처하다
- **get out of hand** 과도해지다, 위협을 주다
  - when the mob was threatening to **get out of hand**
    군 중들의 소요가 걷잡을 수 없이 커질 상황에 처하다
- **cuff** [kʌf] 명 (긴 장갑의) 손목 윗부분, (상의나 셔츠의) 소맷동
- **impetuous** [impétʃuəs] 형 성급한, 충동적인
- **Jean Baptiste pursued a policy which is typical of his whole career**
  장 바티스트는 그의 모든 삶에서 나타나는 전형적인 가치관을 계속해서 보여주었다
- **white heat** 백열, 뜨겁게 달궈진 상태
  - Ready when at **white heat** of passion to take the most extreme measures
    극도로 분노한 상황에서는 가장 극단적인 방법도 서슴없이 선택할 준비가 되어 있고
- **in calmer moments full of enthusiasm for the Rights of Man and the well-being of his fellows**
  좀 더 침착할 때에는 인간의 권리와 동료들의 복지에 대한 열정으로 가득 차
- **harangue** [həræŋ] 동 열변을 토하다
- **the iniquity of kingship** 왕정체제의 부당함
- **stand by somebody** ~의 곁을 지키다, 변함없이 지지하다
  - yet **standing** firm **by his colonel**, because in former days he had done him a kindness
    그러면서도 예전에 그에게 친절하게 대해주었다는 이유로 (상관인) 대령의 곁을 끝까지 지켰다
- **mutineer** [mjùːtəníər] 명 폭도, 항명자
- **pursued his way towards success** 성공을 향해 달려갔다
- **general of division** 사단장
- **he owed his advancement to the way in which he handled his men**
  그의 승진은 사람을 다루는 방법 덕분이었다
- **Naturally great neither as tactician or as strategist**
  날 때부터 천재성을 가진 책략가나 전술가가 아니었지만
- **impart** [impάːrt] 동 나누어 주다, 전해주다
- **magnetism** [mǽgnətìzəm] 명 매력, 사람을 끄는 힘

spired others with his own self-confidence. But with all this self-confidence there was blended in his character a curious strain of hesitation. Again and again during his career he let "I dare not" wait upon "I would." Gascon to the backbone, full of craft and wile, with an eye ever on the future, at times he allowed his restless imagination to conjure up dangers instead of forcing it to show him the means to gain his end. When offered the post of general of brigade, and again when appointed general of division, he refused the step because he had divined that Jacobin would persecute Girondist, that ultra-Jacobin would overthrow Jacobin, and that a reaction would sweep away the Revolutionists, and he feared that the generals of the army might share the fate of those who appointed them. After his magnificent attack at Fleurus, he was at last compelled to accept promotion by Kléber, who rode up to him and cried out, "You must accept the grade of general of brigade here on the field of battle, where you have so truly earned it. If you refuse you are no friend of mine." Thereon Bernadotte accepted the post, considering that he could, if necessary, prove that he had not received it as a political favour. The years 1794-6 saw Bernadotte on continuous active service with the Army of the Sambre and Meuse, now in the Rhine valley, now in the valley of the Danube. Every engagement from Fleurus to Altenkirchen added more and more to his reputation with

- **strain** [strein] 명 (성격·태도상의 특별한) 요소
- **blend in** 조화를 이루다
  - But with all this self-confidence there was **blended in** his character a curious strain of hesitation.
  그러나 이런 자기 확신은 우유부단한 그의 별난 성격과 조화를 이루고 있었다.
- he let "I dare not" wait upon "I would."
  그는 "내가 감히"가 "할 수 있다"로 바뀔 때까지 기다렸다
- **Gascon to the backbone** 뼛속까지 가스코뉴인인
- **craft** [kræft, krɑːft] 명 교활, 술책
- **wile** [wail] 명 간계, 계략
- **with an eye ever on the future** 눈은 항상 미래를 바라보며
- **imagination** [imædʒənéiʃən] 명 상상력, 상상의 산물
- **conjure up** (상상으로) 만들어내다, 출현시키다
- **instead of forcing it to show him the means to gain his end**
  억지로 상상력을 동원해 자신의 목적을 달성할 수 있는 방법을 떠올리는 대신
- **he refused the step** 그는 승진을 거절했다
- **persecute** [pə́ːrsikjùːt] 동 박해하다, 학대하다
- **reaction** [riːǽkʃən] 명 반동, 복고운동
- **sweep away** 일소하다, 휩쓸어가다
  - a reaction would **sweep away** the Revolutionists
  반동세력이 혁명가들을 모두 숙청해버릴 것이다
- he feared that the generals of the army might share the fate of those who appointed them
  그는 군대의 장군들이 그들을 임명해준 사람들과 같은 운명에 처해질 것 같아 두려웠다
- **magnificent attack at Fleurus** 플뢰뤼 전투에서 훌륭한 공격
- where you have so truly earned it
  (전장에서) 정당하게 장군의 직위를 얻은 것이다
- prove that he had not received it as a political favour
  그가 정치적인 배려로 장군의 직위를 얻은 것이 아니라는 것을 증명하다

the authorities and to his hold on the affection of his men. "He is the God of armies," cried his soldiers, as they followed him into the fire-swept zone. His courage, personality and physical beauty captivated all who approached him. Tall, erect, with masses of coal black hair, the great hooked nose of a falcon, and dark flashing eyes indicating Moorish blood in his veins, he could crush the soul out of an incipient revolt with a torrent of cutting words, and in a moment turn the mutineers into the most loyal and devoted of soldiers. During the long revolutionary wars he always kept before him the necessity of preparing for peace, and found time to educate himself in history and political science. It was with the reputation of being one of the best divisional officers of the Army of the Sambre and Meuse, and a political power of no small importance, that, at the end of 1796, Bernadotte was transferred with his division to the Army of Italy, commanded by Bonaparte. From their very first meeting friction arose. They were like Cæsar and Pompey, "the one would have no superior, the other would endure no equal." Bonaparte already foresaw the day when France should lie at his feet; he instinctively divined in Bernadotte a possible rival. Bernadotte, accustomed to the adulation of all with whom he came in contact, felt the loss of it in his new command, where soldiers and officers alike could think and speak of nobody save the conqueror of Italy. Yet neither could

- **authority** [əθɔ́ːriti, əθár-/əθɔ́r-] 명 지휘권, 권한, 권위
- **his hold on the affection of his men** 병사들의 사랑을 받음
- **captivate** [kǽptəvèit] 동 매혹시키다
  - His courage, personality and physical beauty **captivated** all who approached him.
    그의 용기와 인격, 그리고 잘생긴 외모는 다가가는 모든 사람들을 매혹시켰다.
- **masses of coal black hair** 숱이 많은 짙은 검정의 머리카락
- **Moorish blood in his veins** 그의 몸속에 흐르는 무어인의 피
- **incipient** [insípiənt] 형 시초의, 발단의
- **torrent** [tɔ́ːrənt, tár-/tɔ́r-] 명 급류, 여울, (감정의) 연발
- **cutting** 형 (말 등이) 남의 가슴을 찌르는
  - he could crush the soul out of an incipient revolt with a torrent of **cutting** words
    정곡을 찌르는 말을 끊임없이 쏟아내 반역하려는 생각조차 못하게 했다
- **turn the mutineers into the most loyal and devoted of soldiers**
  반란군들을 가장 충성스럽고 헌신적인 병사들로 바꾸어 놓았다
- **he always kept before him the necessity of preparing for peace**
  그는 항상 다가올 평화에 대비할 필요성을 느끼고 있었다
- **a political power of no small importance** 적지 않은 정치적 역량
- **From their very first meeting friction arose** 첫 만남부터 마찰이 일어났다.
- **the one would have no superior, the other would endure no equal**
  한 명은 그보다 뛰어난 사람이 없었고, 다른 한 명은 자신에 필적하는 사람을 용납하지 않았다
- **instinctively** [instíŋktivli] 부 본능적으로, 직감적으로
  - he **instinctively** divined in Bernadotte a possible rival
    그는 베르나도트가 잠재적인 경쟁자임을 본능적으로 알아차렸다
- **adulation** [ædʒəléiʃən] 명 지나친 찬사, 과찬, 아첨
- **accustomed to the adulation of all with whom he came in contact**
  그와 만나는 사람들 모두의 찬사를 받는 데에 익숙한
- **felt the loss of it in his new command**
  그의 새 사령관은 그런 찬사 따위는 하지 않는 사람이라는 것을 느꼈다
- **nobody save the conqueror of Italy**
  이탈리아의 정복자(나폴레옹) 이외에 그 누구에 대해서도

afford to break with the other, neither could as yet foretell what the future would bring forth, so amid an occasional flourish of compliments, a secret and vindictive war was waged between the two. As commander-in-chief, Bonaparte, for the time being, held the whip hand and could show his dislike by severe reprimands. "Wherever your division goes, there is nothing but complaints of its want of discipline." Bernadotte, on his side, anxious to win renown, would appeal to the "esprit" of his soldiers of the Sambre and Meuse, and would spoil Bonaparte's careful combinations by attempting a frontal attack before the turning movement was effected by the Italian divisions. By the end of the campaign it was clear to everybody that there was no love lost between the two. After Leoben Bonaparte was for the moment the supreme figure in France. As plenipotentiary at Leoben and commander-in-chief of "the Army of England" he could impose his will on the Directory. Bernadotte, in disgust at seeing the success of his rival, for some time seriously considered withdrawing from public life, or at any rate from France, where his reputation was thus overshadowed. Among various posts, the Directory offered him the command of the Army of Italy, but he refused them all, till at last he consented to accept that of ambassador at Vienna. Vienna was for the time being the pole round which the whole of European politics revolved, and accordingly there was great

- **bring forth** 낳다, 산출하다, (열매를) 맺다
- **so amid an occasional flourish of compliments**
  이따금 화려한 미사어구로 칭찬을 늘어놓는 가운데에
- **vindictive** [vindíktiv] 혱 원한을 품은, 앙심 깊은
  - a secret and **vindictive** war was waged between the two
  둘 사이에 은밀하고도 원한 깊은 전쟁이 벌어졌다
- **Wherever your division goes, there is nothing but complaints of its want of discipline.**
  당신의 사단은 어디를 가든지 기강이 흐트러져 있다는 불만 밖에 들리지 않는다.
- **esprit** [esprí:] 명 정신, 재기, 재치
- **would spoil Bonaparte's careful combinations**
  보나파르트의 신중한 연합작전을 망쳐버리려고 했다
- **frontal** [frʌ́ntəl] 혱 정면의
- **there was no love lost between the two**
  둘 사이에는 잃어버릴 만한 애정조차 없다
- **After Leoben** 레오벤 조약 후(1797년 캄포 포르미오 조약에 앞서 프랑스와 오스트리아가 체결한 조약)
- **figure** [fígjər/-gər] 명 유명인사, 거물
- **plenipotentiary** [plènipəténʃəri, –ʃièri] 명 전권대사
- **the Army of England** 영국 방면군(영국 침략을 위한)
- **in disgust at seeing the success of his rival**
  경쟁자의 성공을 혐오스럽게 지켜보며
- **for some time seriously considered withdrawing from public life**
  한동안 공직생활에서 은퇴하는 것을 심각하게 고려했다
- **overshadow** 동 빛을 잃게 하다, 볼품없게 하다
- **pole round which the whole of European politics revolved**
  모든 유럽의 정치문제가 활발히 논의되는 중심 무대

possibility there of achieving diplomatic renown. But scarcely had the new ambassador arrived at his destination when he heard of Bonaparte's projected expedition to Egypt. He at once determined to return to France. He felt that his return ought to be marked by something which might appeal to the populace. Accordingly he adopted a device at once simple and effective.

Jacobin at heart when his interest did not clash with his principles, he had from his arrival at Vienna determined to show the princes and dignitaries of an effete civilisation that Frenchmen were proud of their Revolution and believed in nothing but the equality of all men; he refused to conform to court regulations and turned his house into a club for the German revolutionists. His attitude was of course resented, and there was considerable feeling in Vienna against the French Embassy. It only required, therefore, a little more bravado and a display of the tricolour on the balcony of the Embassy to induce the mob to attack the house. Immediately this occurred Bernadotte lodged a complaint, threw up his appointment, and withdrew to France as a protest against this "scoundrelly" attack on the honour of his country and the doctrine of the equality of men.

- **there was great possibility there of achieving diplomatic renown**
  거기에는 외교적 명성을 쌓을 큰 가능성이 있었다
- **scarcely ~when** ~하자마자
  - But **scarcely** had the new ambassador arrived at his destination **when** he heard of Bonaparte's projected expedition to Egypt.
  그러나 새 대사(베르나도트)는 목적지에 도착하자마자, 보나파르트가 예정한 이집트 원정에 대해 들었다.
- **populace** [pápjələs/pɔ́p-] 명 민중, 대중
  - He felt that his return ought to be marked by something which might appeal to the **populace**
  그는 자신의 귀환을 통해 민중들의 마음을 끄는 무언가를 남겨야겠다고 생각했다
- **device** [diváis] 명 계획, 방책
- **Jacobin at heart when his interest did not clash with his principles**
  가슴 속으로 자코뱅 당원이었던 그는 자신의 신념이 자신의 이익과 상충되지 않는다는 것을 알게 되자
- **dignitary** [dígnətèri/-təri] 명 (정부의) 고관
- **effete** [efíːt] 형 정력이 다한, 쇠약해진
  - an **effete** civilisation 쇠약해진 문명(오스트리아를 말함)
- **Frenchmen were proud of their Revolution and believed in nothing but the equality of all men**
  프랑스인들은 혁명에 자부심을 가지고 있고, 그들과 다른 것은 단지 모든 인간이 평등하다는 것을 믿을 뿐이라는 것이다
- **conform** [kənfɔ́ːrm] 동 따르다, 순응하다
  - **conform** to court regulations 궁중 법도에 따르다
- **bravado** [brəváːdou] 명 허장성세, 허세
- **tricolour** 명 삼색기(프랑스 국기)
  - a display of the tricolour on the balcony of the Embassy
  대사관 발코니에 삼색기를 걸어놓음
- **to induce the mob to attack the house**
  폭도들이 대사관을 공격하도록 유인하기 위해

다음 장에 해설 계속

JEAN BAPTISTE BERNADOTTE, KING OF SWEDEN FROM AN ENGRAVING AFTER THE PAINTING BY HILAIRE LE DRU

- **lodge** [lɑdʒ/lɔdʒ] 동 제출하다, 제기하다
- **scoundrelly** 형 비열한, 불한당의
    - as a protest against this "scoundrelly" attack on the honour of his country and the doctrine of the equality of men

    그의 조국의 명예와 인간평등 이념을 "비열하게" 공격한 것에 대한 항의로

On his arrival at Paris he found the Directory shaken to its foundation. Sièyes, the inveterate constitution-monger, who saw the necessity of "a man with a head and a sword," greeted him joyfully; the banishment of Pichegru, the death of Hoche, the disgrace of Moreau, and the absence of Bonaparte had left Bernadotte for the moment the most important of the political soldiers of the Revolution. Acting on Sièyes's advice, Bernadotte refused all posts offered him either in the army or in the Government and awaited developments. Meanwhile he became very intimate with Joseph Bonaparte, who introduced him to his sister-in-law, Désiré Clary. The Clarys were merchants of Marseilles, and Désiré had for some time been engaged to Napoleon Bonaparte, who had jilted her on meeting Josephine. Désiré, very bitter at this treatment, accepted Bernadotte, as she said in later life, "because I was told that he was a man who could hold his own against Napoleon." This marriage was a master-stroke of policy; it at once gave Bernadotte the support of the Bonaparte family, for Bonaparte in his way was still fond of Désiré, and at the same time it gave Bernadotte a partner who at bottom hated Napoleon with a rancour equal to his own. After the disasters in Italy and on the Danube, on July 2, 1799, Bernadotte, thinking the time was come, accepted the post of Minister of War. He speedily put in the field a new army of one hundred thousand men, and by his

- **foundation** [faundéiʃən] 명 근거, 기초
  - he found the Directory shaken to its **foundation**
  총재정부가 그 뿌리부터 흔들리고 있다는 것을 알아챘다
- **inveterate** [invétərit] 형 상습적인, 뿌리 깊은, 완강한
- **constitution** [kùnstətjúːʃən/kɔ́n–] 명 헌법
- **monger** [mʌ́ŋgər] 명 세상에 널리 퍼뜨리는 사람
  - the inveterate constitution-monger 고집스러운 헌법주의자
- **a man with a head and a sword** 문무(文武)를 겸비한 인물
- **banishment** 명 추방
- **had left Bernadotte for the moment the most important of the political soldiers of the Revolution**
  베르나도트를 그 순간 가장 중요한 혁명기의 정치군인으로 남겨두었다
- **development** [divéləpmənt] 명 상황의 전개, 사태의 추이
- **his sister-in-law, Désiré Clary** 그의 처제인 데지레 클라리(조제프 보나파르트는 데지레의 언니인 쥘리 클라리와 결혼함)
- **be engaged to** ~와 약혼하다
  - Désiré had for some time been engaged to Napoleon Bonaparte
  데지레는 한동안 나폴레옹 보나파르트와 약혼한 사이였다
- **jilt** [dʒilt] 동 차버리다
- **hold one's own** 자기 위치를 고수하다, 견디다
  - because I was told that he was a man who could **hold his own** against Napoleon
  그(베르나도트)가 나폴레옹에게도 꺾이지 않는 사람이라고 들었기 때문이다
- **master-stroke** 명 (성공적인 결과를 가져오는) 절묘한 행동
- **in his way** 그 나름대로, 꽤
- **rancour** [rǽŋkər] 명 깊은 원한, 증오
  - it gave Bernadotte a partner who at bottom hated Napoleon with a **rancour** equal to his own
  자신만큼이나 깊은 원한을 가지고 나폴레옹을 혐오하는 배우자를 주었다
- **He speedily put in the field a new army of one hundred thousand men**
  그는 재빨리 10만 명의 새로운 병력을 전장에 투입했다

admirable measures for the instruction of conscripts and for the collection of war material he was in no small way responsible, not only for Masséna's victory of Zurich, but, as Napoleon himself confessed, for the triumph of Marengo.

His term of office, however, was short, for his colleagues intrigued against him. Sièyes desired a man who would overthrow the Directory and establish a dictatorship: Barras was coquetting with the Bourbons. Bernadotte himself talked loudly of the safety of the Republic, but had not the courage to jump with Sièyes or to crouch with Barras. Oppressed by doubt, his imagination paralysed his action, and his personality, which only blazed when in movement, became dull. Still trusting his reputation and thinking that he was indispensable to the Directory, he tendered his resignation, hoping thus to check the intrigues of Sièyes and Barras. To his surprise it was at once accepted, and he found himself a mere nonentity.

On September 14th Bernadotte resigned, on October 9th Napoleon landed at Fréjus. During the Revolution of the 18th Brumaire Bernadotte remained in the background. Desiring the safety of France by the reorganisation of the Directory, hating the idea of a dictatorship, jealous of the success of his rival, he

- **conscript** [kánskript/kɔn-] 명 징집병
- **for the collection of war material** 전쟁 물자의 징발을 위해
- **in no small way responsible** 막중한 임무를 띤
- **term** [təːrm] 명 기간, 기한
- **intrigue against** ~에 대해 음모를 꾸미다
- **coquette** [koukét] 동 아양을 부리다, 꼬리치다
- **crouch** [krautʃ] 동 몸을 구부리다, 웅크리다, 굽실거리다
  - but had not the courage to jump with Sièyes or to **crouch** with Barras
    그러나 시에예스처럼 적극적으로 도약하거나 바라스처럼 몸을 굽힐 용기가 없었다
- **Oppressed by doubt, his imagination paralysed his action**
  의심만 하면서 갖은 상상으로 인해 차마 행동에 옮기지 못했다
- **blaze** [bleiz] 동 타오르다, 불꽃을 일으키다
- **dull** [dʌl] 명 둔한, 더딘
  - his personality, which only blazed when in movement, became **dull**
    행동으로 옮길 때에만 열정적이었던 그의 성격은 둔해지고 말았다
- **indispensable** [ìndispénsəbəl] 형 절대 필요한, 불가결의
- **hoping thus to check the intrigues of Sièyes and Barras**
  시에예스와 바라스의 음모를 저지하기 위해서
- **To his surprise it was at once accepted**
  놀랍게도 그의 사임은 즉각 수리되었다
- **nonentity** [nanéntəti/nɔn-] 명 보잘 것 없는 사람
- **remain in the background** 표면에 나타나지 않다
  - During the Revolution of the 18th Brumaire Bernadotte remained in the background.
    브뤼메르의 18일 쿠데타 중에 베르나도트는 어떤 역할도 하지 않은 채 가만히 있었다.

refused to join the stream of generals which hurried to the feet of the conqueror of Italy and Egypt.

Bonaparte, who could read his soul like a book, attempted to draw his rival into his net, but, as ever, the Gascon could not make up his mind. At first he was inclined to join in the conspiracy, but at last he refused, and told Bonaparte that, if the Directory commanded him, he would take up arms against those who plotted against the Republic. Still, even on the eventful day he hesitated, and appeared in the morning among the other conspirators at Bonaparte's house, but not in uniform, thinking thus to serve both parties.

During the years which succeeded the establishment of the Consulate, Bernadotte waged an unending subterranean war against Napoleon. Scarcely a year passed in which his name was not connected with some conspiracy to overthrow the First Consul. Of these Napoleon was well advised, but Bernadotte was too cunning to allow himself to be compromised absolutely. However much he might sympathise with the conspirators and lend them what aid he could, he always refused to sign his name to any document. Accordingly, although on one occasion a bundle of seditious proclamations was found in the boot of his aide-de-

- he refused to join the stream of generals which hurried to the feet of the conqueror of Italy and Egypt

  서둘러 이탈리아와 이집트의 정복자(나폴레옹)의 발 아래로 모여드는 장군들의 대열에 참가하길 거부했다
- who could read his soul like a book

  그의 속마음을 훤히 꿰뚫어 볼 수 있었던
- draw his rival into his net 그의 경쟁자를 포섭하다
- conspiracy [kənspírəsi] 명 음모, 모반
- plot [plɑt/plɔt] 동 음모를 꾸미다

  - if the Directory commanded him, he would take up arms against those who **plotted** against the Republic

  만약 총재정부가 명령하기만 한다면, 그는 공화국을 전복시키려는 이들(나폴레옹 일파를 말함)에 대항해 무기를 들 것이다
- even on the eventful day he hesitated 거사일에도 그는 망설였다
- thinking thus to serve both parties

  이런 식으로 양다리를 걸칠 생각을 하면서
- subterranean [sʌ̀btəréiniən] 형 지하의, 숨은

  - Bernadotte waged an unending **subterranean** war against Napoleon

  베르나도트는 나폴레옹에 대항해 끊임없이 은밀한 전쟁을 벌였다
- Scarcely a year passed in which his name was not connected with some conspiracy to overthrow the First Consul.

  1년이 지나도록 제1집정관을 타도하려는 몇몇 음모에 그의 이름은 거론되지 않았다.
- well advised 분별 있는, 잘 알고 있는
- cunning [kʌ́niŋ] 형 교활한, 약삭빠른
- be compromised 위태롭게 되다
- sympathise(ze) [símpəθàiz] 동 공감하다, 찬성하다
- he always refused to sign his name to any document

  그는 늘 (음모에 관한) 어떤 문서에도 서명하기를 거부했다
- seditious [sidíʃəs] 형 선동적인
- boot [buːt] 명 마차의 짐칸

camp's carriage, the charge could not be brought home. On another occasion, when it was proved that he had advanced twelve thousand francs to the conspirator Cerrachi, he could prove that it was the price he had paid the artist for a bust. In spite of the fact that no definite proof could be brought against him, the First Consul could easily, if he chose, have produced fraudulent witnesses or have had him disposed of by a court-martial, as he got rid of the Duc d'Enghien. Napoleon waited his time. He was afraid of a Jacobin outbreak if he made a direct attack against him. Further, Bernadotte had a zealous friend and ally in Joseph Bonaparte. So when pressed to take stern measures against his enemy, Napoleon always refused to do so, partly from policy, partly because of his former love for Désiré, and partly from the horror of a scandal in his family, which might weaken his position when he seized the imperial throne. Accordingly he attempted in every way to conciliate his rebellious subject, and at the same time to place him in positions where he could do no political harm. Together with Brune and Marmont, he made him a Senator. He offered him the command of the Army of Italy, and, when Bernadotte refused and demanded employment at home, he posted him to the command of the division in Brittany, with headquarters at Rennes. But the First Consul found that Rennes, far off as it was, was too close to Paris; accordingly he tried to

- **the charge could not be brought home** 혐의가 확실치 않았다
- **advance** [ædvǽns, -vάːns, əd-] 통 송금하다, 선불하다
- **bust** [bʌst] 명 흉상(胸像), 반신상
  - he could prove that it was the price he had paid the artist for a **bust**
  흉상을 제작하기 위해 조각가에게 지불했던 돈이라고 증명할 수 있었다
- **fraudulent** [frɔ́ːdʒulənt] 형 사기의, 부정한
  - the First Consul could easily, if he chose, have produced **fraudulent** witnesses or have had him disposed of by a court-martial
  제1집정관이 마음만 먹는다면 손쉽게 가짜 증인을 만들거나 군법재판에 회부해 그를 처형할 수 있었다
- **Duc d'Enghien** 앙갱 공작(부르봉 가문 출신으로 1804년 날조된 나폴레옹 암살음모 때문에 체포되어 처형당함)
- **Further, Bernadotte had a zealous friend and ally in Joseph Bonaparte**
  게다가 베르나도트에게는 열성적인 친구이자 협력자인 조제프 보나파르트가 있었다
- **stern** [stəːrn] 형 단호한, 강경한
- **partly from policy, partly because of his former love for Désiré, and partly from the horror of a scandal in his family**
  정치적인 고려와 옛 애인인 데지레에 대한 정, 그리고 그의 집안에 추문이 생길까 하는 두려움에서
- **which might weaken his position when he seized the imperial throne**
  그가 황제로 즉위할 때 자신의 입지를 약화시킬 것이다
- **he attempted in every way to conciliate his rebellious subject**
  그는 이 역심을 품은 신하와 화해하기 위해 모든 시도를 다했다
- **demanded employment at home** 국내에서 복무하기를 원했다
- **Rennes, far off as it was, was too close to Paris**
  멀리 보낸다고 보냈지만, 렌은 파리와 너무 가까이 있었다

tempt his Jacobin general by important posts abroad. He proposed in succession the embassy at Constantinople, the captain-generalcy at Guadaloupe, and the governorship of Louisiana, but Bernadotte refused to leave France. At last, early in 1803 Napoleon nominated him minister to the United States. Three times the squadron of frigates got ready to accompany the new minister, but each time the minister postponed his departure. Meanwhile war broke out with England, and Bernadotte was retained in France as general on the unattached list, owing to the efforts of Joseph.

On the establishment of the Empire Napoleon included Bernadotte's name among the number of the Marshals, partly to please his brother Joseph and to maintain the prestige of his family and partly, as in the case of Augereau, Masséna and Jourdan, to win over the staunch republicans and Jacobins to the imperial régime. For the moment the Emperor achieved his object. The ex-Jacobin, proud of his new title and luxuriating in his lately acquired estate of Grosbois, was actually grateful; but still, Gascon-like, he wanted more and complained he had not enough to maintain his proper state. Napoleon, hearing of this from Fouché, exclaimed: "Take from the public treasury enough to put this right. I want Bernadotte to be content. He is just beginning to say he is full of

- **tempt** [tempt] 동 마음을 끌다, 유혹하다
  - he tried to **tempt** his Jacobin general by important posts abroad
    그(나폴레옹)는 이 자코뱅당 장군(베르나도트)을 해외의 중요한 직책으로 유혹하려 했다
- **minister** [mínistər] 명 (국가를 대표하는) 공사(公使)
- **squadron** [skwádrən/skwɔ́d-] 명 소함대
- but each time the minister postponed his departure
  그러나 매번 이 공사(베르나도트)는 출발을 지연시켰다
- **unattached** 형 명령 대기의
  - Bernadotte was retained in France as general on the **unattached** list, owing to the efforts of Joseph
    조제프의 노력 덕분에 베르나도트는 예비 장군의 자격으로 프랑스에 남아있게 되었다
- included Bernadotte's name among the number of the Marshals
  원수들의 명단 속에 베르나도트의 이름을 포함시켰다
- partly to please his brother Joseph and to maintain the prestige of his family
  형인 조제프를 기쁘게 하려는 의도와 가문의 위신을 지키려는 뜻에서
- **win over** 자기편으로 끌어들이다, 설득하다
  - to **win over** the staunch republicans and Jacobins to the imperial régime
    완고한 공화주의자와 자코뱅 당원들을 제국의 정권 안에 포섭하기 위해서
- **luxuriate** [lʌgʒúərièit, lʌkʃúər-] 동 탐닉하다, 즐기다
- **grateful** [gréitfəl] 형 감사하고 있는, 고마워하는
- he wanted more and complained he had not enough to maintain his proper state
  그는 더 많은 것을 원했고, 그의 신분에 걸맞은 생활을 유지하기 위해 충분치 않다고 불평했다
- **exclaim** [ikskléim] 동 큰 소리로 말하다, 외치다
- **put right** 바로잡다, 정돈하다
  - Take from the public treasury enough to **put** this **right**.
    국고에서 충분한 돈을 꺼내서 그의 요구를 들어주어라.
- He is just beginning to say he is full of attachment for my person
  이제야 그가 내 사람이 되고 싶다고 말하는구나

attachment for my person; this may attach him more." But a few days later the Marshal revealed his true feelings when, talking of Napoleon to Lucien, he said, "There will be no more glory save in his presence and by his side and through his means, and unfortunately all for him."

Though the Emperor had promoted him to honour, it was no part of his scheme to allow to remain in Paris a man who, as Talleyrand said, "was capable of securing four cut-throats and making away with Napoleon himself if necessary, a furious beast, a grenadier capable of all and everything, a man to be kept at a distance at all cost." Accordingly the Marshal very soon found himself sent to replace Mortier in command of the "Army of Hanover."

For fifteen months Bernadotte administered Hanover, and the subtle courtesy he showed to friend and foe alike made him as usual the adored of all with whom he came in contact. But whatever he did, the Emperor still suspected him, and gave the cue to all, that Bernadotte was not to be trusted and was no soldier. Napoleon always took care that Bernadotte should never have under his command French soldiers. His troops in 1805 were Bavarians; in 1807, Poles; in 1808, a mixture of Dutch and Span-

- when, talking of Napoleon to Lucien
  뤼시앵(나폴레옹의 동생)에게 나폴레옹에 대한 이야기를 하면서
- There will be no more glory save in his presence and by his side and through his means, and unfortunately all for him.
  나폴레옹의 면전에서나 좌우, 그의 돈, 유감스럽게도 그에 대한 모든 것에서 벗어나는 것이 가장 영광스러운 일이다
- it was no part of his scheme to allow to remain in Paris
  그를 파리에 머무르게 할 계획은 전혀 없었다
- **secure** [sikjúər] 동 확보하다, 손에 넣다
  - was capable of **securing** four cut-throats
    능히 네 명의 암살자 정도는 확보할 수 있었다
- **make away with** 죽이다, 제거하다
- a man to be kept at a distance at all cost
  어떤 희생을 치르더라도 꼭 멀리 떼어 놓아야 하는 남자
- sent to replace Mortier in command of the "Army of Hanover"
  모르티에를 대신해 하노버군의 지휘관으로 임명되었다
- **administer** [ædmínəstər, əd-] 동 지배하다, 통치하다
- **subtle** [sʌ́tl] 형 솜씨 있는, 교묘한
- **courtesy** [kə́ːrtəsi] 명 공손함, 예의바름, 호의
  - the subtle **courtesy** he showed to friend and foe alike
    친구나 적에게 모두 교묘하게 호의를 보여주다
- **adore** [ədɔ́ːr] 동 숭배하다, 존경하다
- **cue** [kjuː] 명 암시, 넌지시 알림
- Bernadotte was not to be trusted and was no soldier
  베르나도트는 믿을 수 있는 자가 아니며 군인도 아니다
- Napoleon always took care that Bernadotte should never have under his command French soldiers
  나폴레옹은 베르나도트가 절대 프랑스군을 지휘하지 못하도록 늘 주의를 기울였다

iards; and in 1809, of Poles and Saxons. Berthier, working out the Emperor's ideas, and himself also hating Bernadotte, took care that in the allotment of duties the disagreeable and unimportant tasks should fall to the Marshal. In spite of the inferiority of his troops, Bernadotte as usual distinguished himself in the hour of battle. At Austerlitz, at the critical moment, he saw that unless the centre was heavily supported Napoleon's plan of trapping the Russians must fail, so without waiting orders he detached a division towards the northern slopes of the plateau, and thus materially assisted in winning the day. But though quickwitted and alert on the battlefield, he never shone in strategy. In the movements which led up to a battle he was always slow and inclined to hesitate, and his detractors seized on this fault to declare, with Napoleon's connivance, that he was a traitor to the Emperor and to France. An incident of the campaign of 1806 gave the Marshal's enemies an excellent opening for showing their dislike. Napoleon, thinking he had cornered the whole Prussian army at Jena on the night of October 13th, sent orders to Bernadotte to fall back from Naumburg and get across the Prussian line of retreat. In pursuance of these orders the Marshal left Naumburg at dawn on the morning of the 14th and marched in the direction of Apolda, which he reached, in spite of the badness of the roads, by 4 p.m., and thereby captured about a thousand prisoners. But

- **Berthier, working out the Emperor's ideas, and himself also hating Bernadotte**
  황제의 생각을 잘 이해하고 그 자신도 베르나도트를 몹시 싫어했던 베르티에
- **allotment** 몡 분배, 할당
- **disagreeable** [dìsəgríːəbəl] 혱 마음에 들지 않은, 하기 싫은
- **inferiority** [infiərió(ː)rəti, -ár-] 몡 열등, 열세, 조악(粗惡)
- **Bernadotte as usual distinguished himself in the hour of battle**
  베르나도트는 늘 그렇듯이 전장에서 뛰어난 활약을 했다
- **unless the centre was heavily supported Napoleon's plan of trapping the Russians must fail**
  중앙을 대대적으로 지원하지 않으면 러시아군을 함정에 빠뜨리려는 나폴레옹의 계획이 실패할 것이다
- **he detached a division towards the northern slopes of the plateau**
  그는 사단 하나를 고원의 북쪽 비탈로 파견했다
- **materially** 튀 현저하게, 크게
- **quickwitted** 혱 약삭빠른, 재치 있는
- **shine** [ʃain] 동 두드러지다, 빼어나다
  - But though quickwitted and alert on the battlefield, he never shone in strategy.
  전장에서 재치 있고 날랬지만, 그는 결코 뛰어난 전략가가 되지는 못했다.
- **lead up to** ~로 이끌다, ~에 이르다
- **detractor** [ditræktər] 몡 비방하는 사람, 중상하는 사람
- **seized on this fault to declare** 이 잘못을 빌미로 ~라고 공언했다
- **connivance** [kənáivəns] 몡 묵인, 묵과
- **corner** [kɔ́ːrnər] 동 구석에 밀어붙이다, 궁지에 빠뜨리다
  - thinking he had **cornered** the whole Prussian army at Jena on the night of October 13th
  10월 13일 밤 예나에서 그는 모든 프로이센군을 궁지에 몰아넣었다고 생각하고
- **to fall back from Naumburg and get across the Prussian line of retreat**
  나움부르크에서 물러나 프로이센군의 퇴각로를 차단하라고

Napoleon had been mistaken in his calculations; the main Prussian force was not at Jena, but at Auerstädt, where it was most pluckily engaged and beaten by Davout, who at once sent to ask aid of Bernadotte; but the Marshal, according to Napoleon's definite orders, pursued his way to Apolda. The Emperor, to vent his dislike against Bernadotte and to cover up his own mistake, asserted that he had sent him orders to go to Davout's assistance, but a careful examination of the French despatches proves that no such document existed; in fact, the official despatches completely exonerate Bernadotte. Before the campaign was finished, Napoleon had to give the Marshal the praise he merited, when, aided by Soult and Murat, he at last forced Blücher to surrender with twenty-five thousand men and all the Prussian artillery at Lübeck. At Eylau Bernadotte's ill luck once again pursued him, for the staff officers sent to order him to march to the field of battle were taken by the enemy. This misfortune gave another opportunity to his detractors, and again the Emperor lent his authority to their false accusations. While secretly countenancing every attack on the Marshal, the Emperor, for family reasons, was loth to come to an open breach. On June 5, 1806, he had created him Prince of Ponte Corvo, a small principality in Italy wedged in between the kingdom of Naples and the Papal States; his reason for so doing he explained in a letter to his brother Joseph, the King

- **the main Prussian force was not at Jena, but at Auerstädt**
  프로이센의 주력은 예나가 아닌, 아우에르슈테트에 있었다
- **pluckily** [부] 용기 있게, 대담하게, 단호하게
  - where it was most **pluckily** engaged and beaten by Davout
    프로이센군은 매우 용감하게 싸웠지만, 다부 원수에게 패했다
- **who at once sent to ask aid of Bernadotte**
  (다부 원수는) 즉시 베르나도트의 도움을 요청했다
- **definite** [défənit] [형] 확실한, 명확한
- **vent** [vent] [동] (감정 등을) 드러내다, (분노를) 터뜨리다
  - to **vent** his dislike against Bernadotte and to cover up his own mistake
    베르나도트에 대한 혐오를 드러내고, 자기 자신의 잘못을 덮기 위해
- **assert** [əsə́ːrt] [동] 단언하다, 강력히 주장하다
- **he had sent him orders to go to Davout's assistance**
  다부를 지원하러 가라는 명령을 내렸다
- **despatch(=dispatch)** [명] 긴급 공문서
- **exonerate** [igzánərèit/-zɔ́n-] [동] 결백을 증명하다
  - the official despatches completely **exonerate** Bernadotte
    공식적인 명령 문서들은 베르나도트의 무죄를 완벽하게 증명해 주었다
- **pursue** [pərsúː/-sjúː] [동] 귀찮게 따라다니다, 끊임없이 괴롭히다
- **the Emperor lent his authority to their false accusations**
  황제는 그들이 부당하게 (베르나도트를) 비난하는 데에 자신의 권력을 빌려주었다
- **countenance** [káuntənəns] [동] 묵인하다, (은근히) 지지하다
- **be loth to(=be loath to)** ~을 싫어하다
- **come to an open breach** 공개적인 불화로 비화되다
- **Prince of Ponte Corvo** 그에게 폰테 코르보 공작의 작위
- **wedge** [wedʒ] [동] 끼어들게 하다, 밀어 넣다
  - **wedged** in between the kingdom of Naples and the Papal States
    나폴리 왕국과 교황령 사이에 꼭 끼인

of Naples. "When I gave the title of duke and prince to Bernadotte, it was in consideration of you, for I have in my armies many generals who have served me better and on whose attachment I can count more. But I thought it proper that the brother-in-law of the Queen of Naples should hold a distinguished position in your country." It was for this reason also that, after the treaty of Tilsit, the Emperor presented the Prince with vast domains in Poland and Hanover.

During the interval between the peace of Tilsit and the outbreak of the war with Austria in 1809, the Prince of Ponte Corvo returned to his duty of administering Hanover. Pursuing his former policy of ingratiating himself with everybody, he renewed his old friendships with all classes, and gained the goodwill of his neighbours in Denmark and Swedish Pomerania, showing a suavity which was in marked contrast to rigid disciplinarians of the school of Davout. Such conduct, however, did not gain the approval of the Emperor, whose policy was, by enforcing the continental system, to squeeze to death the Hanseatic towns, which were England's best customers.

The Marshal was so keenly aware of the displeasure of the Emperor and the hatred of many of his advisers, especially of

- When I gave the title of duke and prince to Bernadotte, it was in consideration of you

  내가 베르나도트에게 공작의 작위를 하사한 것은 형(조제프)을 생각했기 때문이었다
- **count on** ~을 의지하다, 기대하다
  - many generals who have served me better and **on** whose attachment I can **count** more

    나를 더 잘 섬기고 그들의 애정을 더 기대할 수 있는 많은 장군들
- the brother-in-law of the Queen of Naples

  나폴리 왕비의 제부(弟夫)(당시 조제프는 나폴리의 왕이었음)
- **distinguished** [distíŋgwiʃt] 형 눈에 띄는, 고귀한
- the treaty of Tilsit

  틸지트 조약(1807년 프랑스와 프로이센, 러시아가 맺은 강화 조약)
- **ingratiate onself with** ~의 비위를 맞추다, 환심을 사다
- gained the goodwill of his neighbours in Denmark and Swedish Pomerania

  그의 이웃인 덴마크와 스웨덴령 포메라니아와 우호적인 관계를 가졌다
- **suavity** [swάːvəti, swǽv-] 명 유화, 온화
- **marked** 형 명료한, 두드러진, 저명한
- **disciplinarian** [dìsəplənέəriən] 명 엄격한 교사
  - a suavity which was in marked contrast to rigid **disciplinarians** of the school of Davout

    다부 원수 학교의 엄격한 선생님들과는 분명히 대조되는 온화함
- **squeeze to death** 압살하다, 눌러 죽이다
- **Hanseatic** [hæ̀nsiǽtik] 형 한자 동맹의
  - to squeeze to death the **Hanseatic** towns, which were England's best customers

    영국의 최대 고객인 한자 동맹의 도시들을 압살하기 위해
- **keenly** [kíːnli] 부 날카롭게, 예민하게
  - Marshal was so **keenly** aware of the displeasure of the Emperor and the hatred of many of his advisers, especially of Berthier, the chief of the staff,

    원수는 황제의 불쾌함과 그의 많은 조언자들, 특히 수석참모인 베르티에의 증오를 너무나도 잘 알고 있었기 때문에

Berthier, the chief of the staff, that he actually asked to be placed on half pay at the commencement of the campaign of 1809, but the Emperor refused his request. He had determined to end the unceasing struggle between himself and Bernadotte. The battle of Wagram gave him his opportunity. On the first day of the battle, the Marshal had severely criticised, in the hearing of some of his officers, the methods the Emperor had adopted for crossing the Danube and attacking the Archduke Charles, boasting that if he had been in command he would by a scientific manœuvre have compelled the Archduke to lay down his arms almost without a blow. Some enemy told the Emperor of this boast. On the next day Bernadotte's corps was broken by the Austrian cavalry and only saved from absolute annihilation by the personal exertion of the Marshal and his staff, who, by main force, stopped and re-formed the crowd of fugitives. The Emperor arrived on the scene at the moment the Marshal had just succeeded in staying the rout, and sarcastically inquired, "Is that the scientific manœuvre by which you were going to make the Archduke lay down his arms?" and before the Marshal could make reply continued, "I remove you, sir, from the command of the army corps which you handle so badly. Withdraw at once and leave the Grand Army within twenty-four hours; a bungler like you

- He had determined to end the unceasing struggle between himself and Bernadotte.

  황제는 자신과 베르나도트의 끝없는 다툼을 종식시키기로 결심했다.

- the Marshal had severely criticise, in the hearing of some of his officers

  원수는 그의 장교들이 들을 수 있는 곳에서 심한 혹평을 했다

- **boast** [boust] 동 자랑하다, 떠벌리다
- **scientific** [sàiəntífik] 형 숙련된, 노련한
- **lay down one's arms** 무기를 버리다, 항복하다
- **without a blow** 힘들이지 않고, 쉽게
  - if he had been in command he would by a scientific manœuvre have compelled the Archduke to lay down his arms almost **without a blow**

    만약 그가 지휘했더라면, 노련한 솜씨로 (카를) 대공을 손쉽게 항복하도록 만들었을 것이다
- **exertion** [igzə́ːrʃən] 명 노력, 분발
  - only saved from absolute annihilation by the personal **exertion** of the Marshal and his staff

    원수와 그의 참모들의 개인적인 활약으로 전멸당하는 것만은 막았다
- **fugitive** [fjúːdʒətiv] 명 도망자, 탈주자
  - by main force, stopped and re-formed the crowd of **fugitives**

    주력군을 이용해 탈영병이 대량으로 발생하는 것을 멈추게 하고 이들을 재편성했다
- **rout** [raut] 명 참패, 패주
  - the Marshal had just succeeded in staying the **rout**

    원수는 계속해서 패주하고 있을 뿐이었다
- **sarcastically** [sɑːrkǽstikəli] 부 빈정거리며, 비꼬며
- **before the Marshal could make reply continued**

  원수가 뭐라고 대답을 하기도 전에 계속해서 말했다
- **bungler** [bʌ́ŋɡələr] 명 서투른 사람

is no good to me." Such treatment was more than the Marshal's fiery temperament could stand, and accordingly, contrary to all military regulations and etiquette, he issued a bulletin without the authority of the Emperor praising the Saxon troops, and thus magnifying his own importance. The Emperor was furious, and sent a private memorandum to the rest of the Marshals declaring that, "independently of His Majesty having commanded his army in person, it is for him alone to award the degree of glory each has merited. His Majesty owes the success of his arms to the French troops and to no foreigners... To Marshal Macdonald and his troops is due the success which the Prince of Ponte Corvo takes to himself." It seemed as if Bernadotte's career was finished.

The Emperor found he had no longer any reason to fear him, and for the moment determined to crush him completely. So when he heard that Clarke had despatched the Prince to organise the resistance to the English at Flushing, he at once superseded him by Bessières. But the prospect of an alliance by marriage with either Russia or Austria once again caused the Emperor to reflect on the necessity of avoiding scandal and discord in his own family; accordingly he determined to try and propitiate the Marshal by sending him as his envoy to Rome. To a born intriguer like Bernadotte, Rome seemed to spell absolute exile, and

- Such treatment was more than the Marshal's fiery temperament could stand
  그런 조치는 불같은 원수의 성격으로 견딜 수 없는 것이었다
- contrary to all military regulations and etiquette
  군율과 예의에 모두 어긋나게
- he issued a bulletin without the authority of the Emperor praising the Saxon troops
  황제의 허가도 없이 작센군의 공적을 칭찬하는 공보를 발표했다(당시 작센군은 베르나도트가 지휘하고 있었는데, 일개 원수가 마음대로 공을 치하했다는 뜻)
- **magnify** [mǽgnəfài] 통 과장하다, 크게 보이게 하다
- **independently of** ~와는 별개로, 관계없이
- it is for him alone to award the degree of glory each has merited
  각자에게 그 공적에 합당한 영광을 수여하는 것은 오직 그(황제) 혼자뿐이다
- To Marshal Macdonald and his troops is due the success which the Prince of Ponte Corvo takes to himself.
  폰테 코르보 공작이 가로챈 성공은 응당 막도날 원수와 그의 군대에 돌아가야 할 것이다.
- for the moment determined to crush him completely
  우선 그를 완전히 파멸시키기로 결심했다
- **supersede** [sùːpərsíːd] 통 ~의 지위를 빼앗다, ~에 대신하다
- **prospect** [práspekt/prɔ́s–] 명 예상, 기대, (장래의) 가망
  - the **prospect** of an alliance by marriage with either Russia or Austria
    러시아나 오스트리아와의 결혼동맹 가능성
- **reflect on** 곰곰이 생각하다, 심사숙고하다
- **propitiate** [prəpíʃièit] 통 달래다, 녹이다, 화해시키다
- **envoy** [énvɔi, áːn–] 명 외교 사절, 특사
- **spell** [spel] 통 ~을 의미하다, ~한 결과가 되다
  - Rome seemed to **spell** absolute exile
    로마로 파견되는 것은 의심할 여지없는 추방을 의미하는 것이었다

accordingly, in the lowest of spirits, he set about to find excuse to delay his journey, little thinking that fortune had turned and was at last about to raise him to those heights of which he had so long dreamed. Long before, in 1804, at the time of the establishment of the Empire, he had secretly visited the famous fortune-teller, Mademoiselle Lenormand, who had told him that he also should be a king and reign, but his kingdom would be across the sea. His boundless ambition, stimulated by Southern superstition, had fed itself on this prophecy, even when the breach with Napoleon seemed to close the door to all hope.

In May, 1809, a revolution in Sweden had deposed the incapable Gustavus IV. and set up as King his uncle Charles, Duke of Sudermania. The new King, Charles XIII., was old and childless. Accordingly the question of the succession filled all men's minds. With Russia pressing in on the east and Denmark hostile on the west, it was important to find some one round whom all might rally, by preference a soldier. It was of course obvious that France, the traditional ally of Sweden, dominated Europe. Accordingly the Swedes determined to seek their Crown Prince from the hands of Napoleon. Now, of all the Marshals, Bernadotte had had most to do with the Swedes. At Hamburg he had had constant questions to settle with the Pomeranians. At the

- **in the lowest of spirits** 극도로 의기소침하여
- **little thinking that fortune had turned and was at last about to raise him to those heights of which he had so long dreamed**
  운명이 뒤바뀌어서 마침내 그가 그렇게 오랫동안 꿈꾸어왔던 그런 높은 위치로 자신이 추대될 것이라는 생각은 거의 하지 않은 채(왕이 될 줄은 생각지도 못했다는 뜻)
- **fortune-teller** 몡 점쟁이, 점술가
- **he also should be a king and reign, but his kingdom would be across the sea**
  그 역시 왕이 되겠지만, 그의 왕국은 바다 건너에 있을 것이다
- **boundless** [báundlis] 혱 무한한, 끝없는
- **stimulate** [stímjəlèit] 동 자극하다, 격려하다
- **superstition** [sù:pərstíʃən] 몡 미신, 미신적 관습
- **feed on** ~에 쏠리다, 매달리다
  - had fed itself on this prophecy 이 예언에 매달렸다
- **even when the breach with Napoleon seemed to close the door to all hope**
  나폴레옹과의 불화로 모든 희망의 문이 닫혀버린 것처럼 보였을 때에도
- **set up as King his uncle Charles, Duke of Sudermania Duke of Sudermania**
  그(폐된 왕 구스타브 4세)의 삼촌인 쉐데르만란드 공작 칼을 왕으로 세웠다
- **Accordingly the question of the succession filled all men's minds.**
  따라서 후계 문제가 모두의 관심사였다.
- **With Russia pressing in on the east and Denmark hostile on the west**
  동쪽에서는 러시아가 압박하고, 서쪽에서는 덴마크와 적대관계였기 때문에
- **rally round** ~주위로 모이다
  - some one *round* whom all might *rally*
  주위로 힘이 결집될 수 있는 인물
- **by preference** 되도록
- **seek their Crown Prince from the hands of Napoleon**
  나폴레옹의 결정에 따라 그들의 왕세자를 구하다
- **do with** ~와 관계가 있다
- **constant** [kánstənt/kɔ́n–] 혱 성실한, 변하지 않는
- **settle with** ~와 화해하다, 해결을 보다

time of Blücher's surrender at Lübeck he had treated with great courtesy certain Swedish prisoners. It seemed therefore to the Swedish King's advisers that the Prince of Ponte Corvo, the brother-in-law of King Joseph, the hero of Austerlitz, was the most suitable candidate they could find. Napoleon, however, was furious when he heard that a deputation had arrived to offer the position of Crown Prince of Sweden to Bernadotte. Too diplomatic to refuse to allow the offer to be made, he set to work at once secretly to undermine the Marshal's popularity in Sweden, and while pretending to leave the decision to Bernadotte himself, assured his friends that the Marshal would never dare to accept the responsibility. But Napoleon had miscalculated. Some kind friend informed the Marshal of what the Emperor had said, and, as Bernadotte himself admitted, it was the taunt, "He will never dare," which decided him to accept the Swedish offer. Before the Crown Prince elect quitted France the Emperor attempted to place on him the condition that he should never bear arms against him; but Bernadotte, foreseeing the future, refused to give any such promise, and at last the Emperor gave in with the angry words, "Go; our destinies will soon be accomplished!"

The Crown Prince took with him to Sweden his eldest son, who had curiously, by the whim of his godfather, Napoleon, been

- **he had treated with great courtesy certain Swedish prisoners**
  그는 몇몇 스웨덴 포로들을 아주 정중하게 대우했다
- **the most suitable candidate they could find**
  그들이 찾을 수 있는 가장 적합한 후보자
- **deputation** [dèpjətéiʃən] 몡 대리, 대표, 대표단
- **diplomatic** [dìpləmǽtik] 몡 외교의, 외교상의
  - Too **diplomatic** to refuse to allow the offer to be made
  단순히 거절하기에는 외교적으로 너무 민감한 사안이었기 때문에
- **set to work** 일에 착수하다, 작용하기 시작하다
- **undermine** [ʌndərmáin] 통 (명성 따위를) 훼손하다
- **while pretending to leave the decision to Bernadotte himself**
  베르나도트 자신이 결정하도록 맡겨두는 척하면서
- **assured his friends that the Marshal would never dare to accept the responsibility** 원수가 감히 그런 책임을 떠맡지 않을 거라고 분명히 확신했다
- **as Bernadotte himself admitted** 베르나도트 자신이 인정했듯이
- **taunt** [tɔːnt, tɑːnt] 몡 비웃음, 조롱
  - it was the **taunt**, "He will never dare," which decided him to accept the Swedish offer
  "그는 절대로 그렇게 하지 못할 거야"라는 비웃음 때문에 그는 스웨덴의 제의를 받아들이기로 마음먹었던 것이다
- **place on him the condition that** 그에게 ~라는 조건을 붙였다
- **foresee** [fɔːrsíː] 통 예견하다
- **refused to give any such promise** 어떤 확답도 주지 않았다
- **"Go; our destinies will soon be accomplished!"**
  "가버려라. 우리의 운명은 곧 정해질 것이다!"
- **curiously** [kjúəriəsli] 뷔 이상하게도, 기묘하게
- **whim** [hwim] 몡 변덕, 일시적인 생각
  - by the **whim** of his godfather, Napoleon, been named Oscar
  그의 대부인 나폴레옹의 일시적인 생각으로 오스카르라는 이름이 지어졌다

named Oscar. But his wife, Désiré, could not tear herself away from Paris, where she had collected a coterie of artists and writers; her salon was greatly frequented by restless intriguers like Talleyrand and Fouché. Woman of pleasure as she was, the gaiety of Paris was the breath of her nostrils. Accordingly the Crown Princess remained behind, as it were the hostage for the Prince's good behaviour, but in reality a spy and secret purveyor of news hostile to Napoleon.

On landing in Sweden the Crown Prince took all by storm. His good looks, his affability, his great prestige and his apparent love for his new country created an enthusiasm almost beyond belief. But while everything seemed so favourable the crafty Gascon from the first foresaw the dangers which beset his path. Napoleon hated him. Russia looked on him with distrust and desired to absorb Sweden. England and the other Powers mistrusted him as the tool of the Emperor. Accordingly, the moment he landed at Gothenburg the Prince clearly defined the line he intended to pursue, exclaiming, "I refuse to be either the prefect or the custom-house officer of Napoleon." This decision meant a complete reversal of Swedish foreign policy and a breach with France. Fortunately for Bernadotte the old King, Charles XIII., was only too glad to leave everything to his adopted son. Since it was impossi-

- **could not tear herself away from Paris** 파리에서 떠날 수 없었다
- **coterie** [kóutəri] 명 (사교계의) 쟁쟁한 사람들, 동아리, 동인
- **gaiety** [géiəti] 명 유쾌, 쾌활, 환락
- **the breath of one's nostrils** 꼭 필요한 것, 즐기는 것
- **as it were** 말하자면, 소위
  - the Crown Princess remained behind, **as it were** the hostage for the Prince's good behaviour
  왕세자비(데지레)는 파리에 남았는데, 말하자면 베르나도트의 행동을 제약하는 인질인 셈이었다
- **purveyor** [pərvéiər] 명 퍼뜨리는 사람
  - but in reality a spy and secret **purveyor** of news hostile to Napoleon
  그러나 실제로는 나폴레옹에 대한 적대적인 소문을 비밀리에 퍼뜨리는 첩자였다
- **On landing in Sweden** 스웨덴에 도착하자마자
- **take all by storm** 모두의 마음을 사로잡다
- **beyond belief** 믿을 수 없는, 놀라운
- **crafty** [kræfti, kráːf-] 형 교활한, 간악한
- **beset** [bisét] 동 포위하다, 에워싸다, (길 등을) 막다, 봉쇄하다
  - foresaw the dangers which **beset** his path
  그의 앞날을 막고 있는 위험을 예견했다
- **absorb** [æbsɔ́ːrb, -zɔ́ːrb] 동 흡수하다, 병합하다
- **clearly defined the line he intended to pursue**
  그가 추구하려는 노선을 분명하게 정했다
- **prefect** [príːfekt] 명 장관, 지사(知事)
  - I refuse to be either the **prefect** or the custom-house officer of Napoleon.
  나는 나폴레옹의 총독이나 세관 관리가 되기를 거부한다.
- **reversal** [rivə́ːrsəl] 명 반전, 역전, 역행
- **only too glad to** 기꺼이 ~하는

ble to make a complete volte face in a moment, the Crown Prince was content to allow the Swedes to taste to the full the misery of trying to enforce the continental system. For he knew what disastrous effect a war with England would have on Swedish trade, and he foresaw that his subjects would soon be glad to accept any policy whereby their sea-borne commerce might be saved. While the Swedes were learning the folly of fighting the mistress of the sea, the Crown Prince had time to make his plans, so that when the moment arrived he might step forward as the saviour of the country. It was quite clear that a breach with France must mean the loss of Pomerania and all hope of regaining the lost provinces on the southern shores of the Baltic. But Bernadotte determined to find in Norway a quid pro quo for Pomerania. To force Russia, the hereditary foe of Sweden, to make her hereditary ally, Denmark, grant Norway to Sweden, would be a master-stroke of diplomacy, while an alliance with Russia would guarantee the Swedish frontiers and would bring peace with England, because Russia was on the point of breaking with the continental system. The Swedes would thus gain Norway and recover their sea-borne trade, while the Crown Prince would be acknowledged as the legitimate heir of the royal house of Vasa and no longer regarded as an interloper, a mere puppet of Napoleon.

- **volte face** 180도 변화, 전향, 변절
- **to taste to the full the misery of trying to enforce the continental system**
  대륙봉쇄를 강요하려는 시도 때문에 발생한 끔찍한 결과를 모두 맛보는 것
- **For he knew what disastrous effect a war with England would have on Swedish trade**
  영국과의 전쟁이 스웨덴의 무역에 어떤 재앙을 불러왔는지 잘 알았기 때문에
- **whereby their sea-borne commerce might be saved**
  그들의 해상무역을 살릴 수만 있다면
- **folly** [fáli/fɔ́li] 명 어리석음, 우둔, 어리석은 행위
- **the mistress of the sea** 바다의 여왕(영국을 말함)
- **saviour** [séivjər] 명 구세주, 구조자
- **It was quite clear that a breach with France must mean the loss of Pomerania and all hope of regaining the lost provinces on the southern shores of the Baltic.**
  프랑스와의 불화는 포메라니아의 상실과 발트해 남부 해안의 잃어버린 영토를 되찾을 모든 희망을 잃어버리는 것을 의미했다.
- **quid pro quo** [kwìd-prou-kwóu] 명 ~에 대한 보상
- **hereditary** [hərédətèri/-təri] 형 세습의, 물려받은
  - To force Russia, the **hereditary** foe of Sweden, to make her hereditary ally, Denmark, grant Norway to Sweden
    숙적인 러시아를 이용해 전통적인 동맹국인 덴마크의 영토 노르웨이를 스웨덴에게 할양하도록 만든 것
- **master-stroke** 명 훌륭한 솜씨
- **on the poing of ~ing** ~하려는 순간에, 바야흐로 ~하려고
  - was **on the point of breaking** with the continental system
    대륙봉쇄를 파기하려는 순간이었다
- **legitimate** [lidʒítəmit] 형 합법의, 정당한
- **interloper** [ìntərlóupər] 명 침입자

Success crowned the efforts of the elated Gascon. The Czar, with the prospect of a French invasion at his door, was delighted beyond measure to find in Sweden an ally instead of a foe. In August, 1812, he invited the Crown Prince to Russia and the treaty of Åböwas signed, whereby Russia promised to lend her aid to Sweden to gain Norway as the price of her help against France; a little later a treaty was concluded between England and Sweden. The Crown Prince returned from Åböfull of relief; not only was he now received into the inner circle of legitimate sovereigns, but the Czar had actually volunteered that if Napoleon fell "I would see with pleasure the destinies of France in your hands." Alexander had kindled a flame which never died as long as Bernadotte lived. The remainder of his life might be summed up as an effort to gain the crown of France, followed by a period of vain regrets at the failure of his hopes.

On returning to Stockholm the Crown Prince found himself surrounded by a crowd of cosmopolitan admirers, the most important of whom was Madame de Staël, who regarded him as the one man who could restore France to prosperity. His flatterers likened him to Henry IV. and harped on the fact that he also came from Béarn. But in France men cursed the traitorous Frenchman who was going to turn his sword against his country,

- **elated** [iléitid] 형 의기양양한, 우쭐대는, 신이 난
  - Success crowned the efforts of the **elated** Gascon.
  의기양양한 가스코뉴인은 노력한 보람이 있어 성공적으로 왕위를 이어받았다.
- **with the prospect of a French invasion at his door**
  프랑스의 침입이 목전에 다가왔다고 예상했기 때문에
- **beyond measure** 몹시, 대단히
- **the treaty of Åbö** 오보 조약(1809년 스웨덴이 러시아에게 핀란드를 양도한 조약)
- **Russia promised to lend her aid to Sweden to gain Norway as the price of her help against France**
  프랑스에 대항하여 도와주는 대가로 러시아는 스웨덴이 노르웨이를 얻을 수 있도록 협조할 것을 약속했다
- **received into the inner circle of legitimate sovereigns**
  (유럽 정치에서) 합법적인 군주들 중 하나로 받아들여졌다
- **volunteer** [vàləntíər/vɔ́l-] 통 자진해서 말하다
- **if Napoleon fell "I would see with pleasure the destinies of France in your hands."**
  만약 나폴레옹이 몰락한다면 "그대의 손에 프랑스의 운명이 정해지는 것을 기쁘게 지켜볼 것이오(프랑스 왕이 되도록 도와주겠다는 뜻)."
- **kindle a flame** 불을 붙이다, (정열 등이) 타오르게 하다
- **sum up** 요약하다
  - might be **summed up** as an effort to gain the crown of France
  프랑스 왕위를 차지하려는 노력으로 요약될 수 있다
- **followed by a period of vain regrets at the failure of his hopes**
  그의 바람이 실패하면서 쓸데없는 아쉬움의 기간이 뒤따른
- **cosmopolitan** [kàzməpálətən/kɔ̀zməpɔ́l] 형 국제적인, 전 세계의
- **liken** [láikən] 통 ~에 비유하다, 견주하다
  - **likened** him to Henry IV 그를 앙리 4세(프랑스 부르봉 왕가의 시조)에 견주었다
- **harp** [hɑːrp] 통 장황하게 말하다, 되풀이해서 말하다
- **he also came from Béarn** 그 역시 베아른에서 왔다(베아른은 가스코뉴 지방의 일부로 베르나도트와 앙리 4세 모두 이 곳 출신임)

and his name was expunged from the list of the Marshals and from the rolls of the Senate, while the Emperor bitterly regretted that he had not sent him to learn Swedish at Vincennes, the great military prison. When, in accordance with his treaty obligations, early in 1813 the Crown Prince of Sweden landed at Stralsund to take part in the war against Napoleon, his position was a difficult one. The one object of the Allies was to overthrow Napoleon, the one object of the Crown Prince was to become King of France on Napoleon's fall. The Allies therefore had to beat the French troops, but the Crown Prince would ruin his hopes if French soldiers were beaten by the troops under his command. It was clear that Napoleon could only be overcome by the closest co-operation of all the Allies. Accordingly the Czar and the King of Prussia summoned the Crown Prince to a conference at Trachenberg in Silesia and did their best to gratify his pride. The plan of campaign was then arranged, and the Prince returned to command the allied forces in Northern Germany. At St. Helena the Emperor declared that it was Bernadotte who showed the Allies how to win by avoiding all conflict with himself and defeating the Marshals in detail. With great bitterness he added, "He gave our enemies the key to our policy, the tactics of our armies, and showed them the way to the sacred soil of France." Be this as it may, his conduct during the campaign justified the suspi-

- **expunge** [ikspʌndʒ] 동 지우다, 삭제하다
- **roll** [roul] 명 명부, 출석부
- **the Emperor bitterly regretted that he had not sent him to learn Swedish at Vincennes the great military prison.**
  황제는 그의 스웨덴어 공부를 위해 (스웨덴 대신) 뱅센의 거대한 군감옥에 처넣지 않은 것을 뼈저리게 후회했다.
- **in accordance with his treaty obligations** 오보(Åbö) 조약의 의무에 따라
- **to take part in the war against Napoleon**
  대(對)나폴레옹 전쟁에 참전하기 위해
- **to become King of France on Napoleon's fall**
  나폴레옹이 몰락한 뒤에 프랑스의 왕이 되는 것
- **but the Crown Prince would ruin his hopes if French soldiers were beaten by the troops under his command**
  그러나 프랑스군을 자신의 손으로 직접 격파하지 않으면 왕세자의 희망은 물거품이 되고 말 것이다
- **the closest co-operation** 최고로 긴밀한 연합작전
- **conference** [kánfərəns/kɔ́n-] 명 회담, 협의
- **did their best to gratify his pride**
  그의 자부심을 충족시켜주기 위해서 최선을 다했다
- **defeat in detail** 각개격파하다
  - by avoiding all conflict with himself and **defeating** the Marshals **in detail**
    나폴레옹 자신과의 대결은 피하고 원수들의 군대를 각개격파하는 방법으로
- **showed them the way to the sacred soil of France**
  그들에게 신성한 프랑스 땅으로 들어올 수 있는 길을 보여주었다
- **suspicion** [səspíʃən] 명 혐의, 의심

cion with which he was regarded by friend and foe. Only three times did the Prince's army come in contact with the forces of the Emperor. At Grosbeeren and Dennewitz, where his divisional officers fought and won, the Prince kept discreetly in the rear. At Leipzig he held back so long that the French army very nearly escaped. It was the taunt of his chief of the staff, "Do you know that the soldiers say you are afraid and do not dare to advance?" which at last forced him into battle. But while thus he offended his allies, he gained no respect from his former countrymen. He had always believed that his presence alone was sufficient to bring over the French troops to his side, but his first attempt ought to have shattered this delusion. At Stettin, during the armistice, he entered the fortress and tried to seduce the governor, an ex-Jacobin and erstwhile friend. As he left the town a cannon was fired and a ball whistled past his ear. He at once sent a flag of truce to demand an explanation for this breach of the etiquette of war, whereon his friend the ex-Jacobin replied, "It was simply a police affair. We gave the signal that a deserter was escaping and the mainguard fired." In spite of this warning and many other indications, Bernadotte failed to understand how completely he had lost his influence in France, and while the Allies were advancing on Paris his secret agents were busy, especially in Southern France, trying to win the people to his cause. Keep-

- **by friend and foe** 적도 친구도
- **Only three times did the Prince's army come in contact with the forces of the Emperor.**
  왕세자의 군대는 황제의 군대와 단지 3번 싸웠을 뿐이다.
- **discreetly** [diskríːtli] 📖 신중하게
  - the Prince kept **discreetly** in the rear
  왕세자는 신중하게 후방에 물러나 있었다
- **hold back** 주저하다, 망설이다
  - At Leipzig he **held back** so long that the French army very nearly escaped.
  라이프치히에서 그는 너무 오래 주저하다가 프랑스군이 거의 다 도망가도록 만들었다.
- **offend** [əfénd] 📖 불쾌하게 하다, 감정을 상하게 하다
  - But while thus he **offended** his allies, he gained no respect from his former countrymen.
  그러나 이런 행동에 연합국들은 불쾌해 했고, 옛 동포들에게서도 아무런 존경을 받지 못했다.
- **his presence alone was sufficient to bring over the French troops to his side**
  그의 존재만으로도 충분히 프랑스군이 넘어올 것이다
- **shatter** [ʃǽtər] 📖 산산히 부수다
- **delusion** [dilúːʒən] 📖 잘못된 생각, 망상
- **seduce** [sidjúːs] 📖 부추기다, 속이다, 꾀다
- **erstwhile** [ə́ːrsthwàil] 📖 예전의
- **a ball whistled past his ear** 탄환 하나가 그의 귀를 스쳐갔다
- **explanation** [èksplənéiʃən] 📖 설명, 해명, 해석
- **We gave the signal that a deserter was escaping and the mainguard fired.**
  탈영병이 달아나고 있다고 신호를 보내 정문 경비병이 발사한 것이다(베르나도트를 탈영병 취급한 것임).
- **failed to understand how completely he had lost his influence in France**
  프랑스에서 그가 얼마나 완전히 영향력을 잃었는지 이해하지 못했다
- **cause** [kɔːz] 📖 대의명분, ~을 하기 위한 운동

ing well in the rear of the invading armies, he entirely neglected his military duties and passed his time listening to the reports of worthless spies. The result of his intrigues was that he quite lost touch with the trend of events at the front, and when Paris fell, instead of being on the spot, he was far away. The Czar, long disgusted with his delays, no longer pressed his suit, and finding an apparent desire for a Bourbon restoration, accepted the return of that house. So when the Crown Prince came to Paris he found nothing for it but to make his best bow to the Bourbons and slink away home to gain what comfort he could in the conquest of Norway. Thus once again was Sièyes' saying proved correct: "He is a blackbird who thinks himself an eagle."

On his return home his Swedish subjects gave their Crown Prince a very warm welcome. They knew of none of his intrigues or tergiversations, they only saw in him the victorious conqueror of Napoleon, who, by his successful campaigns, was bringing peace and prosperity to Sweden, by his diplomacy had acquired Norway, and by his clever huckstering had gained twenty million francs for ceding to France the isle of Guadaloupe, of which Sweden had never taken possession, and another twelve millions for parting with the lost Pomeranian provinces. But in spite of his popularity at home the Crown Prince had much to make him

- **Keeping well in the rear of the invading armies**
  연합군의 후방을 잘 지켜야 하는 임무에도 불구하고
- **passed his time listening to the reports of worthless spies**
  가치도 없는 첩자들의 보고를 듣는 데에 시간을 허비했다
- **lose touch with** ~와 연락이 끊어지다, 현실 감각이 없다
  - he quite **lost touch with** the trend of events at the front
    전방에서 일어나고 있는 사건의 흐름을 완전히 놓치고 말았다
- **when Paris fell, instead of being on the spot, he was far away**
  파리가 함락될 때 그 현장에 서 있는 대신, 멀리 떨어져 있었던 것이다
- **long disgusted with his delays** 그가 머뭇거리는 데에 오랫동안 넌더리가 난
- **no longer pressed his suit**
  더 이상 (베르나도트를 프랑스 왕으로 앉히는 것을) 추진하지 않았다
- **restoration** [rèstəréiʃən] 명 복고, 부흥
- **nothing for it but to** ~외에는 별 도리가 없는
- **make his best bow to the Bourbons**
  부르봉 왕가의 사람들에게 정중하게 인사하다
- **slink** [sliŋk] 동 살며시 도망치다
- **blackbird** 명 지빠귀, 찌르레기
  - He is a **blackbird** who thinks himself an eagle.
    그는 자신을 독수리라고 생각하는 참새에 불과했다.
- **tergiversation** [tə̀:rdʒivərsèiʃən] 명 변절, 핑계
- **they only saw in him the victorious conqueror of Napoleon**
  그들은 단지 그를 나폴레옹에 대한 승리자로 여겼다
- **huckster** [hʌ́kstər] 동 행상하다, 팔러 다니다
- **gained twenty million francs for ceding to France the isle of Guadaloupe, of which Sweden had never taken possession** 스웨덴이 한 번도 소유하지 않았던 과들루프 섬을 프랑스에 양도하고 2천만 프랑을 받았다(1813년 영국은 프랑스로부터 과들루프 섬을 빼앗아 15개월간 스웨덴에 임시로 양도했음)
- **for parting with the lost Pomeranian provinces**
  포메라니아 지방을 상실하는 대가로(1814년 노르웨이에 대한 보상으로 덴마크에 양도)

anxious abroad. At the Congress of Vienna a strong party backed the claims of the deposed Gustavus IV., and it was only the generous aid of the Czar which defeated this conspiracy. Further, the attitude of the Powers clearly showed him how precarious was the position of an intruder among the hereditary rulers of Europe. Consequently, when Napoleon returned from Elba the Prince exclaimed: "The cause of the Bourbons is for ever lost," and for a moment thought of throwing in his lot with the Emperor. But the sudden defeat of Murat came as a warning, and he hastened to offer the aid of twenty-six thousand troops to the Allies. Though outwardly in accord with them, the Crown Prince secretly hoped for the victory of Napoleon; to his intimates he proclaimed that "Napoleon was the first captain of all ages, the greatest human being who had ever lived, superior to Hannibal, to Cæsar, and even to Moses." Whereat the Crown Princess, who had at last rejoined her husband in Sweden, replied: "You ought to exclude Moses, who was the envoy of God, whereas Napoleon is the envoy of the Devil."

The news of Waterloo once again drove the Prince's ideas into their old current. Surely France must now recognise that he alone could save her; but the second restoration dashed his hopes to the ground. Yet hope springs eternal in the human breast, and

- **a strong party backed the claims of the deposed Gustavus IV.**
  강력한 세력이 폐위당한 구스타브 4세의 스웨덴 왕위요구를 지지했다.
- **it was only the generous aid of the Czar which defeated this conspiracy**
  이 음모는 (러시아) 차르의 관대한 도움으로서 간신히 분쇄할 수 있었다
- **precarious** [prikéəriəs] 형 불확실한, 믿을 수 없는, 불안한
  - how **precarious** was the position of an intruder among the hereditary rulers of Europe
  유럽의 정통 지배 가문이 아닌 침입자의 위치가 얼마나 불안한 것인지
- **The cause of the Bourbons is for ever lost.**
  부르봉 가문의 대의명분은 영원히 상실되었다.
- **for a moment thought of** 잠시 동안 ~을 고려했다
- **he hastened to offer the aid of twenty-six thousand troops to the Allies**
  그는 서둘러 연합국에 2만 6천 명의 병력을 제공했다
- **outwardly** [áutwərdli] 부 외견상으로는, 밖으로는
  - Though **outwardly** in accord with them
  비록 겉으로는 그들(연합국)과 함께 했지만
- **proclaim** [prouklèim, prə-] 동 선언하다, 분명히 말하다
- **the greatest human being who had ever lived**
  지금까지 살아왔던 인간들 중에서 가장 뛰어난 사람
- **exclude** [iksklú:d] 동 몰아내다, 제외하다, 빼다
  - You ought to **exclude** Moses, who was the envoy of God, whereas Napoleon is the envoy of the Devil.
  모세는 (비교 대상에서) 제외해야 해요. 그는 하느님의 사자이지만, 나폴레옹은 악마의 사자이니까요.
- **the second restoration**
  2번째 왕정복고(나폴레옹의 백일천하 이후 부르봉 왕가가 다시 왕권을 잡음)
- **dash ~to the ground** 땅에 내동댕이치다, 분쇄하다

Bernadotte, year by year, watched the trend of French politics with an anxious eye. Even as late as the Revolution of 1830 he still thought it was possible that France might call him to be her ruler, and he never lost the chance of doing the Bourbons an ill-turn. In spite of these intrigues, save for an appeal lodged in 1818 against the high-handed conduct of the Quadruple Alliance in interfering between Sweden and Denmark, Bernadotte's European career really ended with the fall of Napoleon. As Charles XIV. he ascended the Swedish throne on February 18, 1818, on the death of his adoptive father. As King he pursued the same policy as Crown Prince, alliance with Russia. His internal policy was based on the principle of maintaining his dynasty at all costs. With this object, in Sweden he ruled more or less as a benevolent despot, consulting his States General as little as possible, paying the greatest attention to commerce and industry, and opening up the mines and waterways of the country. In Norway, however, where the Storthing had long enjoyed great powers, he ruled as a liberal constitutional monarch, and with such good fortune did he and his successors pursue their policy that of all the diplomatic expedients arranged at the Congress of Vienna, the cession of Norway to Sweden stood the test of time the longest, and it was not till 1906 that the principle of nationality was at last enforced in Scandinavia.

- **trend of French politics** 프랑스 정치의 동향
- **with an anxious eye** 간절한 눈빛으로
- **Even as late as the Revolution of 1830**
  1830년 7월 혁명(샤를 10세의 복고 정책에 대항한 혁명) 때까지도
- **lodged an appeal against** ~에 대해 항소하다, 이의를 제기하다
- **high-handed** 혱 고압적인
- **Quadruple Alliance** 4국 동맹
  (오스트리아, 러시아, 프로이센, 영국 4국이 빈체제의 유지를 위해 체결한 동맹)
  - save for an appeal lodged in 1818 against the high-handed conduct of the **Quadruple Alliance** in interfering between Sweden and Denmark
    1818년 4국동맹이 스웨덴과 덴마크 사이에 강압적으로 간섭하려 했을 때, 이에 대해 항의한 것을 제외하고는
- **Bernadotte's European career really ended with the fall of Napoleon.**
  유럽 무대에서 베르나도트의 경력은 사실상 나폴레옹의 몰락과 함께 끝나버렸다.
- **the principle of maintaining his dynasty at all costs**
  무슨 수를 써서라도 그의 왕조를 유지한다는 원칙
- **benevolent** [bənévələnt] 혱 호의적인, 인정 많은
- **despot** [déspət, -pɑt/-pɔt] 명 전제 군주, 독재자
- **consulting his States General as little as possible**
  의회의 자문은 가능한 한 받지 않고
- **open up** ~을 가능하게 하다, 이용할 수 있게 하다
  - **opening up** the mines and waterways of the country
    전국의 광산과 수로를 개발하고,
- **Storthing(=Storting)** [stɔ́ːrtiŋ] 명 노르웨이의 의회
- **expedient** [ikspíːdiənt] 명 수단, 방법
- **stand the test of time** 세월의 시험을 견디다
  - the cession of Norway to Sweden **stood the test of time** the longest
    스웨덴은 오랜 세월 시련을 견디며 노르웨이를 소유했다
- **it was not till 1906 that the principle of nationality was at last enforced in Scandinavia**
  1906년 스칸디나비아에 퍼진 민족주의 이념에 의해 (노르웨이의 독립이) 강요될 때까지 계속되었다.

Though Charles XIV. made no attempt to interfere in European politics, the princes of Europe could never shake off their dislike of him, standing as he did as the one survival of Napoleon's system. When the time came for his son Oscar to seek a bride, the Swedish proposals were met with scorn in Denmark and Prussia, and even in Mecklenburg-Anhalt and Hesse-Cassel. As the Austrian envoy at the Swedish court whispered to his English colleague, "All Europe would see the fall of these people here without regret." Consequently the Swedish King was driven to seek a bride for his son from Napoleon's family, and eventually the young Prince married the daughter of Eugène Beauharnais, the old ex-Viceroy of Italy, Napoleon's stepson.

Charles XIV., a man of regrets, spent the remainder of his life buried in the memories of the past. He seldom got up till late in the day, dictating his letters and receiving his ministers in bed. When he was dressed, he spent some hours going over his private affairs and revising his investments, for he feared to the end that he might be deprived of his crown. In the evening he entertained the foreign representatives and held his courts, after which he passed the small hours of the night with his particular cronies fighting and re-fighting his battles, and proving how he alone could have saved Europe from the misery of the Napole-

- **shake off** 쫓아버리다, 고치다
  - the princes of Europe could never **shake off** their dislike of him
  유럽의 군주들은 결코 그에 대한 혐오를 지울 수 없었다
- **standing as he did as the one survival of Napoleon's system**
  그가 나폴레옹 체제에서 살아남은 자라는 사실 때문에
- **scorn** [skɔːrn] 몡 경멸, 조소
  - the Swedish proposals were met with **scorn** in Denmark and Prussia, and even in Mecklenburg-Anhalt and Hesse-Cassel
  스웨덴의 제안은 덴마크나 프로이센에서는 물론, 메클렌부르크-안할트나 헤세-카셀같은 작은 공국에서조차 멸시를 당했다
- **his English colleague** 영국의 대사(大使)
- **All Europe would see the fall of these people here without regret.**
  이 나라(스웨덴) 국민들이 몰락한다면 모든 유럽이 아무런 양심의 가책 없이 지켜볼 것이오.
- **consequently** [kánsikwèntli/kɔ́nsikwəntli] 젭 따라서 그 결과로
- **the Swedish King was driven to seek a bride for his son from Napoleon's family**
  스웨덴 왕은 어쩔 수 없이 아들의 신부감을 나폴레옹 가문에서 찾아야만 했다
- **Charles XIV.** 칼 14세(베르나도트의 스웨덴 왕호)
- **go over** 점검하다, 거듭 살피다
- **revising his investments** 그의 (개인적인) 투자를 재점검하는
- **for he feared to the end that he might be deprived of his crown**
  그가 죽는 날까지 왕위에서 쫓겨날까 두려워했기 때문에
- **entertained the foreign representatives** 외국 대사들을 식사에 초대했다
- **hold court** 재미있는 이야기를 들려주다, 사람들을 즐겁게 하다
- **crony** [króuni] 몡 친구, 옛 벗
- **how he alone could have saved Europe from the misery of the Napoleonic wars**
  그 혼자 나폴레옹 전쟁의 악몽에서 유럽을 어떻게 구했는지

onic wars. He died on March 3rd, 1844, at the age of eighty, having given his subjects the precious boon of twenty-five years of peace.

In spite of his brilliant career, Bernadotte must ever remain one of the most pathetic figures in history. He stands convicted as a mere opportunist, a man who never once possessed his soul in peace and who was incapable of understanding his own destiny. So much was this the case that in his latter days the old Jacobin, now a crowned King, really believed he was speaking the truth when he said that along with Lafayette he was the only public man, save the Count of Artois, who had never changed since 1789. He saw no inconsistency between the declaration of his youth, "that royalty was a monster which must be mutilated in its own interest," and his speech as an old man to the French ambassador, "If I were King of France with an army of two or three hundred thousand men I would put my tongue out at your Chamber of Deputies." He was Gascon to the backbone, and his tongue too often betrayed his most secret and his most transient thoughts. For the moment he would believe and declare that "Napoleon was not beaten by mere men… he was greater than all of us… the greatest captain who has appeared since Julius Cæsar… If, like Henry IV… he had had a Sully he would have governed empires." Then, thinking of himself as Sully, he would

- **precious** [préʃəs] 형 귀중한, 가치 있는
- **boon** [buːn] 명 혜택, 이익
  - having given his subjects the precious **boon** of twenty-five years of peace
    그의 백성들에게 25년간의 평화라는 아주 귀중한 선물을 주고는
- **pathetic** [pəθétik] 형 애처로운, 애수에 찬
- **opportunist** 명 기회주의자
  - He stands convicted as a mere **opportunist**
    그는 기회주의자에 불과하다는 오명을 쓰고 있다
- **a man who never once possessed his soul in peace and who was incapable of understanding his own destiny**
  단 한 번도 영혼의 평화를 가져보지 못하고 자신의 운명을 이해하지 못했던 사람
- **So much was this the case that** ~는 그런 사례를 잘 보여주고 있다
- **the old Jacobin, now a crowned King**
  한때 자코뱅 당원이자 지금은 왕관을 쓰고 있는 왕(베르나도트를 말함)
- **really believed he was speaking the truth when he said that**
  그가 ~라고 말할 때 자신이 진실을 말하고 있다고 진정으로 믿었다
- **along with Lafayette he was the only public man, save the Count of Artois, who had never changed since 1789.**
  라파예트를 따른 사람들 중 아르투아 백작을 제외하고는 자신이 1789년 이후 결코 변절하지 유일한 공인(公人)이었다
- **He saw no inconsistency between**
  ~과 ~사이에 모순이 있다는 것을 알지 못했다
- **mutilate** [mjúːtəlèit] 동 훼손하다, 불구로 만들다
- **put out one's tongue** 혀를 내밀다, 경멸하다
- **Chamber of Deputies** (프랑스의) 국민회의
- **transient** [trǽnʃənt, -ʒənt, -ziənt] 형 일시적인, 변하기 쉬운
- **Sully** 쉴리(1560~1641, 앙리 4세 시대의 뛰어난 정치가였음)

gravely add, "Bonaparte was the greatest soldier of our age, but I surpassed him in powers of organisation, of observation and calculation." Yet with it all he had many of the qualities which go to make a man great. His personal magnetism was irresistible, he had consummate tact, a keen eye for intrigue, a clear vision to pierce the mazes of political tangles, and considerable strength of purpose backed by an intensely fiery nature. Frank and generous, he inclined naturally to a liberal policy, but his innate selfishness too often conquered his generous principles. It was this conflict between his liberal ideas and his personal interest which caused that fatal hesitation which again and again threatened to spoil his career and which made him so immensely inferior to Napoleon. To gain his crown he willingly threw over his religion and became a Lutheran; to keep his crown he was ready to sacrifice his honour. As a Swedish monarch he thought more of the interests of his dynasty than of the interests of his subjects, but he was far too wily to show this in action. Posing as a patriot King and boasting of his love for his adopted country, he ever remained at heart a Frenchman.

When in 1840 the remains of the great Emperor were transferred to Paris, he mournfully exclaimed to his representative: "Tell them that I who was once a Marshal of France am now only a King of Sweden."

- **gravely** [greivli] 튀 진지하게, 근엄하게
- **but I surpassed him in powers of organisation, of observation and calculation**
  그러나 조직력이나 관찰력, 예측력에서는 내가 그를 능가했다
- **Yet with it all he had many of the qualities which go to make a man great.**
  그런 모든 단점에도 그는 위대한 인물이 되기에 충분한 많은 자질들을 가지고 있었다.
- **irresistible** [irizístəbəl] 형 저항할 수 없는, 매혹적인
- **consummate** [kənsʌ́mət] 형 숙련된, 유능한
- **tact** [tækt] 명 재치, 기지
- **pierce** [piərs] 동 관통하다, 통찰하다
- **tangle** [tǽŋgəl] 명 얽힘, 혼란
  - a clear vision to pierce the mazes of political **tangles**
    복잡하게 얽힌 정치적 문제를 간파할 수 있는 명확한 통찰력
- **considerable strength of purpose** 대단한 의지력
- **intensely** [inténsli] 튀 격렬하게, 맹렬하게
- **innate** [inéit, -́-] 형 타고난, 선천적인
  - his **innate** selfishness too often conquered his generous principles
    그는 선천적인 이기심 때문에 자신의 관대한 원칙(자유주의)을 자주 무시했다
- **It was this conflict between his liberal ideas and his personal interest which caused that**
  그의 자유로운 사상과 개인적인 욕심에서 오는 갈등 때문에 ~한 문제가 야기되었다
- **which made him so immensely inferior to Napoleon**
  그를 나폴레옹보다 한참 뒤떨어지게 만들었던
- **willingly threw over his religion and became a Lutheran**
  기꺼이 자신의 종교를 버리고 루터교로 개종했다
- **pose** [pouz] 동 ~인 체하다, 가장하다
- **he ever remained at heart a Frenchman**
  마음속으로 그는 항상 프랑스인이었다
- **remain** [riméin] 명 유해
- **mournfully** [mɔ́ːrnfəlli] 튀 슬픔에 잠기어, 탄식하며
- **I who was once a Marshal of France am now only a King of Sweden**
  한때는 프랑스 제국의 원수였던 내가 지금은 스웨덴 국왕에 불과하다